IMPROVING WRITING K–8

Strategies, Assessments, and Resources

Second Edition

Susan Davis Lenski
Illinois State University

Jerry L. Johns
Northern Illinois University, Emeritus

KENDALL/HUNT PUBLISHING COMPANY
4050 Westmark Drive   Dubuque, Iowa 52002

Reading Resources by Susan Davis Lenski and Jerry L. Johns
Improving Reading: Strategies and Resources (3rd ed.)
Reading & Learning Strategies for Middle Grades through High School (2nd ed.)
Teaching Beginning Readers: Linking Assessment and Instruction (2nd ed.)
(with Laurie Elish-Piper)
Comprehension and Vocabulary Strategies for the Primary Grades (with Roberta L. Berglund)

Books by Jerry L. Johns
Basic Reading Inventory (8th ed.)
Spanish Reading Inventory
Fluency (with Roberta L. Berglund)
Content Area Reading Strategies (with Roberta L. Berglund)

Author Addresses for Correspondence and Workshops

Susan Davis Lenski
Campus Box 5330
Normal, IL 61790-5330
Illinois State University
E-mail: sjlensk@ilstu.edu
309-438-3028

Jerry L. Johns
2105 Eastgate Drive
Sycamore, IL 60178
E-mail: jjohns@niu.edu
815-895-3022

Address for Orders
Kendall/Hunt Publishing Company
4050 Westmark Drive
P.O. Box 1840
Dubuque, IA 52004-0810

Telephone for Orders
800-247-3458

Website
www.kendallhunt.com

Sample writings reprinted with permission of authors.

Interior Photos: Bonnie Stiles

ISBN 0-7575-0788-3

Printed in the United States of America
10 9 8 7 6 5 4 3 2 1

Contents

Preface

Who will use this book?

Practicing teachers, prospective teachers, and professionals who fulfill special resource roles will appreciate the user-friendly approach we have taken in presenting the second edition of *Improving Writing K–8: Strategies, Assessments, and Resources*. The book is grounded in solid knowledge about writing. It will be used in college and university courses as well as for school district inservices and staff development programs.

What are some of the unique characteristics of this book?

Please note the subtitle—Strategies, Assessments, and Resources. These three topics form the heart of this book, providing teachers with all the background needed to help students improve their writing skills. The variety of strategies, assessment ideas, and resources will meet diverse student needs. Following is a brief outline of the unique features of this book and how these three topics are presented.

Strategies	*Assessments*	*Resources*
• Concise description of writing instruction in Chapter 1 • Overview of each chapter • Boxed teaching goals in Chapters 2–6 • Background information for teaching goals • Step-by-step instructional plan • Expanded instructional ideas • Useful, practical activities	• Teacher self-assessments • Student self-assessments • Rubrics • Practical evaluative ideas • Reproducible assessment pages • Brief assessment tips	• Reproducible student worksheets • Transparency masters • Teacher examples • Student examples • Technology Tips referencing specific websites • Lists of books • Lists of websites • Appendix • Reference section • Index

Is the book easy to use?

Yes! We have published several other books and teachers have complimented us on the organization, content, and presentation.

The organization of *Improving Writing* is similar to our successful and well-received earlier resources for teachers. In short, we have listened to people who teach, plan to teach, or function in various resource roles.

Introducing Writing

Goal — To help students develop a basic understanding of writing.

Section 2.1

BACKGROUND

Young children experiment with writing long before they enter school. Picking up a crayon, marker, or pencil and making scribbles on paper is fascinating for a two- or three-year-old child. A more formal introduction to writing occurs when children enter kindergarten. They are no longer in complete control of their writing, and often what is presented conflicts with concepts and ideas that they have developed at home. Since children have a definite set of unique experiences with writing before formal instruction begins, teachers must be sensitive to the tension that this can create. When their teachers provide children with many examples of writing, model how to write, and think aloud as they write, young children become accustomed to more formal ways of expressing themselves.

When children enter kindergarten, signing in may be their first introduction to a specific purpose for writing. When teachers use the names on the sign-in sheet to check attendance, children begin to understand that writing their names represents them and their presence at school. It also demonstrates the fact that what they write can be read by others and translated into talk.

The morning message can be a powerful vehicle for reinforcing the relationship between reading, writing, and speaking (Mariage, 2001). It also provides early experiences with concepts of print and high frequency words. When teachers begin their day by conveying a message through writing, children begin to see that writing is a form of communication. This concept is what we build upon as we guide children through their development as writers.

The use of literature is an important component in children's introduction to writing. When children are excited about a story that they have heard and are given the opportunity to write like an author, it can become an important pathway into their literacy development. In addition, working with language in terms of rhythm, rhyme, or repeating patterns provides models that encourage children to experiment with various ways of expressing themselves.

When teachers present many examples of writing, young children begin to understand the purposes and functions of writing. When teachers model how to write, use write alouds, and provide examples of writing structure through literature, children begin to experiment with using writing to express themselves.

I SeThre TRTLS

I See three turtler

I see three turtles.

Teachers can model writing in various ways.

17

Teaching Strategy 1

Section 2.1

SIGNING IN

Harste, Woodward, and Burke (1985) sum up beginning writing instruction with these words, "Let them 'sign in,' please!" (p. 22). Researchers have found that the letters in a child's first name play an important part in his or her literacy development. Name writing empowers emergent writers and provides an entry point through which they gain insights into written language (Clay, 1975). Clay reminds us that a child's "name is likely to be the most highly motivating word to want to write" (p. 46). Therefore, it is an excellent place to begin a child's instruction. Most children learn to write their names before attempting to write almost anything else. They first recognize the initial capital letter as "their name" and pay little attention to what comes after it. This initial letter is generally the first one that children associate with a sound. Later, as children's name writing improves, they begin to notice the other letters in their names and use them to create new words. From there, children's writing usually expands to include the names of their classmates and other familiar words.

Directions

1. Prepare a large, unlined sheet of paper with the date at the top. Place it on a table that is easily accessible to children. Provide plenty of sharpened pencils.

2. Explain to children that when they come into the classroom you want them to write their name on a sign-in sheet. Demonstrate by holding up the paper and writing your name at the top. Tell them that you will know who is at school each day by reading the names on the sheet.

3. Since some kindergarten children are unable to write their names or may know only a part of their names, be sure to stand at the table and note the order the children sign in until you are able to read or recognize each name. Read the names on the sign-in sheet aloud once children are settled on the rug. This demonstrates the importance of writing your name and the idea that writing can be translated into spoken language.

4. Have children take over calling attendance once they begin to show an interest. You may need to assist them in reading the names at first; however, this activity provides a strong incentive for children to begin to recognize classmates' names.

5. Keep the dated sign-in sheets and assess them periodically through the year. They provide valuable information on children's developing awareness of print.

6. Conference with children throughout the year on what they have accomplished. Point out the progress that children have made in writing their names. The information from the sign-in sheets provides the teacher with direction for instruction that moves children along in their development.

7. Have children respond to yes/no questions along with signing in once the sign-in routine is familiar. Simply add two columns to the right of the sign-in sheet with yes and no headings and write a question at the top. Have children check or make a mark to indi-

18

How to use this book

In a few minutes, you can learn to use *Improving Writing*.

A **Quick Reference Guide for Teaching and Assessment Goals** appears on the inside front cover.

Choose a specific goal and locate it on the page number listed. Each chapter has several teaching goals arranged in the same basic format:

- Chapter overview
- Numbered section heading (2.1, 2.2)
- Highlighted teaching goal
- Background information

- Numbered teaching strategies
- Additional ideas and activities
- Resources throughout
- Assessments throughout

The **teaching goal** for section 2.1 is highlighted.

Background information related to achieving the goal is provided.

Teaching strategies are provided for each goal. They are clearly numbered.

Resources in the form of student examples or overhead masters are given with many of the strategies.

 **ICON** indicates group exercises.

Websites are listed throughout the book. Because the websites change often, we cannot ensure their accuracy.

The **appendix** provides easy reference to valuable resources in the teaching of writing.

Word to the wise teacher

 Now it's up to you to use *Improving Writing K–8: Strategies, Assessments, and Resources* (2nd ed.) to energize and strengthen your writing program. As you use the book, please consider the following invitation.

You're invited to share an example of student writing (with signed permission), a teaching idea, or activities that we might be able to use in future editions.

You can find our addresses on the copyright page. We value your input!

Sue & Jerry

About the Authors

Susan Davis Lenski is a Professor at Illinois State University, in the Department of Curriculum and Instruction, where she teaches undergraduate and graduate courses in reading, writing, language arts, and literacy theory. Dr. Lenski brings 20 years of experience as a public school teacher to her work as a professor, writer, and researcher. During her years as a teacher, Dr. Lenski developed a writing program that balances different types of writing instruction. She has presented this program to many teachers through staff development programs and graduate courses. As a result of suggestions from practicing teachers, Dr. Lenski has revised and expanded her program, which forms the basis for this book.

Dr. Lenski has been recognized for her work by a variety of organizations. For her work in schools as a teacher, she received the Nila Banton Smith Award and led her school to receive an Exemplary Reading Program Award, both from the International Reading Association. In Illinois, Dr. Lenski was inducted into the Illinois Reading Council Hall of Fame, and at Illinois State University, Dr. Lenski was named Outstanding Researcher. As a result of her practical experience and her grounding in theory, Dr. Lenski is a popular speaker for professional development programs and has consulted in the United States, Canada, and Guatemala. She has presented her work at numerous scholarly conferences, has published more than 50 articles in state and national journals, and has coauthored eight books.

Jerry L. Johns, Distinguished Teaching Professor Emeritus of Northern Illinois University, was the 2002–2003 president of the International Reading Association. He has been recognized as a distinguished professor, writer, and outstanding teacher educator. He has taught students from kindergarten through college and serves as a professional development consultant and speaker to schools and professional organizations. His more than 700 presentations and professional development sessions involved travel throughout a majority of the United States and to 12 countries.

Dr. Johns is a past president of the Illinois Reading Council, College Reading Association, and Northern Illinois Reading Council. He has received recognition for outstanding service to each of these professional organizations and is a member of the Illinois Reading Council Hall of Fame. Dr. Johns has served on numerous committees of the International Reading Association and was a member of the Board of Directors. He has also received the Outstanding Teacher Educator in Reading Award from the International Reading Association and the Champion for Children Award from the HOSTS Corporation.

Acknowledgments

We take pleasure in thanking the following individuals who shared ideas, compiled resources, edited our writing, and offered support and encouragement during the writing of this book. We also thank Eve Dinardi for her cheerful assistance with some typing.

Dawn Andermann
Christina Basham
Liz Beardmore
Rachel Becknell
Cheryl Benes
Pam Bloom
Jenny Bolander
Carol Burger
Julie Byrd
Becky Cockrum
Sharon Cuningham
Donna Deatherage
Trina Dotson
Shelley Fritz
Susan Giller
Barb Glover
Robin Gran
Mary Ann Gregg
Wendy Hagenbuch
Jan Herman
Lynda Hootman
Jane Jackson
Annette Johns

Jan Karcher
Sandy Leffler
Fran Lenski
Joyce Madsen
Julie McCoy
Cindy McDowell
M. Kristiina Montero
Marla Moore
Barbara O'Connell
LaShawn Pierce
Laurie Reddy
Rebecca Rhodes
Marilyn Roark
Gretchen Schmidt
Lin Scott
Barbara Short
Bonnie Stiles
Kari Tangel
Pamela Tow
Isabelle Townsend
Tammy Tripp
Brenda Vercler
Jill Veskauf
Sally Wallace

Improving Writing Instruction

"I love being a writer. What I
can't stand is the paperwork."

—Peter DeVries

OVERVIEW

Writing instruction in elementary schools has improved dramatically over the past 30 years. The changes in instruction have been the result of research on the process of writing (e.g., Emig, 1971; Graves, 1975). This research has influenced the way teachers think about writing and how they teach writing in schools. For example, many teachers are now providing students with more frequent authentic writing experiences. And many teachers are helping students learn how to write for real reasons and specific audiences. Teachers are also helping students understand that writing is a process—not just a product.

Although writing instruction has definitely improved over the past three decades, expectations for students' writing have in-

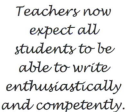

Teachers now expect all students to be able to write enthusiastically and competently.

creased even more. Teachers now expect all students to be able to write enthusiastically and competently. National expectations have been defined by national standards—one of which states that students will be able to "employ a wide range of strategies as they write and use different writing process elements appropriately to communicate with different audiences for a variety of purposes" (International Reading Association & National Council of Teachers of English, 1996). In order for students to meet this ambitious standard, teachers will need to spend more time helping students learn the skills, strategies, and subtleties of writing. According to a recent Writing Commission report, teachers should double the time they spend in writing instruc-

What can a teacher do to help this student meet the National Standards?

tion (www.writingcommission.org). New ideas about writing instruction can help teachers meet this goal.

Writing: A Process, an Art, and a Craft

No matter what kind of writing curriculum or program you currently use, writing instruction in your class can be improved. To improve writing instruction in your class, you need to address all three of the components of writing: the process, the art, and the craft.

The Process

You will need to help students learn that writing is a process. That means that you should help students understand that writing requires planning, drafting, revising, and editing.

The Art

As students experience the stages of writing, you should teach them that a piece of writing is a work of art; it is a creation. Therefore, you need to make room in your writing program for students to experience the magic and mystery of writing. You can do this by organizing the contexts of writing so that students experience the freedom that allows the art of writing to emerge.

The Craft

Writing is also a craft. Writing can be the intentional act of using knowledge about words, sentences, and paragraphs. These skills can be learned through a balanced instructional program that includes a variety of types of writing activities, experiences, and instructional lessons. A balanced writing program can help students learn the many organizational patterns, traditions, rules, and conventions that govern writing.

When you address the process of writing in its contexts through a balanced writing program, you are teaching writing as a process, an art, and a craft. Consequently, your writing instruction will be improved.

The Writing Process

To improve writing instruction, teachers need to have a basic knowledge of the writing process. (See Figure 1.) Writing has been described as a recursive process with five stages (Emig, 1971; Graves, 1975). The five stages in the writing process are prewriting, drafting, revising, editing, and sharing.

Five Stages of Writing
Prewriting
Drafting
Revising
Editing
Sharing

Prewriting/Planning

Writers begin their writing tasks by prewriting or planning their pieces of writing. During the prewriting stage, writers consider their purposes for writing, determine the forms that their writing will take, and identify their audiences. Writers can choose to outline their ideas during the prewriting stage, they can map their ideas on a graphic organizer, or they can think through ideas in their minds.

Drafting

After writers have a plan for writing, they usually write their first drafts. When drafting pieces of writing, writers record their thoughts and ideas, often referring to their writing plans.

The Writing Process

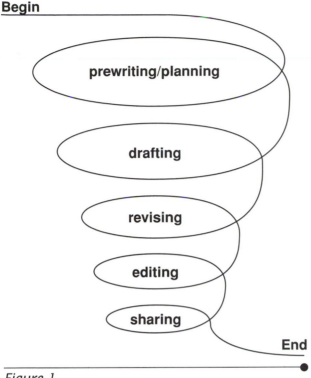

Figure 1

From Susan Davis Lenski and Jerry L. Johns, *Improving Writing K–8: Strategies, Assessments, and Resources,* (2nd ed.). Copyright © 2004 by Kendall/Hunt Publishing Company (1-800-247-3458, ext. 4 or 5). May be reproduced for noncommercial educational purposes.

During drafting, writers might decide to periodically address the conventions of writing such as spelling and word usage, but the primary purpose of the drafting stage is to write down thoughts and ideas.

Revising

After a piece of writing is drafted, writers often begin revising their writing. While revising, writers reread their pieces, looking carefully at the substance of their writing. Writers may rework their writings at this stage, rewriting passages or sentences to make their meanings more clear. Writers may revise their pieces of writing many times. In fact, well-known authors often revise drafts hundreds of times before editing.

Editing

When revision is complete, writers edit their writings. In order for an audience to be able to read and understand a piece of writing, it needs to be written using the conventions of the language in which it is written. Final drafts, therefore, should be edited to conform very closely to Standard English.

Sharing

The final stage in the writing process is sharing the writing with an audience. Writing is meant to be read. Because sharing is a vital component of the writing process, many writers submit their works in some type of published form. In the case of students, publishing could mean a class book, a display, or an electronic file.

Recursive Nature of the Writing Process

Writing is a composing process that is shaped by the decisions writers make as they identify their writing purposes, decide upon forms, and clarify their thoughts and ideas (Dyson & Freedman, 1991). Writing is like cooking soup, designing a web page, or painting a picture. It follows specified steps but allows for spontaneity. The process of writing, therefore, has five stages that are followed in order in some instances or are adapted to fit the contexts of writing. The process of writing is recursive.

Writing is generally a bit messy.

Writers know that completing a piece of writing is rarely as neat as many people infer from the writing process. Writing is generally a bit messy. That's because the writing process is recursive. When writing, writers move back and forth between writing stages as necessary. Sometimes a piece of writing takes little or no revision or editing; sometimes writers begin the process by drafting; sometimes writers edit as they write. Therefore, it's important for teachers to realize that the five-stage writing process represents a *model* of writing. Writers often use all five stages, but they will not necessarily follow every stage in order as they write.

Writing is a creative process.

Contexts for Writing

The process used for writing is shaped by its contexts (Hayes, 1996; Schneider, 2001). (See Figure 2.) Because the process of writing is embedded with a writer's decisions, every writing event is unique and individual. Writing, however, is shaped by three factors: the social contexts in which writers find themselves, the physical contexts of writing, and the individual contexts consisting of motivation, knowledge, and ability.

What Contexts Shape Writing?
Social
Physical
Individual

Social Contexts

Writing occurs in specific social contexts.

CURRICULUM AND LOCAL OR STATE MANDATES. In schools, teachers' writing assignments and students' purposes for writing may be influenced by a curriculum and local or state mandates.

AUDIENCES. Students in schools write for slightly different purposes than do other writers. Students often write for an audience of teachers rather than selecting their own audiences.

WRITING COMMUNITY. Students participate in a different type of social community from most writers. Students in schools are a part of a large community of learners, often 20 to 35 other students. In this community, writing may be highly valued or writing may be neglected. The community of learners may have a high degree of interest and energy, or the class may be quiet and passive. As the leader of the learning community, the teacher may be an enthusiastic writer, or the teacher may dread writing.

All of these factors influence the social contexts of the writing community.

Physical Contexts

A second context for writing is the physical context. Writing occurs in a physical environment and can be influenced by that environment.

CLASSROOM. The physical environment in a classroom could be noisy or quiet; it could be bright or dark; it could be crowded or roomy.

WRITERS' TOOLS. Writers' tools are also a part of the physical context of writing. Some writers work better at a keyboard. Others need a specific type or size of pen. Many writers have other individual preferences: sharp #2 pencils, purple ink, lined paper.

The physical contexts of writing are an important piece in the writing process. In order to compose a piece of text, writers frequently need their physical environments to accommodate their individual writing preferences.

Individual Contexts

Most of all, writing is individual. The individual contexts for writing consist of the writer's motivation, knowledge, experiences, and abilities. Although writing is influenced by its social and physical contexts, it is primarily an individual process.

MOTIVATION. Writers come to a writing event with their own goals and purposes. Even though the goals and purposes for students' writings are frequently influenced by teachers, writers also have their own agendas.

KNOWLEDGE. In addition to their goals and purposes, writers bring knowledge to each writing event. Students will bring a range of

Contexts for Writing

SOCIAL CONTEXTS

- Curriculum
- Local or state mandates
- Audiences
- Writing community

PHYSICAL CONTEXTS

- Classroom
- Writers' tools

INDIVIDUAL CONTEXTS

- Motivation
- Knowledge
- Experiences
- Abilities

Figure 2

Is writing valued or neglected in your classroom?

knowledge about other genres and contents. For example, if you were asking students to write fairy tales, some students would have lots of experience hearing and reading fairy tales while others would have less experience with this genre. If students were writing a fictional story set in a forest, students with prior knowledge about the animals, plants, and weather of a forest would have more knowledge about the content than other students would. Therefore, the knowledge about genres and contents that students bring to a writing event influences their ability to write a specific piece.

EXPERIENCES. Students will bring different experiences to writing. Some students have experienced positive, enthusiastic writing programs that have encouraged them to write. Other students may not be so lucky. They may have experienced writing instruction that is narrowly focused and even punitive. While students who have had positive experiences with writing may not always be the best writers in your class, their experiences with writing are different from students who have had negative writing experiences. These differences in experiences also can influence students' writings.

ABILITIES. Students bring different inherent abilities to writing assignments. Some students are more fluent than are other students. While some students gush words, others struggle to find words to express simple thoughts. Al-

though the ability to write fluently can be learned, students bring individual talents and abilities to writing assignments.

In conclusion, writers bring *themselves* to each writing event. They bring their attitudes and abilities, their successes and their failures, their enthusiasms and their dislikes. Writing is an individual process that is highly influenced by contexts for writing.

Balanced Writing Instruction

Writing instruction should include many different kinds of writing experiences, activities, and strategies. Teachers can improve their writing instruction by providing students with a balance of instructional activities (Fletcher & Portalupi, 2001). Balanced writing instruction takes into account different types of writing students need to learn along with a variety of components that are essential to writing. (See Figure 3.)

One way to describe a balanced writing program is to compare writing instruction to the preparation for running a race. When training for a 10k race, for example, runners will not run the same distance at the same speed every day. Instead, they vary their training regime based on their needs. Runners organize their training programs so that they run at a steady pace for a set number of miles several times a week to build a base for improvement. They spend another day or two practicing skills by running on a track, running up hills, or increas-

Do your students have the tools they need to begin a writing assignment?

Balanced Writing Instruction

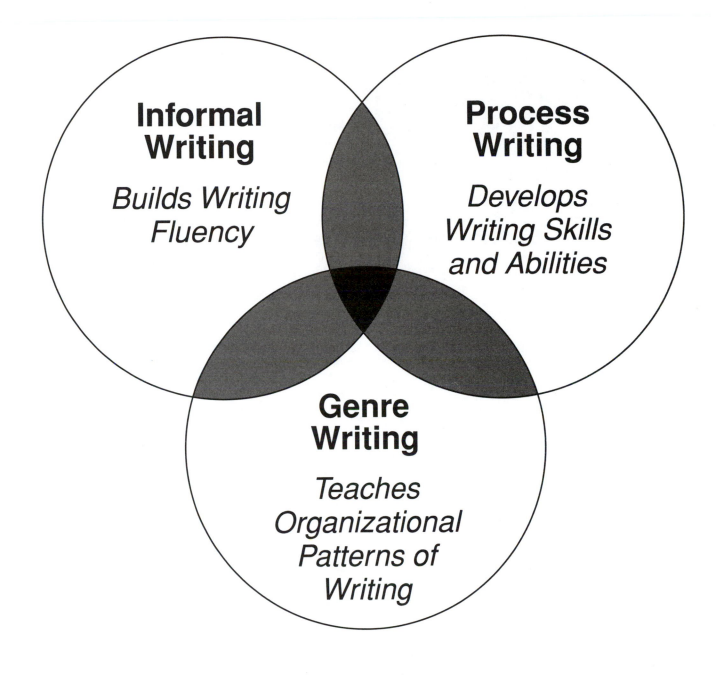

Informal Writing

Builds Writing Fluency

Process Writing

Develops Writing Skills and Abilities

Genre Writing

Teaches Organizational Patterns of Writing

Figure 3

Will your students become writing winners?

Merely assigning informal writing activities to students will not help them learn how to become better writers. Again, comparing writing to running a race, at one time runners believed that if they ran long, slow distances in practice they would become expert runners. On race day, however, these runners found that they ran more slowly than they had intended. Runners need to build their running skills by timing splits and running hills. Teaching students how to write is very similar. If students spend all of their time practicing writing, they will not make as much improvement as if they had a writing coach, or a mentor.

Process Writing

When people learn new skills, they generally need others who are more knowledgeable to help them improve in specific areas. Writing is a skill to be learned as well as a craft. Writers, therefore, need writing mentors (Dorn, French, & Jones, 1998). Process writing works best as students learn the skills of writing while experiencing the writing process. While students write, they need teachers to help them refine their pieces of writing by helping them set purposes, identify topics, and locate audiences. Teachers can also help students develop their knowledge of the craft of writing by showing them how to develop their own writing styles, by helping them revise their writing, and by assisting with editing. Helping students learn the craft of writing during the writing process is an important function of a balanced writing program.

ing their distances. Finally, runners compete in races to chart their progress. As in running, a writing program should include a variety of activities to improve students' writing abilities.

Generally, there are three types of writing assignments that teachers should consider as they develop a balanced writing program—informal, process, and genre.

> *A writing program should include a variety of activities to improve students' writing abilities.*

Informal Writing

Informal writing is the kind of writing that people participate in to discover their thoughts and feelings, to learn new content, or to respond to other pieces of writing. Informal writing provides practice with transforming ideas into words. Using the running analogy, informal writing is like running miles with no stopwatch and no coach. It builds a base of experiences in order to move to the next level of proficiency.

Genre Writing

The final component of a balanced writing program is teaching the organizational patterns of writing. Writing is governed by rules and conventions. These rules apply not only to the conventions of language but also to the patterns of

Writing Instruction

http://www.mcps.k12.md.us/curriculum/english/comp_effect_rwinstr.htm

This site presents components of effective reading and writing instruction K–8.

writing. Writing is often structured in common writing genres:

- personal experience stories
- fictional writing
- expository writing
- persuasive writing

Although most long pieces of writing include passages of more than one organizational structure, teaching students the common organizational patterns of writing helps them understand various ways to organize ideas.

Using the running analogy, once a runner has run lots of miles to build up a running base and has developed running skills by running splits or hills, the runner is ready for a race. Before running a race, however, the runner should become aware of the rules of the race. For example, to begin a race, typically a gun fires or someone shouts "Go." Then the runners take off down the course, heading for the finish line. They are timed as they cross the finish line and are given their race times. Let's say a runner is unfamiliar with the structure of a race. The runner begins when the starting gun fires, but then she notices a stone in her shoe. She thinks back to training sessions when she would take out the stone and begin the run a second time. Think about the absurdity of this runner stopping and yelling, "Wait a minute. I'd like to start again." It wouldn't happen.

The running analogy illustrates the need for teachers to teach students the accepted structures of writing. In addition to giving students practice writing and helping students build their repertoire of skills, teachers also need to teach students the organizational patterns of writing that are accepted in our society.

Writing Synergy

All of the components of a balanced writing program work in conjunction with each other

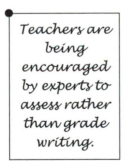

Three Types of Writing Assignments
Informal
Process
Genre

Teachers are being encouraged by experts to assess rather than grade writing.

to help students write. They can be called synergetic, because each component of a balanced writing program supports and extends other components in a variety of ways. For example, informal writing is a good activity in itself. Participating in informal writing activities can help writers generate ideas and clarify thoughts. In turn, these ideas and thoughts can be the basis for developing writing topics. Another example is that when writers learn the organizational patterns of writing, they can use their knowledge about writing genres to make decisions about writing purposes, forms, and audiences. Writing activities are synergetic—another reason why a writing program should include a variety of writing activities (Fletcher & Portalupi, 2001).

Writing Assessment

As teachers develop a balanced writing program based on knowledge about their students, the writing process, and the contexts of writing, they also need to consider how they will assess writing. Writing used to be graded after students completed a piece of writing. Teachers judged writing by marking the errors and assigning a grade. Currently, however, teachers are being encouraged by experts to assess rather than grade writing (Tchudi, 1997). The assessment standards developed by the International Reading Association and the National Council of Teachers of English (1994) best describe the essentials of writing assessment.

These assessment standards are challenging. While it may be difficult to address all of these standards in a writing program, teachers can periodically implement writing assessments that conform to the standards developed by these two large professional literacy organizations. Through the use of different types of assessments, such as self-reports, checklists, and rubrics, teachers can begin assessing writing rather than grading writing.

Assessment Standards for Writing

1. The interests of the students are paramount in assessment.
2. The primary purpose of assessment is to improve teaching and learning.
3. Assessment must reflect and allow for critical inquiry into curriculum and instruction.
4. Assessment must recognize and reflect the intellectually and socially complex nature of writing and the important roles of school, home, and society in literacy development.
5. Assessment must be fair and equitable.
6. The consequences of an assessment procedure are the first, and most important, consideration in establishing the validity of the assessment.
7. The teacher is the most important agent of assessment.
8. The assessment process should involve multiple perspectives and sources of data.
9. Assessment must be based in the school community.
10. All members of the educational community—students, parents, teachers, administrators, policy makers, and the public—must have a voice in the involvement, interpretation, and report of assessment.
11. Parents must be involved as active, essential participants in the assessment process.

A Writing Community

A writing community is a place where both teachers and students write. In a writing community, writing is initiated for real reasons and is produced for real audiences. Ideally, all writers—teachers and students—engage in meaningful writing activities that improve their writing abilities. In order for a writing community to exist, however, the cognitive, affective, social, and physical conditions of writing must be addressed (Dyson, 2001).

To build a writing community, teachers need to address all of the various aspects of writing. Teachers should first become writing role models by writing for their own purposes. Teachers need to write with students, write for students, write for themselves, and write outside the school day. Students should know that their teachers are writers. Knowing that teachers are active participants in the writing community can bolster students' affective feelings about writing. Students identify with teachers who are writing role models (Frank, 2003).

Having teachers as writers in the writing community is fundamental to a strong writing program. Teachers need to encourage students to take part in the writing community by encouraging students to write. Teachers can show the value of writing by writing their own pieces, but they also can structure lessons that make writing fun for students. Teachers need to encourage students to write and to think of themselves as writers.

> *Thinking writers are more strategic writers.*

The Importance of the Teacher

When teachers are faced with various ideas about writing, they may become confused by the different ideas that are presented. Despite the changes in writing instruction that followed the process writing movement, many teachers hold to traditional views about writing (Strickland, Bodino, Buchan, Jones, Nelson, & Rosen, 2001). Further, the new pressures of mandated testing have made some teachers wonder about the place of process writing. Some teachers, therefore, use traditional methods, others are attracted to process writing, and still others combine writing workshops with writing tests (Wolf & Wolf, 2002). Although these variations in writing instruction across schools and classrooms seem disconcerting, research indicates that how teachers approach instruction is more important than what approach they use (Pollington, Wilcox, & Morrison, 2001).

Finally, teachers need to view writing as part of an overall language arts curriculum. Writing cannot be taught without a strong connection to reading, speaking, listening, and viewing (Barrs, 2000). Although teachers can provide time for writing and explicit instruction in writing, they also need to weave writing through other subjects and language processes so students understand that writing is a tool that they can use to discover their own thoughts and to communicate effectively with others.

Conclusion

Writing is a process, an art, and a craft. To improve writing instruction, teachers need to allow students to experience writing so the art of writing can flourish. The art of writing is the creative component that mysteriously

happens. It can't be taught, but it can be encouraged by providing an atmosphere that encourages creativity. Teachers can orchestrate an atmosphere of creativity by becoming writing role models and by creating a community of writers in their classrooms. Additionally, teachers can join their own community of learners by becoming involved in a professional organization such as those listed in the Appendix. By becoming members of a professional organization, teachers can join other professionals in learning how to strengthen their instructional writing programs.

Writing is also a craft. Teachers can teach the craft of writing through a balanced writing program and a variety of lessons. Students need to learn how to discover their thoughts and feelings through writing, to develop the content of their writing, to understand the structures of writing, and to refine language to conform to Standard English. Teachers can provide students with instructional activities that facilitate this type of learning.

These students have formed a community of writers.

Emergent and Developing Writers*

Bonnie Stiles

OVERVIEW

The term emergent writing covers a range of ages and abilities—from children just learning to hold a crayon and making a mark on a page to children writing letters that represent the sounds in a word they want to write. The term clearly describes the stage of writing in which children are just learning what writing is all about and how to go about it. At this stage of development, children should be

> Writing is an integral part of literacy learning for young children.

provided with experiences that demonstrate that writing is an important form of communication used throughout our society for many purposes. They also need to participate in activities that help them to recognize the reciprocal relationship between reading and writing.

Developing writers are beginning to understand and explore different forms, purposes, and func-

---

* For this chapter, I chose to use the term children instead of students to highlight the differences between beginning writers and those in the primary and intermediate grades who are polishing and perfecting their writing skills. Emergent and developing writers are just beginning to learn what writing is, what it does, and how to go about it. These children have different developmental needs than do older students, and those needs require different approaches for instruction.

tions of writing about the end of first grade and into second grade. These children are steadily making progress toward becoming independent writers and are ready for instruction and guidance on how to improve their craft.

Early experiences lay the foundation for future literacy development (Clay, 1975). For teachers of children in the primary grades, this means that much of their time, energy, and instruction needs to focus around literacy activities. The International Reading Association (IRA) and the National Association for the Education of Young Children (NAEYC) felt strongly enough about the importance of early literacy to join together to create a statement about developmentally appropriate practices for teaching young children to read and write (1998). They state that "although reading and writing abilities continue to develop throughout the life span, the early childhood years—from birth through age eight—are the most important period for literacy development" (p. 196).

The IRA and NAEYC (1998) also note that children acquire important knowledge of the alphabetic principle through *both* reading and writing and that writing helps children attend to print in a more focused way. This means that teachers need to teach writing with the same time, energy, and resourcefulness as they do reading. They need to provide young children with demonstrations of how writing works, opportunities to practice new skills, and guidance to move children along in their development. Young children also need encouragement to continue their natural desire to communicate through writing (Rog, 2001).

Writing is an integral part of literacy learning for young children and, therefore, needs to be a daily event. Writing on a daily basis encourages children to explore writing as a means of communication and expression. Daily writing, however, should not be interpreted to mean drills on letter recognition or handwriting practice. It means providing opportunities for children to learn about and use the tools they need to become writers. It means providing time to experiment with new ideas, skills, strategies, and structures so that children

Do you look for positive signs of improvement?

Writing is meant to be shared.

develop into confident, motivated writers (Raines & Canady, 1990).

Donald Graves (1983) suggests that teachers must create a need for learning within children, similar to the need to learn to speak as infants. When teachers frequently and clearly illustrate that writing is an important form of communication and provide meaningful experiences that demonstrate this importance, children will not need coaxing to write. Providing children with a

Young children enjoy writing.

Writing that communicates a message

sense of audience and with authentic reasons to communicate with different audiences develops a need within them to say things in a way that can be understood. When children feel that what they say is important to others, writing becomes important to them.

One way to stress importance is to honor the writing of emergent and developing writers. Graves (1983) reminds us that writing is meant to be shared, so children should have many opportunities to read their own writing. Providing time during the school day for them to share their writing with you, classmates, other school personnel, and parents is an important part of writing instruction. Time for teachers and children to respond to one another's writing is also important and emphasizes the fact that each person's writing is important.

The classroom environment is another important component of a teacher's literacy program. The environment can create learners willing to risk trying new skills, or it can foster learners who are afraid to attempt anything that they know they can't do well (Csak, 2002). Accepting children's writing, at whatever stage

it may be, provides young writers with the freedom to learn and grow without reservation. Approximations should be celebrated as the milestones they truly are, each bringing children along in their development. Looking for positive signs of improvement rather than looking for what is lacking encourages children to try new things.

This chapter provides strategies that help move emergent and developing writers through various stages of their development. For the emergent writers entering kindergarten, strategies are provided that help children develop a basic understanding of writing. From the importance of children writing their names, to understanding the teacher's message each morning, to slipping into the role of author, these strategies provide children with opportunities to experience writing and its purposes. Teaching strategies are then offered to help emergent writers become actively involved in writing. These strategies encourage children to participate in writing activities with strong teacher support. The teaching strategies for late emergent and early writers are designed to help children gain independence as writers. These strategies encourage children to use the knowledge, skills, and strategies they have learned with teacher support as needed. The teaching strategies provided for developing writers help them explore new genres and improve the quality of their writing. A teaching strategy on conferencing is also included which provides ideas for holding productive writing conferences with both developing and emergent writers. Assessment strategies end the chapter. When combined with the assessment ideas offered throughout the chapter, these strategies provide teachers with a variety of assessments, which enable them to develop a comprehensive view of children's writing development.

Handwriting for Kids

www.geocities.com/creadman/handwrite/

This site is for students just learning how to write. It provides tracing guides and practice worksheets for printing and cursive writing.

Introducing Writing

Goal • *To help students develop a basic understanding of writing.*

BACKGROUND

Young children experiment with writing long before they enter school. Picking up a crayon, marker, or pencil and making scribbles on paper is fascinating for a two- or three-year-old child. A more formal introduction to writing occurs when children enter kindergarten. They are no longer in complete control of their writing, and often what is presented conflicts with concepts and ideas that they have developed at home. Since children have a definite set of unique experiences with writing before formal instruction begins, teachers must be sensitive to the tension that this can create. When teachers provide children with many examples of writing, model how to write, and think aloud as they write, young children become accustomed to more formal ways of expressing themselves.

When children enter kindergarten, signing in may be their first introduction to a specific purpose for writing. When teachers use the names on the sign-in sheet to check attendance, children begin to understand that writing their names represents them and their presence at school. It also demonstrates the fact that what they write can be read by others and translated into talk.

The morning message can be a powerful vehicle for reinforcing the relationship between reading, writing, and speaking (Mariage, 2001). It also provides early experiences with concepts of print and high frequency words. When teachers begin their day by conveying a message through writing, children begin to see that writing is a form of communication. This concept is what we build upon as we guide children through their development as writers.

The use of literature is an important component in children's introduction to writing. When children are excited about a story that they have heard and are given the opportunity to write like an author, it can become an important pathway into their literacy development. In addition, working with language in terms of rhythm, rhyme, or repeating patterns provides models that encourage children to experiment with various ways of expressing themselves.

When teachers present many examples of writing, young children begin to understand the purposes and functions of writing. When teachers model how to write, use write alouds, and provide examples of writing structure through literature, children begin to experiment with using writing to express themselves.

Teachers can model writing in various ways.

Harste, Woodward, and Burke (1985) sum up beginning writing instruction with these words, "Let them 'sign in,' please!" (p. 22). Researchers have found that the letters in a child's first name play an important part in his or her literacy development. Name writing empowers emergent writers and provides an entry point through which they gain insights into written language (Clay, 1975). Clay reminds us that a child's "name is likely to be the most highly motivating word to want to write" (p. 46). Therefore, it is an excellent place to begin a child's instruction. Most children learn to write their names before attempting to write almost anything else. They first recognize the initial capital letter as "their name" and pay little attention to what comes after it. This initial letter is generally the first one that children associate with a sound. Later, as children's name writing improves, they begin to notice the other letters in their names and use them to create new words. From there, children's writing usually expands to include the names of their classmates and other familiar words.

Directions

1. Prepare a large, unlined sheet of paper with the date at the top. Place it on a table that is easily accessible to children. Provide plenty of sharpened pencils.

2. Explain to children that when they come into the classroom you want them to write their names on a sign-in sheet. Demonstrate by holding up the paper and writing your name at the top. Tell them that you will know who is at school each day by reading the names on the sheet.

3. Since some kindergarten children are unable to write their names or may know only a part of their names, be sure to stand at the table and note the order the children sign in until you are able to read or recognize each name. Read the names on the sign-in sheet aloud once children are settled on the rug. This demonstrates the importance of name writing and the idea that writing can be translated into spoken language.

4. Have children take over calling attendance once they begin to show an interest. You may need to assist them in reading the names at first; however, this activity provides a strong incentive for children to begin to recognize classmates' names.

5. Keep the dated sign-in sheets and assess them periodically through the year. They provide valuable information on children's developing awareness of print.

6. Conference with children throughout the year on what they have accomplished. Point out the progress that children have made in writing their names. The information from the sign-in sheets provides the teacher with directions for instruction that move children along in their development.

7. Have children respond to yes/no questions along with signing in once the sign-in routine is familiar. Simply add two columns to the right of the sign-in sheet with *yes* and *no* headings and write a question at the top. Have children check or make a mark to indi-

cate their answers. Be sure to read the questions orally and demonstrate how you want them to respond. Some sample questions are listed below.

Do you like watermelon?
Do you have a brother?
Is your favorite color blue?
Would you like to eat your lunch outside today?

8. Later in the year, you may want to ask questions that require children to write an answer in the form of a word or phrase. Children can also help generate questions that they would like their classmates to answer. Simple questions that might be asked include their favorite food, story, animal, color, and so on.

9. Once children are able to respond to these questions, you may want to have them answer more complex questions, such as asking whether they prefer chocolate or strawberry ice cream.

10. Use the reproducible that follows for your sign-in sheet when children are ready to answer a question, along with writing their names each morning.

11. An example of a sign-in sentence activity follows on page 20.

Assessment

The information provided by sign-in sheets should be used in conjunction with other assessments to provide a full, rich picture of children's writing development. By dating and then comparing sheets at various times throughout the year, important information can be attained not only on name writing but also on fine motor development, spatial relationships, letter formation, and the use of uppercase and lowercase letters. Informal observation can provide information on children's willingness to participate, to read and write words, and to ask and answer questions.

Sign-In Sheet for _____

Date _____

	Yes	No

I hAv pink hP.

Teaching Strategy 2

Section 2.1

The morning message (Kawakami-Arakaki, Oshiro, & Farran, 1989) is a valuable activity for early readers and writers. It provides an opportunity for children to observe concepts of print such as directionality, return sweep, punctuation, and capitalization. It provides the opportunity for children to recognize high-frequency words, to recognize spelling patterns, and to understand that writing communicates meaning. It is also a powerful demonstration of the relationship between reading and writing.

Directions

1. Explain to children that you have something to tell them but that you want to tell them in writing. Comment as follows.

   We are having a special visitor today. I am going to write a sentence about our special guest, and I want you to help me read it.

2. Proceed to write each word of the message, stretching it out as you write. Have children read each word before proceeding to the next. The message can contain something about the day ahead, a special event, a visiting guest, or anything of interest. This is usually done first thing in the morning. An example is shown below.

   Tim's mom is coming to visit today. She is bringing Tim's new kitten for us to see. The kitten's name is Fluffy.

3. Have children read the entire message once it is complete. Point to each word as it is read. Then have individuals come up to point and read. Discuss the message.

4. Use the morning message as a regular part of your morning routine to demonstrate concepts of print such as where we begin reading, how we move from left to right as we read, how to move from one line to the next for a return sweep, where capital letters are used, how to space, what a letter, word, and sentence are, and what kinds of punctuation we use.

5. Make the message more of a challenge. Once the morning message is an established routine, write it without verbalizing. Have children read the message as you write it. They will begin to recognize more and more words as the year progresses. In time, have children help compose the message and assist in the writing. You can also lengthen the message to make it more of a challenge, as in the example below.

Today we are going to visit the school garden to check on our vegetables. We will take our gardening tools and gloves so that we can weed the garden. We will also need the watering cans so we can give our plants some water. We will check to see if any of the vegetables are ready to eat!

6. Expand the morning message by adding a list of activities in which children will participate that day. Limit these to activities you do every day so children will see the same list over and over again.

Today we are writing to our grandparents to invite them to visit us during Grandparents Week. Look at our chart to see if you have all of the parts you need for a friendly letter. Then get an envelope from the writing center, fold your letter, and put it in my basket.
Today we will have these activities:

- *Reading,*
- *Centers,*
- *Writing Workshop,*
- *Math, and*
- *Science.*

7. Have children begin to write this list of activities for you as the school year progresses. Progress to having them take over the writing of the list.

8. Use the reproducible that follows to plan your morning messages each week.

Assessment

This activity provides an excellent opportunity to observe children's development. You will be able to observe their growing control over concepts of print as they volunteer to read, and later write, the morning message each day. You will also note gains in their recognition of letters, sounds, and words as the year progresses.

Morning Messages

For the Week of _____

Monday	
Tuesday	
Wednesday	
Thursday	
Friday	

Innovations on a familiar story involve changing parts of the existing text by substituting new words, phrases, or sentences. Don Holdaway (1970) tells us that "it is the richness of the instructional literature that will influence and characterize the written output of the children. Once inbuilt, a literacy structure becomes a resource of expression" (p. 161). The repeating pattern or rhyme of many children's books can become the vehicle by which children "role-play as an author" (p. 161). Using memorable literature that children enjoy and relate to can become a pathway into literacy for emergent writers.

Directions

1. Begin with a story that children have enjoyed during shared reading.

2. Suggest that the class or group make up their own version of the story using the predictable pattern, rhyme, or rhythm of the story.

3. Reread the story and discuss the characters, theme, illustrations, repeated phrases, rhymes, ending, and so on. Ask children for suggestions to change one aspect of the story, such as the main character. For example, after reading *Alexander and the Terrible, Horrible, No Good, Very Bad Day* (Viorst, 1972) children may want to change the main character to that of a classmate, teacher, or a famous person.

    We have read the story Alexander and the Terrible, Horrible, No Good, Very Bad Day *this week. Today I thought we might write our own version of the story by changing a few things. Instead of writing about Alexander, we might write about whom? Yes, Michael Jordan would make a great character for our new story!*

4. Changing another aspect of the story, such as a repeated line, also provides a new direction. An example follows.

    If we write our story about Michael Jordan, are we going to have his day be terrible, like Alexander's? Sandy suggests that we make Michael Jordan's day a terrific one instead of a terrible one. What words could we use to describe a terrific day? Good! Wonderful, awesome, and terrific will work well. Now let's rewrite the line that repeats throughout the book using the words from our list. Michael Jordan had a wonderful, awesome, terrific, very good day.

5. After deciding on the elements you want to change, have children begin to brainstorm ideas to use in the story. In the example used above, you might say the ideas that follow.

    Now that we know our story will be about Michael Jordan's very good day, we need to think of things that he might do during that day. Remember that Alexander did lots of things during his terrible day like losing his marble, going to his father's office, buying new shoes, and having to wear his railroad pajamas. What kinds of things should we have Michael Jordan doing? [Students suggest golfing, practicing basketball, working out, signing autographs, and playing in a basketball game.]

6. Write your Innovation on a chart as children share their ideas. Read your story together to see if there are any changes that need to be made. This chart can be hung in the classroom and used during free time or center time.

7. Rewrite the Innovation as a Big Book, having pairs of children illustrate each page. In this way, children become both the authors and illustrators. Include a title page that includes the name of each child.

8. Assemble the pages and bind the book. Include a library pocket and card inside the front cover and a page at the end of the book for parents to write comments. If parents write comments about the book on the special comment page, be sure to share them with the class. Invite the children to read the book during their free time or during center time by placing it in the reading center or library corner.

9. Use the Big Book for shared reading to work on concepts of print, letter and sound recognition, sight words, and so on.

10. Remember that changing one word or phrase in the story may require a number of other changes to maintain meaning, as well as the rhythm, rhyme, or pattern of the story.

11. Use the reproducible that follows to plan changes for your Innovations.

12. Two examples of students' writings follow on pages 27–28.

Assessment

Informal observations during this activity can provide information on the level of children's involvement, willingness to take risks, and their creativity. Children's oral language can also be assessed, as well as their understanding of print concepts, literary structure, and literary language.

Innovation for _____

● _____

Change:

Main character _____

Theme _____

_____

Ending _____

Other _____

Use:

Repeated phrase _____

_____

Rhyme _____

Pattern _____

Rhythm _____

Other _____

Notes:

The Great Enormous Potato

By
Bryce Billard

One day Gouo planted a potato. It grew so big that he could not get it out. He called Dylan. They pulled and pulled, but they could not get it out. So Dylan called Alex. They could not get it out, so Alex called Bryce. They pulled and pulled, but they could not get it out. So Bryce called He-man. They pulled and pulled but could not get it up. So He-man called Bryan, They pulled and pulled, but they could not get it out. So Bryan called the Bat. They pulled and pulled and they got it out. They cooked it into a potato stew.

The Little Yellow Chick

By
Matthew Garrison

Once upon a time the little yellow chick decided to make a pumpkin pie. So he asked his friends the frog, toad, and rooster, "Who will get the flour?"

"Hop it," said the frog.

"Ribbit," said the toad.

"Cock-a-doodle-doo," said the rooster.

"So I will do it myself," said the little yellow chick. "Who will help me get some pumpkins?"

"Not me," said the frog.

"No way," said the toad.

"Oh, forget it," said the rooster.

"Then I will do it myself," said the yellow chick. "Who will help me bake the pie?"

"No!" they all said.

"Who will help me eat the pie?" said the yellow chick.

"We will," said the friends.

"I will let you all in," said the yellow chick, and they all ate the pie.

Getting Started

Goal • To help students become actively involved in writing.

BACKGROUND

Once children begin to understand the purposes and functions of writing, they become more actively involved in actual writing. Teacher guidance and support are crucial as emergent writers begin to explore and use writing as a form of expression. As they learn more about writing through modeling and demonstration, children need to have opportunities to become active participants in the act of writing.

Language-experience stories demonstrate the connection between reading and writing as children see their thoughts translated into words on a page. Children are encouraged to participate in writing about things that are familiar to them. As you write what the child says, concepts such as letter-sound correspondence, left-to-right movement, and one-to-one matching become clear. Children struggling with beginning reading activities also benefit by using their own language as instructional material for reading (Christensen, 2002).

Interactive writing provides young writers with the opportunity to "share the pen" and write with varying degrees of teacher support. This teaching strategy establishes a risk-free venue that allows children to contribute what they know and understand. It is also a means of demonstrating new strategies and skills that children may be ready to learn. Also, concepts of print such as left-to-right progression, spacing, letter recognition, letter-sound relationships, and return sweep are modeled as you and children compose and write together.

> *Shared writing provides a format for small or large group instruction.*

Shared writing provides a format for small or large group instruction. Children are drawn into the act of writing because the story or information is written on large charts or pieces of paper that are easy for children to see, even within a large group. Texts are composed and written together, so children can see how thoughts and ideas are translated into writing. They problem solve with you to write clearly and include important information. Structure and sequencing are also demonstrated and reinforced through shared writing activities.

Activities that involve children in actual writing are the next step in the process of shaping young writers (Bradley, 2001). Your guidance and support are crucial as emergent writers begin to explore and use writing as a form of expression. As they learn more about writing through modeling and demonstration, children need many opportunities to participate in scaffolded writing activities.

Are you involving students in actual writing?

Animal Diaries

www.tesan.vuurwerk.nl/diaries/

This site is for K–6 grade students. It allows them to meet authors and illustrators, send virtual postcards, read stories and poems about animals, color pictures, and much more.

Teaching 1 Strategy
LANGUAGE-EXPERIENCE APPROACH (LEA)

The language-experience approach (LEA) is based on the language and experiences of children (Stauffer, 1970). Using a familiar experience, a child dictates a story. The teacher acts as a scribe, writing down what the child says using his or her exact language. The connection between reading and writing is emphasized as the child sees the oral sentences translated into writing. The child is able to read the text more successfully because it is based on his or her own experiences and written in his or her own language. Don Holdaway (1970) states that "a major insight for the beginning reader must be that written language is talk written down. By developing reading materials from the children's own language about matters of which they had real experience . . . a bridge would be built between familiar language and printed symbols" (p. 29).

Directions

1. Use the language-experience approach with individual children. In this way the child's exact language can be used and will not confuse other children when it varies from Standard English. To get started you might say as follows.

   What would you like to write about today? Did you do something special this week? Yes, you went camping with your dad. Would you like to write about that?

2. Discuss the topic with the child and generate ideas and vocabulary the child will be able to use in dictation. This discussion allows the child to organize ideas and extend understanding.

   What would you like to write about your camping trip? Where did you go camping? In your backyard? Could we write that in your story?

3. Ask the child to generate sentences based on the things discussed. Take down the child's dictation on lined paper, using the child's exact language, even if it is grammatically incorrect. (Remember, when the child attempts to read the story, he or she is likely to say it in exactly the same way that it was dictated. Using any other wording will only confuse the child.) Say each word slowly, as you write it. Then reread the sentence and have the child read it with you.

4. Continue in this manner, taking down the child's dictation and reading over what has been written. Help the child think about what has already been said and prompt him or her to add information where needed, as in the following example.

   Let's read what we have written so far. (Point to each word as you read.) I went camping with my dad. We slept in our backyard. *Okay, what else did you do? Did you eat anything while you were camping?*

5. Once the text is finished, read the story aloud and have the child read it with you. Then have the child read it independently.

6. Have the child illustrate the story. The text and illustration can be glued onto a larger piece of construction paper or it can be made into a book.

7. Use this story as a reading text to help the child understand that his or her thoughts can be said aloud, written down, and read.

8. Copy the child's story on sentence strips. During center time, the child can read the story and reassemble it in the correct order. Also, individual sentences can be cut apart, word by word. The child can then reassemble the sentence in the correct order. The sentence can be glued onto paper or reused.

9. When working with struggling readers and writers, using their own words as a reading text can make the learning process much easier, providing the support needed for them to succeed. However, the language-experience approach is just a stepping stone to help the child understand what reading and writing are all about. When the child has made the connection, progress to predictable emergent texts for reading instruction.

10. Use the reproducible that follows to guide you as you work with a child using the language-experience approach.

Assessment

Informally, the teacher can assess the child's ability to construct grammatically correct sentences, to express ideas orally, and to sequence a story. Letter/sound knowledge and word recognition can be assessed when the story is used as a reading text. Also, if the child is asked to reassemble a cut-up sentence, the teacher can assess how well he or she can reconstruct it word by word.

Language Experience Story

1. Use this approach one-on-one.

2. Have the child choose a familiar topic such as a trip, a book read aloud, a family member, and so on.

3. Discuss the topic and then take down the child's dictation using his or her exact language.

4. Reread the story together. Then have the child read it alone.

5. Have the child illustrate the text.

6. Use the story as a reading text.

7. Copy the story onto sentence strips for the child to sequence using a pocket chart.

8. Cut apart one of the child's sentences so it can be reassembled, word by word.

Interactive writing is an activity in which the teacher and children "share the pen" as they create a text (Pinnell & McCarrier, 1994). Generally, this activity begins with a common experience or a familiar story. Together, teacher and children compose and write the text. In this activity, teachers are able to provide information on letters/sounds and other concepts of print that children are still unsure of, yet allow them to be successful by applying the knowledge they do have. Because the teacher scaffolds their writing, children can create a text that they would not be able to do on their own. The composition is then read and reread often, usually during shared reading. It can also be posted in the room to become part of a print-rich environment.

Directions

1. Choose a common experience or a familiar story to use as the basis for your interactive writing. An example might be a recent field trip, a special event such as a birthday, a visitor to the class, or a favorite or recent story.

2. Tape a piece of butcher paper or tagboard on the chalkboard or bulletin board.

3. Compose a text to extend their understanding, summarize, or comment on their favorite part of the story or event.

   We have just finished a story about a special penguin. I would like to write about this story with your help. Who would like to tell me what happened in the story? Mary said that Tacky saved the other penguins. Let's write that together.

4. "Share the pen" as you write the text, drawing upon the children's and your combined knowledge of the letters and sounds that comprise each word of the sentence or sentences that you want to construct.

   Who knows what letter/sound the word, Tacky, begins with? T. That's right, Sarah. Would you come up and write a T on our paper? Great. Now what comes next? What makes the a sound that comes after the T in T-a-ck-y. Anyone? How about Annabelle? Do you know what letter begins your name? That's right, an a, and that's the same letter and sound that comes next in Tacky's name. Would you come up and write an a after the T? Now, for the next part of the word we need two letters that make one sound. Does anyone know what two letters make the /k/ sound? Okay, Jackie, I'm sure that you know because these two letters are in your name. That's right ck! Please come up and write them. Now, the end of the word Tacky sounds like the name of the letter e, but that's really not the letter that it ends with. The letter it really ends with sometimes borrows the sounds of several other letters, like i and e. Does anyone know what this letter might be? No, well then I will write it up here at the end of our word. It is a y, but in some words it sounds different. Think about the word my. It has a y at the end, but it sounds like an i. I call y a tricky letter because it can really fool us.

5. Demonstrate how to stretch out each word and listen for the sounds that comprise it. In the example above, the first word of the sentence, *Tacky,* is stretched out so that the children can hear and identify each letter/sound in the word, *T-a-ck-y.*

6. Inquire if anyone knows the letter or letters of each sound as it is heard. In the sample above, Sarah volunteers the letter and comes up to write the letter *T*.

7. Ask the volunteer to select a colored marker and write the letter or letters represented by the sound on the butcher paper.

8. Make sure that the letter/letters are correct in both form and case. If not, use corrective tape to cover it and write it correctly with the child. You might make the following statements.

    That was a great try! You wrote a lower case t, but Tacky is a special word. What kind of word is it? Yes, it's a name and we begin someone's name with what kind of letter? That's right, a capital. Let's cover this letter up and write a capital T.

9. Demonstrate where spaces go and emphasize their importance by having a child hold the space between words with his or her hand, as another child writes the letter/letters needed for the next word.

    Okay, we have Tacky written. Now the next word is saved, but before we can write it we need to let our readers know that this is a new word. How do we do that? Right, with a space. Who would like to come up and place their hand after our first word so that we can leave a good space as we write the next word? Sam, would you like to put you hand here to mark the space? Great!

10. Ask a child whose name begins with that letter/sound to come up and write it if other children seem unsure. In the example, the teacher calls on Annabelle to supply the short *a*, knowing that this child knew the first letter and sound of her name. So when no one else volunteered, the teacher drew upon the knowledge of a child who knew the information required but wasn't ready to apply it to a new situation without support.

11. Supply the letter or letters needed if no one knows them. Use a separate color and discuss the letter/letters you add, giving instruction at point of need. In the example, none of the children knew what letter represented the last sound in the word *Tacky*. The teacher used this opportunity to explain a concept that many of the children were probably not ready for. However, children whose names had *Y*s in them or who had experienced this situation might be ready to make this connection.

12. Continue in this manner until the entire text is written. Read the text over together several times, pointing to each word as it is read. Then have individual children read the text, pointing as they read. You can extend this lesson by having children illustrate the text.

13. Post the text in your room to provide children the opportunity to practice reading it during their free time.

14. Use this text during shared reading, drawing children's attention to various letters, words, punctuation, or other concepts of print.

15. To make this experience even more effective, ensure that those children not participating at the board are engaged by having them follow the procedure as described.
    - Stretch out the word being written orally with you.
    - Think of words that begin with the letter being discussed.

- Clap the parts of the word being written.
- Write the word as you stretch it out on individual whiteboards or chalkboards.
- Write the letter _____ (in the air, on their neighbor's back, on their chalkboard or whiteboard, etc.).
- Find the letter _____ on your alphabet chart, or find the letter that comes before or after.
- Make the punctuation mark that you think our sentence needs.

16. Use the reproducible that follows to guide you during your interactive writing.

17. A copy of a student's work is on page 37.

Assessment

If different colored markers are used and noted for individual children, the teacher has a record of what each child contributes. If only two colors are used, one for children and one for the teacher, instruction can be planned for those letters/sounds or concepts that the teacher needed to supply. Note: It is time to discontinue using interactive writing when most of your children can

- Control concepts of print such as left to right progression, return sweep, spacing, and letter formation,
- Stretch out an unknown word and write the sounds heard on a regular basis,
- Compose two or more sentences that represent a complete message, and
- Have some high frequency words that they can use in their writing.

Interactive Writing

1. Jointly compose a sentence or sentences to write.

2. Use different colored markers if you want to keep track of what children know and can apply.

3. "Share the pen" as you write each word, allowing the children to write the letters/sounds that they know.

4. Stretch out words so that children can hear all of the sounds in the words that need to be written.

5. Call on volunteers or children that have the needed letters/sounds in their names. Be sure they know the letters and can write them.

6. Supply any letters or other concepts of print that children do not know. Provide some quick instruction whenever you need to supply information.

7. Remember to emphasize spaces by having children mark them with their hands.

8. Jointly read the text over many times and then put it up for children to read whenever they have the opportunity.

9. Keep all children engaged by having those on the rug or at their seats respond to questions concerning the letters, words, or sentences being written.

From Susan Davis Lenski and Jerry L. Johns, *Improving Writing K–8: Strategies, Assessments, and Resources* (2nd ed.). Copyright © 2004 by Kendall/Hunt Publishing Company (1-800-247-3458, ext. 4 or 5). May be reproduced for noncommercial educational purposes within the guidelines noted on the copyright page.

My Tonsils
By
Jaclyn (Kindergartener)

When I was in the hospital I was scared. The funny gas was the scariest. I had to have funny gas because I had to go to sleep for my surgery. My surgery was for my tonsils.

After the surgery when I woke up I felt very happy because I was glad that it was over. Also, I saw mommy and daddy in my hospital room.

The room was big. The room had a bed, a TV, a remote for the bed to move, a table and a cushy chair.

My throat hurt. I had to take the liquid cherry Tylenol. It was good. After I got home my throat was a little sore.

I'm just glad that I won't have to have my tonsils out again. I don't have any!

SHARED WRITING

In shared writing, the teacher and children "share" the construction of a written text. Using a common experience, the teacher and children discuss and then compose the text. The teacher acts as scribe, modeling correct letter formation, left-to-right movement, top-to-bottom progression, punctuation, capitalization, and spelling. The connection between reading and writing is emphasized as children see the sentences given orally translated into writing. The children read the text more easily because they have the background knowledge needed and are involved in the creation of the text.

 Directions

1. Select a common experience as the basis of your text such as a field trip, a class pet, or a book read aloud. It should be something that all of the children are familiar with and can discuss. To get started you might remark as follows.

   Today we are going to write about Larry, our class guinea pig. Who has something that they would like to say about Larry?

2. Discuss the topic, generating ideas and vocabulary the children will be able to use in their dictation. This discussion allows children to organize their ideas and extend their understanding.

   What would we like to write about in our story? Could we write about the different colors that Larry has on his fur? What are some of the colors we would want to write down? Good! Larry is white, black, and brown. What else could we write about Larry?

3. Ask children to generate sentences based on the things discussed. Then take the children's ideas, combined with items discussed earlier, and jointly compose your shared writing text. (Remember that this text will be used as reading material for the children and, therefore, it should be grammatically correct.) Say each word slowly, as you write it on the chart. Then reread the sentence and have the children read it with you.

4. Continue in this manner, composing, writing and reading over what has been written. As your text grows, help children think about what has already been written and prompt them to add information where needed. An example follows.

   Let's read what we have written so far. (Point to each word as you read.) *Larry is our class pet. He is white, black, and brown. He is very soft and we like to hold him. What else have we learned about Larry? What does he like to do? Yes, he loves to eat! What kinds of things does he like to eat?*

5. Once the text is finished, read the entire story aloud and have the children read it with you. Then have the children read it without your help and then take turns reading the story individually.

6. Have children illustrate the story and display their illustrations in the classroom along with the text. Children can practice reading the text during center time or free time.

7. Use the shared writing text during shared reading to develop sight vocabulary, letter/sound recognition, concepts of print, spelling, and punctuation.

8. As a variation, write the text on sentence strips and use them with a pocket chart. During centers or free time, children can reassemble the sentences in the correct order and check them against the original text.

9. Use the following reproducible to plan your shared writing, along with any observations you make during the activity.

10. An example of shared writing can be found on page 41.

Assessment

Informally, the teacher can assess children's ability to construct grammatically correct sentences, to express themselves coherently, to include appropriate information, as well as to organize and sequence a story. Recognition of specific letters, sounds, and words can also be assessed.

Shared Writing For _____

Topic

Details

Extensions

Illustrations _____ (Individual _____ Group _____)

Reassemble story using pocket chart _____

Observations

Dear Toad,

I made a now suit fore you. It loks lik a rainbow I hop you like it i know you dnnit like your otnr suit bekuse it lokd fany

Yur friend,

Antonio

Gaining Independence

Goal ● *To help students gain independence as writers.*

BACKGROUND

Once children have been actively involved in writing, it is time to guide them toward independence. Teacher modeling and support are still important for emergent writers, but scaffolding allows them to strike out on their own with a built-in safety net. Children still need to see teachers demonstrate how writing is structured and how it functions. They need guidance and gentle nudges to help them along in their development, but they are ready to assume the responsibility of writing for themselves.

> *The goal of any writing program should be to develop effective, independent writers.*

When children begin to write on their own, it is important for teachers to remind children of the strategies and skills introduced during shared and interactive writing and to encourage them to try these new ideas in their own writing. Strategies such as using developmental spelling help emergent writers to get their ideas down on paper without the worry of getting everything just right. It invites them to use what they know and go on without fear of criticism or failure. Developmental spelling also stretches and improves children's letter-sound knowledge each time they write, and it also provides teachers with instructional ideas.

Writing aloud (Routman, 1991) is a strategy that helps young writers understand the processes involved in writing. As teachers model writing for the class, they share their thoughts and concerns aloud as they go through the stages of composition. In this way, emergent writers can observe how an experienced writer decides on a topic, translates thoughts into written words, chooses appropriate words, thinks about spelling, and so on. Teachers also invite children to participate in making decisions about their writing, giving young writers experience in problem solving as they write.

Sequencing writing in a logical fashion is a skill that emergent writers need to see modeled. Once children begin to understand how the order of ideas is important if stories are to make sense, teachers can have children participate in sequencing activities. In this way, children are carefully guided to think about sequencing in their own writing.

Has this child developed independence and confidence as a writer?

The goal of any writing program should be to develop effective, independent writers. When children have had many, many opportunities to observe writing demonstrated and to participate in activities that involve and guide them in writing, they are ready to write on their own. Independent writing is a format that allows emergent and early writers to practice new skills and strategies presented in shared and interactive writing and experiment with new ideas of their own. Independent writing also demonstrates what children know about writing to provide instructional information for the teacher.

Teaching **1** *Strategy*

DEVELOPMENTAL SPELLING

When young children begin to write, they are learning to communicate in an entirely new way. Since they do not have the spelling conventions of their older peers, they need to be encouraged to use what they know to get their ideas down on paper. Developmental spelling provides children with an easy way to do just that. It also offers teachers the opportunity to observe what children know about letters, sounds, concepts of print, sentence structure, punctuation, spacing, and spelling. This form of writing is developmental, building on what they know and helping them to expand their knowledge as they work to communicate their ideas. Knowing where students are in terms of their writing and spelling development provides direction for instruction.

Directions

1. Ask children what it is like when they want to write something and don't know how.

2. Tell them that you have an easy way for them to write what they want to write. Tell them to just write down the word the way it sounds by stretching it out and listening to the sounds. (A good visual for stretching out words is to stretch a slinky as you slowly say a word and write it.)

3. Demonstrate this process by slowly stretching out a word such as *frog* and writing the letter or letters that make each sound by explaining as follows.

   I want to write the word frog, but I'm not sure how. So I'm going to say the word slowly and write down the letters that make each sound. **F,** *that's an f, so I will write the letter f.* **F-R,** *that's an r, so I will write an r next to the f.* **F-R-O,** *that's an o, so I will write an o next to the fr.* **F-R-O-G,** *that's a g, so I will write the letter g next to the fro. That spells frog.*

4. Stretch out the word again, pointing to each letter as you say its sound. Have children confirm that these letters represent the word *frog*.

5. Model writing a sentence using this method of stretching out words and writing what you hear. An example follows.

> *I want to write the sentence The frog sat on a log. Let's see, I know the word the so I will write that first. We just wrote the word frog, so I can write that word, too. Now I need sat. S—A—T. Who knows what I should write for the first sound? Yes, an s is the first letter in sat. Now let's listen for the next sound, S-A-T. That is an a (write it). S-A-**T**, that is a t (write it). Have we written sat? Let's see S-A-T. Yes, I think that says sat. Now we need the word on. **O-N**. What do you hear? Yes, an o and then an n. Good! Let's read our sentence to see what we need, The frog sat on . . . What's next? Yes, we need the word a. How do you think we write that? Just the way it sounds, good! So let's write a and read our sentence, The frog sat on a . . . What do we need now? Yes, we need the word log. Let's stretch it out and write what we hear, **L-O-G**. What is the first letter? Yes, an l (write it). Now listen to the next sound L-**O**-G. What should I write next? Yes, an o makes that sound (write it). Now listen, L-O-**G**. What should I write? Yes, a g. Do we have all the sounds we need to write for log, L-O-G? Did we do it? Let's read the whole sentence, The frog sat on a log. What do we need at the end of our sentence? Good, a period. Now our sentence is complete.*

6. Have children practice using this method to write a caption to a picture or a journal entry.

Budr Flizs
(butterflies)

7. Provide a supportive environment that allows children to take risks. As they write, offer assistance with stretching out words but do not spell them. Encourage children to do their best and praise them for their approximations.

8. Provide many opportunities for children to write and use developmental spelling on a daily basis. Be sure to be available to support and encourage them as they write.

9. Use the following reproducible to help children stretch out words.

10. An example of a child's writing illustrating developmental spelling can be found on page 46.

Assessment

Keeping samples of children's writing from the beginning of the year provides an ongoing record of their progress. Note any new information on their letter/sound recognition, concepts of print, punctuation, spacing, and spelling with each new piece of writing. This provides information on their development as well as a guide for instruction.

SpinAndSpell

www.spinandspell.com/

This site offers an animated spelling game for children ages 4–8.

Stretching Out Words

1. Show a slinky and slowly stretch it out.

2. Now say a word like *cat* slowly, stretching out each sound as you stretch out the slinky (*C-A-T*).

3. Have children tell you what letters they hear as you stretch out *cat*.

4. Write the letters suggested on the chalkboard.

5. Point to each letter as you say its sound. Then blend the sounds together, saying the word. For example, point and say each sound in *c-a-t*, then say *cat*.

6. Ask children to confirm that the word is spelled the way it sounds.

7. Have children practice writing words at their seats as you stretch them out slowly. Have volunteers spell each word for the class and discuss the different ways the word was spelled.

8. Then give the children several words to stretch out and write on their own. Compare spellings by having volunteers tell the class how they spelled each word.

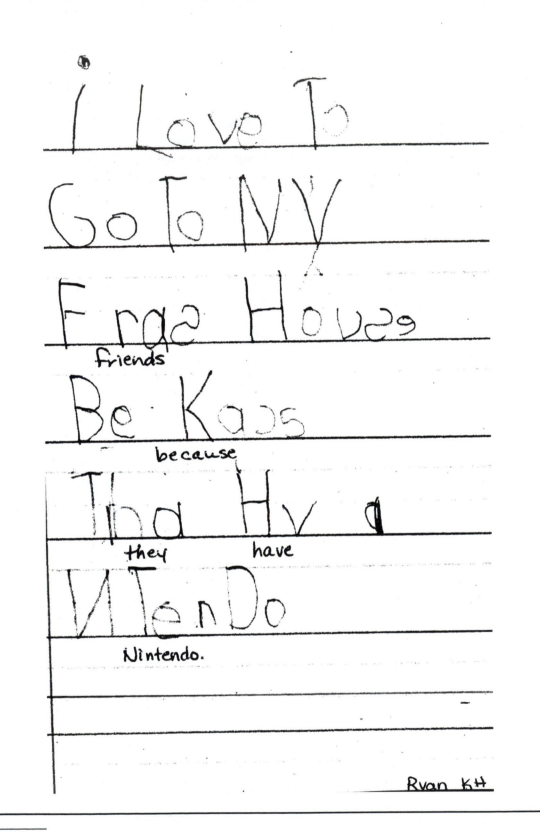

i Love To
Go To MY
Frns Houss
friends
Be Kaus
because
Tha Hv
they   have
VITenDo
Nintendo.

Ryan KH

Teaching Strategy _____

WRITING ALOUD

Regie Routman (1991) aptly calls this think-aloud strategy "writing aloud." Writing aloud provides a vivid model of the thought processes involved in writing. Here the teacher can demonstrate how thoughts can be translated into writing, step by step. This step-by-step thinking aloud clearly demonstrates how a writer goes from the initial thinking and composing stages into actual writing. Children not only see and hear how this process works but also participate in some of the decisions, developing a better understanding of the writing process as well as the problem solving related to writing, such as revising and editing.

Directions

1. Choose an interesting story or personal anecdote, one to which children will be able to relate. Tell your story orally and then discuss with the class what you should write and the order in which you should write it.

   I have just told you about the time that my husband brought home a dog that no one wanted and how our own dog reacted. That was a long story, and I don't think that I want to write all of that, so I need to decide what I want to write. It needs to be long enough to help a reader understand just what happened, but not too long.

2. Ask children for input as you begin composing your story.

   How should I begin my story? What would be a good way to catch the reader's attention? Should I first talk about the dog my husband brought home or about my own dog? I think that the reader needs to know a little about my dog before I write about anything else. What should I say that would help a reader picture what my dog is like?

3. Begin writing once your story has been discussed and children have helped you decide what to include and in what order it should be written. As you write, ask for help with spelling, capitalization, punctuation, and various concepts of print.

   How should I start my first sentence? Does anyone remember what you should do when you first begin a story? Yes, I need to begin my sentence with a capital letter, but I also need to do something else. Yes, I need to indent. I need to push in the first line three fingers and then begin my first sentence. After that I can come all the way out to the edge with my sentences.

4. Think aloud about any strategies that you want to bring to children's attention, as in the following example.

   I'm not quite sure how to spell the word nosey, but that's what I want to say about my dog. So I will write the word the way that I think it sounds and circle it to remind me to check it later. This way I can keep writing and don't have to worry about whether I spelled it right or not. I know that I can come back once I'm finished and look up the circled words that I was not sure about.

5. Purposely include errors that your children should be able to catch. Reread often, asking children if what you have written **makes sense** and **looks right**. Remember to have children explain "why" whenever they suggest a correction.

Let's read over what I've written.

> *I have a dog who doesn't know she's a dog she thinks she is a person and that she's in charge she is very bossy and very nosey.*

Does my story make sense? Does it look right? No? Why not? I did forget to put a capital letter on she. Good! Why do I need to put one there? Yes, it is the beginning of the sentence and I need to let my readers know that by putting a capital letter on the first word. Anything else? Oh yes, I need a punctuation mark at the end of my second sentence. Why? Good! It tells my readers that my sentence is over. I think I will use an exclamation mark here because I want my readers to know that sentence should be emphasized as they read.

6. Review the sequence of the story as you write. Ask children if the story makes sense in the order written. Discuss how important it is to put things in the right order so that a reader can understand just how things happened.

I have written about my dog so that my readers will understand why she treated the new dog the way she did. Now what should I write? What would make sense? Can I write about how she treated the other dog now? No, you're right. First, I need to tell the reader why my husband brought the other dog home and what that dog was like. That way the reader will better understand why things happened the way they did.

7. Once the story is finished, ask children for a good way to end the story. Discuss in what ways writers let us know that the story is over.

8. Read the whole story aloud. Ask children if the story gives a clear "mind picture" of what the dogs were like and what really happened. Explain that adding details or more information helps readers get a better picture in their mind.

Let's read my story.

> *I have a dog who doesn't know she's a dog. She thinks she is a person and that she's in charge! She is very bossy and very nosey. She knows everything that goes on inside and outside our house. No one comes near unless she lets him or her. One day my husband brought home another dog. My dog was not happy having another dog in the house and kept him cornered in the kitchen all day.*

Have I told the story in a way that helps a reader "see" just what happened, or could I explain it a little better? What else could I say about my husband bringing home the new dog? Yes, I could explain why he brought the dog home. The owner couldn't keep him anymore and my husband didn't want the dog to go to the dog pound. So he brought him home. Where would I add those two sentences? Do they help the reader understand the situation better? Good. What else could I add? Do you think I need to tell more about the other dog?

9. Add details suggested and then reread the story. Ask if any words were forgotten or if words were put in that didn't need to be there. Then read the story over and, together, check for problems with spelling, capitalization, punctuation, and so on.

*Now that I have added some information to help my readers get a better picture of what happened that day, I need to be sure that I haven't forgotten any words, capital letters, periods, or misspelled words. Let's read the story again to see if it sounds right and looks right. Tom is not quite sure of my spelling of the word scared, so let's circle that word. Who would like to look it up in the dictionary for me? Anything else? Mary thinks I need to add a word to my last sentence, The great dog was so scared that he stayed in the kitchen the whole day. What word did I forget? Yes, I need to add the word big to make it sound right. Let's read it again, The great **big** dog was so scared that he stayed in the kitchen the whole day. That sounds better!*

10. Discuss an appropriate title for your piece. Remind children that a title should give the reader an idea of what the story is about.

What would be a good title for my story? I need to think about what my story is really about. Who knows? Yes, it is about my little dog bossing around a great big dog. What title would give a reader an idea about my story? The Bossy Dog. That's a great title.

11. Ask children to think about the story overnight. Tell them that sometimes it helps to put your writing away and then come back to it at another time. That way you can think about what you have written and perhaps think of something you might like to change. Reread the story the next day and ask for any additional suggestions that the children might have. Make any changes that you or the class feel would improve your piece.

12. Display the story in the room to use for center time or for children to read during their free time. Return to the story during shared reading or shared writing to discuss concepts of print, sequencing, word study, revising, editing, and so on.

13. Use the following reproducible to guide you as you conduct your write-aloud activity.

Assessment

The discussions resulting from "writing aloud" provide a rich source of information about where children are in their writing development. Note any evidence of growth demonstrated by particular children. For example, a quiet child may begin to feel more comfortable during these group discussions and offer ideas or comments for the first time. Another child might bring up a concept, such as quotations, that they may have seen in their reading but may not have been modeled during prior writing activities. Suggestions offered by children illustrate what they notice and might apply in their own writing. Ideas to focus on during subsequent lessons can also be determined during this activity.

Writing Aloud

1. Tell an interesting story.

2. Discuss the story and plan what to write.

3. Begin putting ideas down on paper.

4. Involve children in the process, asking for input on sequence, description, capitalization, spelling, punctuation, and so on.

5. Circle any words that you and the children are unsure how to spell as you write.

6. Read over the story to be sure that it makes sense and is interesting. Make changes suggested.

7. Check for spelling, capitalization, and punctuation.

8. Decide on a title.

9. Leave the story overnight and return to it the next day to see if there are any other changes needed.

10. Post the story in the room. Use it for centers, free time, and shared reading and writing.

11. Note any evidence of growth demonstrated by individual children or concepts mastered by the class as a whole for future lessons.

Teaching Strategy 3

STORY SEQUENCING

Sequencing is an important component in writing. Young writers need to understand that what they write needs to be in a particular order to make sense. Demonstrating a logical order or progression visually helps to make this concept easier for emergent writers to understand. When pictures are arranged in a logical order, a story can evolve that will make sense. When pictures are arranged in a nonsequential order, a story told in this way would not make sense. This strategy uses visual prompts to clearly demonstrate the need to follow a logical progression when writing.

Directions

1. Using packaged sequencing cards or teacher-made pictures, select three cards that will either tell a story or show the order in which something is done. Be sure pictures are large enough so they can be seen by the entire class.

2. Put magnets on the back of the cards if you have a magnetized chalkboard or use a pocket chart to display the cards. Be sure that the order in which you place the cards is not the correct one.

3. Ask the children to carefully observe the cards and then tell you something about them. You might say something similar to the following example.

   I have some pictures that I would like to use to tell a story. What do you think of my story?

4. Because the pictures are out of order, children should remark that your story doesn't make sense in the order you have it arranged. Go over the order together and discuss how a story would sound using the pictures in this order.

   If I used these pictures to tell a story, how would the story sound? Let's try it. The little boy got dressed, then he woke up, and finally he went to school. Does that make sense? No, it doesn't. How should this story be told?

5. Have children help you to rearrange the pictures in sequential order. Then ask them to help you tell the story again.

   Now that we have put the pictures in a different order, do you think my story will make more sense? Let's see. First the little boy woke up. Next he got dressed. Then he went to school. Does my story make more sense now? Why?

6. Discuss the fact that initially the pictures did not tell the story correctly because the things the little boy did were not in the right order. Emphasize that most things need to happen in a certain order and have children offer other examples. Discuss the fact that stories also need to be written in a certain order to make sense.

7. Tell the children that you would like to write your story now that the pictures make sense. Have children help you compose a sentence for each picture. An example follows.

Sam woke up early in the morning.

Then Sam got his clothes out and got dressed.

When Sam was ready, he got his book bag and walked to school.

8. Point to the words as you have children read the story. Then take away the pictures and have children read the story again to see if it makes sense. Then rearrange the sentences incorrectly and read the story. Discuss how this changes the story and doesn't make sense.

9. Discuss your use of transition words to show order in the story. Ask children to brainstorm other words that might also express order. Start a chart in your room with these ideas and refer to it often. Throughout the year, add to the chart when children come up with new ways to show order.

10. Write your story on chart paper and hang it in the room for children to read. If you write it on sentence strips, you can use them, along with the sequencing pictures, as an independent activity.

11. Model this activity numerous times with different sets of pictures. Work as a class to sequence the pictures and then compose the sentences. When children have a firm grasp on this activity, you can help them assume more control. Sequence the pictures as a class and then assign small groups of children to compose the sentences. When you begin this phase, have each group write a sentence for one of the pictures and then use the sentences from all the groups to compose the story. Later, you can have groups write a sentence for each of the pictures to compose their own stories. As the year progresses, have each child write sentences independently to go with the pictures.

12. As an independent activity, photocopy the pictures used for sequencing and distribute them to children. Duplicate the following page and have children cut out the pictures and paste them in order. Then have children compose their own story in the spaces provided.

13. Later in the year increase the number of pictures that you sequence to challenge children.

14. An example of a piece of student's writing follows on page 55.

Assessment

This activity allows the teacher to observe children as they work through the logical order of a story. As children write sentences, observe and assess their sentence structure, use of transitions, and the match between picture and text.

Story Sequencing Activity

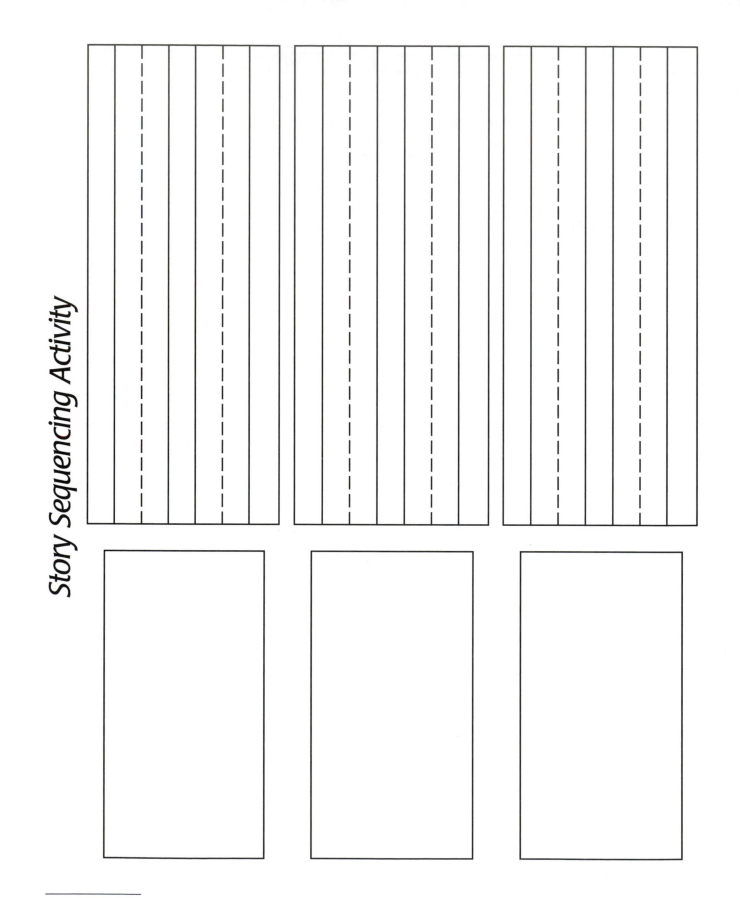

Two Twin Babies

By
Morgan
(second grader)

Once there were two twin babies. I had to babysit them. They went to my bookbag and scattered all my papers. I went to check on them. I said, "No, babies, no!" Next they went to my room. They tried to get my jewelry. But they couldn't get it so they got a chair and they got the jewelry. They started to chew on it. So I said, "No, babies, no!" So they went to my coat and they started to chew on it. I said, "No, babies, no!" So they stopped. So I went to lay down. I turned on the T.V. When they heard the T.V. they came out to watch it with me. I wanted to watch Cartoon Network. They wanted to watch the Di Di Da Da show. So we watched the Di Di Da Da show. The doorbell rang. It was the mom. I was so glad after that. I turned on the Cartoon Network, but it was over!

Independent writing can reveal what children know about the writing process and conventions and provide instructional direction to move them along in their development. It encourages children to practice the skills and strategies presented during such activities as interactive and shared writing and provides a risk-free environment for children to "give it a try." When independent writing is used after shared and/or interactive writing, the teacher can draw attention to the concepts just demonstrated and encourage children to do the same things when they write. Conferencing with children during this activity can provide support, encouragement, and guidance.

Directions

1. Provide a journal, folder, or notebook for children to use for their independent writing. A folder of writing provides evidence of children's progress during the year.

2. Review the concepts and skills used during your interactive or shared writing activity, such as stretching out words and writing the sounds they hear, spacing, punctuation, or capitalization. Remind children that they can do these same things when they write.

3. Allow early kindergarten children to write for 5 to 10 minutes. Expand this time frame throughout the year as you see children staying engaged for longer periods of time. Beginning first graders should begin writing for 10 to 15 minutes. Increase the time as needed.

4. Confer with individual children during the writing time. Be positive! Remember that when children are allowed to try out new strategies or skills without fear of criticism, they are more willing to continue to expend effort and remain engaged.

5. Have the child read his or her message to you. Provide positive feedback on the message to emphasize that meaning is the most important aspect of writing. You might say something like the following example.

    That was great! I know just what happened to you when you went to the dentist.

6. Praise the child for all of the emergent writing behaviors attempted.

    I really like the way you spelled dentist. I can read it because you listened to the sounds and wrote just what you heard.

7. Ask the child if there was anything that he or she had difficulty with or was confused about. Discuss these areas of concern or confusion.

    I can see why the word drill might be difficult to spell. The beginning sounds can sometimes be confusing. Let's listen to some other words that begin like drill and see if we can figure out how it might be spelled.

8. Choose one teaching point to discuss if no concerns or confusions were addressed. Be sure that the teaching point is one that the child is ready for or that was previously demonstrated during other writing activities.

> *Do you remember when we wrote about Tacky? We had trouble with the ending of his name. The word candy is another word that ends with that same letter and sound. Do you remember what that letter was? Why don't you go over to our chart and see if you can find Tacky's name. Yes, it ends with a y. I told you a y sometimes sounds like an e. The word candy ends with a y just like Tacky.*

9. Provide time each day for independent writing. For early kindergarten, provide unlined paper with a large space for illustration. For end of kindergarten and first grade, add top and bottom lines, and a dotted middle line.

10. Use the following reproducible as journal pages for emergent writers in kindergarten or early first grade.

11. An example of a piece of student's writing follows on page 59.

Assessment

Independent writing can provide information about the child's understanding of the function of writing and his or her knowledge of the writing process. The child's use of conventions such as spacing, directionality, spelling, and punctuation can also be assessed. Looking back at the independent writing of the child from the beginning of the year can provide the teacher with important information on growth and development and the child with a sense of accomplishment.

Name _____

One day I went
into my attic
and I steped
on a nail. I
had to get a
bandage and an
elastic wrap.
And I am glad
that I am ok.

Alexis 2nd

Developing Writers

Goal • *To help students grow and develop as writers.*

Section 2.4

BACKGROUND

When children become independent writers, it is time for them to begin to learn more about the craft of writing. Modeling and scaffolding continue to play an important role in working with developing writers. Children must hear their teachers write aloud and see them model new strategies and skills to understand how writers think and work.

Exploring new writing genres helps children to expand their thinking in terms of topics and to develop as writers. Children are naturally curious about the world around them, and many will surprise us with their level of knowledge. Introducing young children to informational writing can motivate and serve to gently move them into beginning research. Informal writing may also be a new writing genre for children. This type of writing flows naturally from science or social studies units conducted throughout the year. For developing writers, informational writing can be used to help assess their understanding of content area concepts or to encourage them to expand their understanding. For emergent writers, it can be as easy as "Tell me what you know about _____."

When developing writers begin to really reflect and think about their writing, they are often frustrated because they are unable to express themselves in a satisfactory way. This is when teachers have that "teachable moment" and can provide children with strategies and skills that will ease their dissatisfaction and move them along in their development as writers. Strategies such as using good leads and endings assist young writers in improving the effectiveness of their writing.

Adding details can also resolve some of the dissatisfaction that children often experi-

> *Audience is an important concept to all writers.*

Children often surprise us with their level of knowledge.

ence with writing. When children want to have their audience understand just what happened at their birthday party or how they helped to find their lost dog, providing assistance in adding detail can help young writers to convey their message in a more satisfactory way. Even emergent writers can begin this process when they add details to their drawings to help their readers better understand what they want to convey.

Audience is an important concept to all writers, and young children should become familiar with writing for specific audiences as soon as they begin to write. They need to understand the differences between writing for themselves, classmates, parents, or those outside of the school or family. Book making is one way to address the issue of audience. When children create a book, they are doing so to present their writing to a specific audience. Different types of books and bindings are naturally geared to different audiences. Small books can be created for personal use or to be shared with family. Larger books can be shared with classmates. More durable books can be added to the classroom library to share with classmates and visitors.

By providing developing writers with the strategies and skills that they need when they need them, we are teaching within Vygotsky's (1962) zone of proximal development. In other words, we are working at the cutting edge of their learning. This zone is where the most effective learning takes place. When teachers know children and provide them with the instruction that they need at the moment they need it, they are providing the most effective and powerful instruction possible.

⌨ *Erin's Children's Poetry Page*

www.cswnet.com/~erin/child.htm

This site allows students to view and read many different poems, ballads, and nursery rhymes.

Teaching **1** *Strategy*
Section 2.4
INFORMATIONAL WRITING

Children are naturally curious about the world around them, and informational writing can capitalize on this curiosity. Graves (1983) suggests that every child is an expert on some topic or can become an expert. Teachers can easily move from language-experience stories and shared writing activities to inviting children to write their own informational pieces. Newkirk (1989) states that "as long as children have access to a variety of non-narrative forms, they will adopt them, just as they adopt other forms of adult behavior" (p. 24). Modeling informational writing is a powerful way to extend and clarify various purposes of writing.

📑 Directions

1. Reread several shared writing pieces that you have completed together. Discuss the idea that these are all based on something real or something that actually happened. Discuss the difference between fact and fiction. Provide several fictional examples (such as talking furniture) versus real things (such as grass, trees, and so on).

2. Using a current need in the classroom or a unit of study or theme you are currently exploring, model how to draw on your knowledge to write an informational piece. Explain to the class that they will be writing about all the things they have learned about a current unit of study (for example, the sun). With input from the children, make a list of the things that you have learned about the sun. You might begin your discussion as described below.

> We have been learning about the sun and working hard to become experts about it. Today we are going to write about what we have learned. We call this a report, because it reports or tells our readers what we know about something. Let's make a list of all of the facts that we know about the sun.

3. Once you have generated your list, talk about each item and decide if you have enough information about each fact to include it in your report. Then decide on a logical sequence in which to write them.

4. Begin writing with child input and discussion.

5. Tell children that once their writing is complete they should read their report and think about any additional information that should be included or anything that should be removed. Then have students make their revisions by using the ideas that follow.
   - Decide if there is enough information to write about each fact.
   - Decide the order of the facts.
   - Write the report.
   - Add an illustration to the report.

6. Encourage children to use this same process to write a report of their own. You might explain as follows.

> We have just written a report about the sun. Now I want you to write one of your own. Remember what we did? We made a list of facts we knew about the sun and then decided in what order to write them. Once we had the order, we began to write our report. Take out a piece of paper and start a list of what you know about the sun. Share your list with a friend. Decide in what order to write about what you have listed. If you need help, you can ask your neighbor or raise your hand. Then begin your report. Don't forget to add illustrations.

7. Circulate around the room, answering questions or providing assistance. Many times children are unaware of how much they know about a topic. Asking a few questions about the topic usually helps them to realize the extent of their knowledge.

8. This first informational piece by children might look very much like the piece you wrote together. If this occurs, encourage children to add information that is not included in the modeled piece. The piece written together is a positive model and one that you want children to emulate. Just encourage them to make it their own by adding knowledge that might not have been included in the original.

9. Informational writing can include many other functional forms, which also need to be modeled. The more authentic the writing, the more children will begin to understand the purpose for this type of writing. Authentic writing might include the following forms.

- Letters
- Posters
- Lists (rules, materials, food, etc.)
- Signs
- Invitations
- Questionnaires
- Notices
- Labels

- Solutions to real problems
- Notes to parents
- Directions (for centers, use of equipment, etc.)
- Charts
- Reports
- Summaries
- Recipes
- Menus

10. Even emergent writers can be asked to "tell me what you know about _____." This might initially be in the form of a drawing, with the child giving dictation. As the school year progresses, children can be encouraged to write about their drawings.

11. Model informational writing very early in the year by making labels, signs, or any of the other items listed above. Then use informational writing throughout the year across the curriculum.

12. The following reproducible can be used by children to organize and review their informational writing.

13. An informational piece written by a kindergarten student follows on page 65 and one written by a first-grade student follows on page 66.

Assessment

One of the most important connections that young writers need to make is that writing serves a purpose. Whether we are writing a letter to a friend or making a list of ingredients for our favorite recipe, writing serves to communicate. Providing models of informational writing can clarify this purpose. Having children write informational pieces can illustrate the extent to which children have made this connection.

Informational Writing

1. Write about something on which you are an expert.

2. Make a list of all of the facts you know about this topic.

3. Do you have enough information to write a report?

4. Decide in what order you will write the facts.

5. Write your report.

6. Read over your report. Then read it to a friend and discuss any information that you should include or remove.

7. Make any changes needed.

8. Add a picture to go with your report.

My report is on _____ .

_____ I have read over my report.

_____ I had a friend read over my report.

_____ I made changes needed.

_____ I made a picture to go with my report.

Said ShArks
Catch

We like fish
Said the sharks
and this is the way
We Catch them.

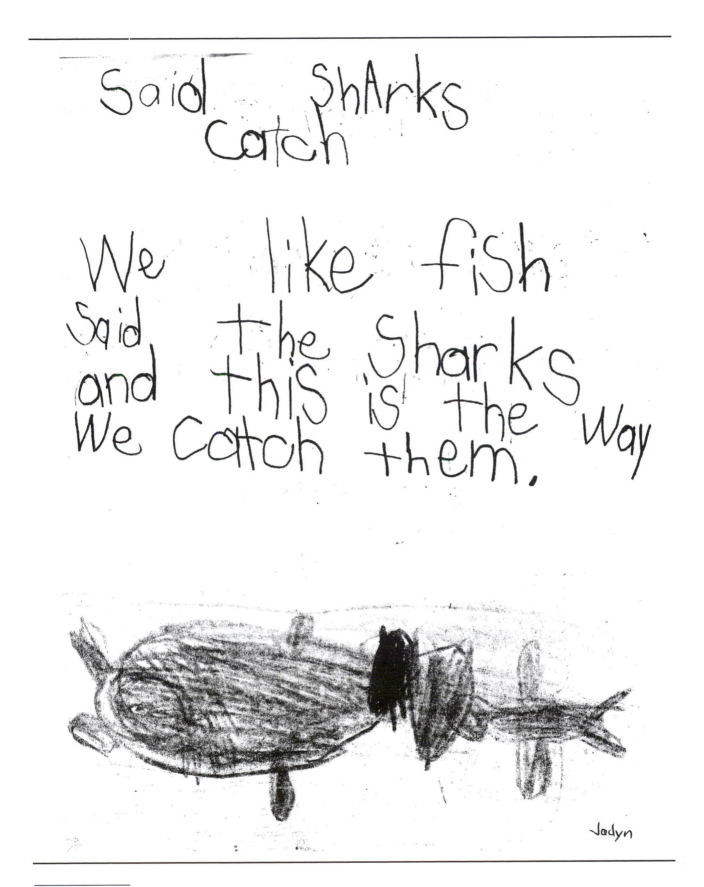

Jadyn

Wolves

By
Kayla Bouchey

When wolf pups are born they usually have two to ten pups in a litter. They weigh about one pound when they are born. When they are one month old, they can get with the rest of the pack. When the pups leave the den, they are looked after by the pack. Through playing, the pups will learn skills that will be important later in their lives.

A pack works together. There are usually two to ten wolves in a pack, but there can be up to twenty. A pack is usually a family group. A family group has a mother, father, and some pups.

The wolves in North America eat mostly moose, deer, caribou, elk, and sheep. They work together to take the animal down. After that, they let the wolf pups eat and then the older ones. The pack sometimes travels up to 100 miles for food.

Wolves are very interesting animals.

LEADS AND ENDINGS

Leads and endings may seem more appropriate for older children, but it is never too early to develop an understanding and appreciation of good leads and endings when writing. Emergent writers know when they hear a good lead or ending and can begin to experiment with them in their writing. Fletcher and Portalupi (1998) state that "teachers can help even emergent writers become aware of how a lead can strengthen a piece of writing" (p. 29). The key, at this early stage, is exposure. Children need to hear and see what good leads and endings sound and look like. They need to see the teacher modeling how to write a good lead and a good ending. When leads and endings become a common topic of discussion, children will begin to point them out as they read and begin to use them in their own writing.

Directions

1. Ask children what it means to *lead* something. Discuss the idea of a lead as something to follow, as in Follow the Leader. Explain that a lead in writing works the same way, in that it leads the reader into the story or book. If the lead is interesting, it will catch the reader's attention. If it catches the reader's attention, he or she will probably want to read the rest.

2. Explain that a lead usually consists of the first line or two of a story, although it could be longer. Select several picture books appropriate for your children that have interesting leads. Read the lead from the first book and ask children if it makes them want to read the book. Discuss the reasons why the sentence grabs their attention or makes them want to know what happens next. Two books with engaging leads are *Fly Away Home* and *The Day the Goose Got Loose*. Additional titles of books with good leads can be found on page 71.

3. Write the lead, word for word, on a chart and hang it so children can easily refer to it as they write.

4. Continue reading leads from the other books selected, discussing what makes them good leads. Add them to the chart. Repeat this process throughout the year, reading good leads and adding them to your chart whenever you find one that you think the children will enjoy.

5. Encourage children to look for good leads as they read throughout the day. When they find a lead that they think others would like to hear, have them share it with classmates. Then add it to the chart.

6. Demonstrate how to select a good lead when conducting a shared writing activity. Discuss the purpose of your piece of writing and what type of lead would work best. Try using the leads listed on your classroom chart whenever you demonstrate writing. Also, try to demonstrate a new lead whenever you feel that the children are ready. Write them on the chart.

7. Tell children that some interesting ways to write leads include the following ones.

- An interesting sentence
- An amazing fact
- A description of the setting, character, or event
- Words spoken by one of the characters
- A question
- The ending

8. Introduce endings in the same way. Help children understand that the last thing you see, do, or hear is usually what you remember. An example might be a movie that you saw where the ending was such a disappointment that it caused you to dislike the entire movie. Discuss any movies or books that you have seen or read that had disappointing endings and how they made them feel. Emphasize that a good ending to their writing is also important because a poor ending can cause readers to feel disappointed, even if they liked the rest of the story.

9. Demonstrate what a good ending sounds like by reading children's books that have strong endings. Repeat the same process that you used for leads by hanging a chart to list good endings that you and the children find. Model using good endings during shared writing or whenever you write for or with the class.

10. Tell children that some interesting ways to end a story might include

- A surprise
- Repeating the beginning of the story
- Words spoken by one of the characters
- A strong emotion.

11. Remind children throughout the year to use interesting, creative leads and good endings when they write.

12. Use the following reproducible to guide you as you introduce children to good leads and good endings.

13. An example of a student's writing that has a good lead and ending follows on page 70.

Assessment

Assess how well children understand the use of good leads and endings by what they demonstrate in their writing. Children will show you what they know. Watch to see which children are taking a risk and using some of the leads and endings on your class charts or experimenting with their own. Also note which children are more hesitant. Conference with children to commend and guide them on their attempts or nudge them to make an attempt.

Leads and Endings

1. Demonstrate only one concept during a lesson, either leads *or* endings.

2. Select several children's books that have strong leads.

3. Read the lead and discuss whether it invites the reader to continue reading and why.

4. Write the lead, word for word, on a chart that is hung for easy reference.

5. Continue reading other examples of good leads. Discuss why they are good leads and list them on your chart.

6. Encourage children to share good leads they find in their own reading. List these on the classroom chart.

7. Demonstrate using strong leads when conducting shared writing activities.

8. Encourage children to use leads from your chart in their own writing.

9. Use this same procedure to encourage the use of strong endings. For each example that is shared, discuss what makes it a good ending and why. Add each to the classroom chart on endings.

10. Repeat lessons on leads and endings throughout the school year. Discuss them whenever you read a good story or write with your class.

The Two Best Friends

By
Tiffany
(second grader)

One fine day, two friends were hanging out at the waterfall. Their names were Brooke and Kayla. They did everything together. One day it was recess. The friends were walking along. They saw a girl named Tiffany. Tiffany was alone, so the two friends walked over to Tiffany and asked, "What is the matter?" "Nobody wants to play with me," said Tiffany. "Then come and play with us," said Kayla. "Really?" said Tiffany. "Sure, come on, " said both girls. "Thank you, Brooke and Kayla." So the two friends became three best friends forever. That's the story of the two best friends who became three best friends.

The End

Children's Books

With Good Leads

 Bates, L. (1975)
Little rabbit's loose tooth
New York: Crown

 Baylor, B. (1974)
Everybody needs a rock
New York: Charles Scribner's Sons

 Borden, L. (1999)
Good luck, Mrs. K!
New York: Simon and Schuster

 Bunting, E. (1991)
Fly away home
New York: Clarion

Burningham, J. (1984)
Grandpa
New York: Crown

Carle, E. (1995)
The very lonely firefly
New York: Philomel

Carlson, N. (1994)
How to lose all your friends
New York: Penguin

 Catalanotto, P. (2001)
Emily's art
New York: Simon and Schuster

 Christelow, E. (2002)
Where's the big bad wolf?
New York: Clarion

 Kellogg, S. (1992)
The Christmas witch
New York: Dial Books for Young Readers

Lindbergh, R. (1990)
The day the goose got loose
New York: Dial

Lovell, P. (2001)
Stand tall, Molly Lou Melon
New York: Scholastic

 McDonald, M. (1999)
The night iguana left home
New York: D K Publishing

McPhail, D. (1997)
Edward and the pirates
New York: Little, Brown

O'Neill, A. (2002)
The recess queen
New York: Scholastic

Park, B. (2001)
Junie B., first grader (at last!)
New York: Random House

Parker, N. W. (1992)
Working frog
New York: Greenwillow

Sendak, M. (1963)
Where the wild things are
New York: Scholastic

Van Allsburg, C. (1985)
The polar express
Boston: Houghton Mifflin

Viorst, J. (1972)
Alexander and the terrible, horrible, no good, very bad day
New York: Simon and Schuster

Ward, C. (1988)
Cookie's week
New York: G. P. Putnam's Sons

Wood, A. (1984)
The napping house
New York: Harcourt, Brace, Jovanovich

With Good Endings

Allard, H. (1977)
Miss Nelson is missing!
Boston: Houghton Mifflin

Burleigh, R. (1999)
Flight: The journey of Charles Lindbergh
New York: Putnam

Cronin, D. (2000)
Click, clack, moo: Cow's that type
New York: Simon and Schuster

De Paola, T. (1978)
The popcorn book
New York: Holiday House

Hutchins, P. (1976)
Don't forget the bacon
New York: Greenwillow

Hutchins, P. (1986)
The doorbell rang
New York: Scholastic

Littledale, F. (1978)
The snow child
New York: Scholastic.

Munsch, R. N. (1965)
Thomas' snowsuit
Toronto, Canada: Annick

Munsch, R. N. (1980)
The paper bag princess
Toronto, Canada: Annick

Numeroff, L. (2002)
If you take a mouse to school
New York: Scholastic

Polacco, P. (1998)
Thank you, Mr. Falker
New York: Philomel

Small, D. (1985)
Imogene's antlers
New York: Crown

Tresselt, A. (1964)
The mitten
New York: Lothop, Lee, & Shepard

Van Allsburg, C. (1985)
The polar express
Boston: Houghton Mifflin

Viorst, J. (1972)
Alexander and the terrible, horrible, no good, very bad day
New York: Simon and Schuster

Wood, A. (1984)
The napping house
New York: Harcourt, Brace, Jovanovich

It is common for emergent writers at the beginning of kindergarten to draw a picture and then, perhaps, to write something. Toward the end of kindergarten and into first grade, children may begin to write their message first and then add a drawing to illustrate it (Graves, 1983). Whether a child's story is told in the drawing alone or in a combination that includes scribbling, mock letters, invented spelling or conventional spelling, drawings are an important part of emergent writing. Therefore, drawings are an excellent way to demonstrate how adding detail to a story aids the reader in understanding the writing. Through conferences and minilessons, young writers learn to self-assess and add information which will encourage them to use words to enrich their message as their writing develops. However, it is important that "teachers recognize that their responsibility is to support the child's own constructions and inventions, not to instruct the child in what to write and how to write it" (Raines & Canady, 1990, p. 83). Teachers of emergent writers need to remember that a gentle nudge is more effective in a child's writing development than attempting to correct his or her writing to perfection.

Directions

1. During individual conferences, ask children to tell you about the story they have written. Encourage them to explain any part of their story that seems unclear.

2. Rephrase what the child said.

3. Discuss certain details from the story and ask where it shows or tells that information. Children may add to their drawings as they discuss details, or you may suggest that they add something to their drawings that would help you to understand the story better, as in the following example.

   You told me in your story that you went to the airport with your family to pick up your grandma. What can you add that will help me to know that you are at the airport? Good, you could add airplanes to your picture. Is there anything else that you would like to add? Yes, the building that you waited in would be good. That's called a terminal. Now I can tell exactly where you were!

4. After children have added one or two details, reflect on what was accomplished. Remind them that they reread their writing and looked at the drawing to see if they had included enough detail to help the reader understand the story.

   What did you just do to make your writing better? You read what you had written and looked at your drawing. Then you decided to add a few things to your drawing. This helped me to understand exactly what happened in your story. When you add details to your writing or your drawing, you are making sure that you have given the reader enough information to understand your story better.

5. Observation may show that a group of children or even the entire class is ready for this strategy. Modify the lesson above by doing a "write aloud" and following a similar procedure.

6. Tell a story and then write it, talking about what you are thinking and doing as you write. Illustrate your story. Reread your story with the children, and look carefully at your illustration. Discuss whether you have given your reader enough information, either in your writing or in your illustration. Add any information that the group feels is needed.

7. Early in the year, limit your lesson to adding details to your drawing. Later, expand your lesson to include adding details to your writing.

8. A variation for developing writers would be to add words or phrases to a particular sentence to create a more detailed or descriptive one. Start with a sentence from a book or one of your own pieces of writing to demonstrate how this process can help create a clearer mental picture or provide more information. Look at the parts of the sentence, such as the subject, verb, or any prepositional phrases. Demonstrate how to add words or phrases that provide more detail or description to the various parts of the sentence. Compare the original sentence with the rewritten one and discuss which one is more effective.

9. Repeat this lesson, having the children add words or phrases to improve a sentence.

10. Challenge children to write a sentence and then add some interesting words or phrases to it. Have them share with a friend or with the class. Remind children that they can add interesting words or phrases whenever they write.

11. Repeat these lessons throughout the year, encouraging children to add details to their own writings/drawings.

12. Use the following reproducible to record when children include details in their writing.

13. An example of a student's piece of writing follows on page 77.

Note

Many emergent writers are still uncertain about the relationship between writing and drawing. Although they may be able to identify the difference in a text or in the writing of another, when they compose they will sometimes combine or confuse the two. Teachers of emergent writers must be sensitive to this possible confusion and allow them to experiment with their own writing until the differences become clear.

Assessment

Adding details is an important strategy in children's development as writers. Observing children's writing provides information on those ready and willing to attempt to add details independently and those who need more instruction or some gentle nudging.

Class Record for Adding Detail

Observations for _____

Date

Children's Names	Adds Detail	Does Not Add Detail

The Case of the Missing Basketball

By
Drew Foster

One day Sean bought a basketball at the sports' department at K-Mart. He set it down to look at a T-shirt. All of a sudden, Sean looked down and his basketball was gone! So Sean called Drew to help him find it. They decided to go to Michael's house to see if he knew where the ball was because Sean had seen him while he was in K-Mart. Michael said that he saw Tyler on his bike with a basketball. So Sean and Drew went over to Tyler's house and asked him if he had Sean's basketball. He said that he had found one in the shoe department at K-Mart, but he didn't know if it was Sean's. Sean looked at the basketball and saw Michael Jordan's sign on it. Then Sean knew that it was his. Drew went home and Sean went back to K-Mart to get his T-shirt.

Making books that children can read and keep is a necessity in the classroom. There are many writings completed within the classroom that teachers will want to save and use as learning materials. Innovations, language-experience stories, shared writing pieces, as well as stories written by individual children can all become a part of the classroom library or a child's personal library when made into a book. There are many types of books and ways to bind them depending on how they will be used. A little book for an individual child requires only folding and stapling to become a treasure to read and reread, both at school and at home. For books that will be used extensively in the classroom, a more durable binding becomes necessary.

Directions for Individual Books

Standard Book—This type of book can be used to record writing for individual children to keep. You can create as many pages for the book as you need, simply by adding more paper.

1. Take a rectangular sheet of blank paper and fold it widthwise (known as a hamburger fold). The paper can be any size that meets your needs.

2. Continue to add paper and fold until you have the number of pages required. Remember that the front and back of each page created can be used for text and illustrations.

3. To add a cover, simply use a piece of card stock or construction paper. Cut to size and fold in a hamburger fold. Have the child add a title and illustrate the cover, if desired. The cover can be laminated to add durability.

4. Place the folded papers inside the cover.

5. Open all of the pages. Use a long-arm stapler, if available, and staple three times from the outside along the fold. If a standard stapler is used, keep the book closed and staple from the outside as close to the fold as possible.

6. Add text and illustrations to each page.

Guess Who?—This book can be used for informational writing, a response to literature, a sequencing activity, and much more.

1. Fold an 8" × 11" piece of paper lengthwise (known as a hot dog fold).

2. Fold it again, this time in a hamburger fold.

3. Crease this fold well.

4. Fold the paper in another hamburger fold and crease.

5. Open the hamburger folds, leaving only the hot dog fold still in place.

6. Holding the fold at the top, cut up the **front side** on the fold lines.

7. Write a word, phrase, question or statement on each "door" created.

8. Have children write or draw their answers or steps beneath each door.

Flip Book—This book is very versatile and can be adapted to use with any curricular area.

1. Using any sized rectangular paper, fold it evenly in a hamburger fold.

2. Take a second piece and again fold it in a hamburger fold. However, this time make the fold off center so that when folded about 1" of the paper sticks out at the bottom.

3. Place this piece **over** the piece folded evenly.

4. Continue to fold pieces, having each piece folded a little more unevenly and put each, in turn, over the others. This creates a stairstep effect. These pages are easily turned by little hands and can have words or illustrations added to the edges that extend out.

5. Use a long-arm stapler, open the folded pieces, and staple several times from the outside.

6. When using a standard stapler, keep pages folded and staple from the outside as close to the fold as possible. If the pages are small enough, you can loosely roll the pages on one side of the fold and slide them into the stapler to staple with the book open.

Accordion Book—This book can be used as an individual book or as a class book, depending on the materials used. It is ideal to use when working on sequencing.

1. Use a legal sized piece of paper.

2. Fold the paper in a hot dog fold.

3. Holding the fold at the top, fold the paper in a hamburger fold.

4. Keeping the hot dog fold at the top, fold the paper in another hamburger fold. Crease well.

5. Open the last hamburger fold. You should have one fold line visible.

6. Hold the paper with the hot dog fold still at the top and the first hamburger fold in your left hand.

7. Take the right-hand corner of the top piece and fold it **toward** you along the visible fold.

8. Take the right-hand corner of the bottom piece and fold it **away** from you along the visible fold. Crease well.

9. Open to reveal a four panel accordion book.

10. Add text and illustrations to each panel, starting on one side and continuing on the back.

Directions for Classroom Books

Book Binding—A more durable, hardcover binding (Graves 1983; Raines & Canady, 1990) is great for books that will be used extensively in the classroom. It can be used both for individual-sized books or Big Books.

1. Cut two pieces of heavy cardboard slightly larger than the paper used for the pages of the book.

2. Lay the two pieces of cardboard side by side.

3. Using wide masking tape, tape the two pieces of cardboard together, leaving a space of about ½ inch between them.

4. Using decorative contact paper, cut a piece that extends about one to two inches beyond the attached cardboard pieces when lying open. If fabric is preferred, use thinned white glue to attach to the cardboard.

5. Fold the four corners over first and then fold in the sides of the contact paper or fabric and secure.

6. Measure and cut a piece of contact paper or fabric to cover the inside and secure the sides folded in.

7. Staple the pages of the book along the left-hand side. Place the stapled edge in the center of the open cover. Attach the pages to the cover using two strips of contact paper or fabric, one in front and one in back.

Accordion Book—As with the smaller accordion book, this type of book is great for sequencing but lends itself to many other uses. It can easily be used as a story starter in the writing center by adding illustrations without text. Children then write the text to accompany the pictures.

1. Use a long piece of tagboard (12" × 18" or longer).

2. Fold the paper in a hamburger fold. Crease.

3. Fold the paper in another hamburger fold. Crease well.

4. Open the last hamburger fold. You should have one fold line visible.

5. Hold the paper with the first hamburger fold in your left hand.

6. Take the right-hand corner of the top piece and fold it **toward** you along the visible fold.

7. Take the right-hand corner of the bottom piece and fold it **away** from you along the visible fold. Crease well.

8. Open to reveal a four piece accordion book.

9. Add text and illustrations to each panel, starting on one side and continuing on the back.

10. If you require more sections, use a longer piece of tagboard and continue to add hamburger folds until you have the desired number of panels.

Laminated Books—If you have access to a laminating machine, this can be a low-cost way to create durable classroom books, both large and small. Laminated books can be used in the classroom library, for shared reading when enlarged, and they can be sent home to share with parents.

1. Using a story created by the class, small group, or individual child, write the text on large 12" × 18" white construction paper. Have children illustrate each page.

2. Create a title page and have the "authors and illustrators" sign their names. This can be decorated, if desired.

3. Using the same paper, create a cover by writing the title and having children decorate it. Add the class name as the authors, for example "Mrs. Day's First Grade," and then the date. A back cover can also be decorated.

4. A page for parents' comments can be added at the back of the book but should not be laminated.

5. Laminate the front and back covers. For added durability, you can also laminate the pages of the book.

6. Punch holes in each sheet along the left side. Space the holes evenly, about one to two inches apart. Be sure the holes line up on each page by using the previous page as a guide.

7. Using strong yarn or string and a large craft needle, begin sewing a zigzag stitch down the side of the book.

8. At the bottom, repeat the process going up. Tie the ends in a bow at the top. This should create a strong crisscrossed binding that can easily be replaced, if necessary.

9. Add a library pocket to the inside of the front cover and place in your classroom library.

10. Create enough classroom books so each child can take one home at the end of the year, if possible.

Assessing Emergent and Developing Writers

Goal ● *To informally assess emergent and developing writers.*

BACKGROUND

Ongoing assessment is an integral part of literacy instruction. Through assessment, teachers learn about their children and the effectiveness of their instruction. Assessment can be part of a cycle that continually informs and guides instruction. As the teacher assesses and analyzes the strengths and weaknesses of children's writing, the information gathered guides instruction to meet children's needs revealed through the assessments.

Including a variety of assessments that reflect how children learn provides a rich, well-rounded picture of children's development. Integrating assessment and instruction provides information on the processes children use to write, as well as on the final product. Encouraging children to reflect and self-assess their writing is important in developing effective and independent writers. In this way, assessment becomes more than just a grade after teaching. It becomes a vehicle through which teachers take children from where they are to where we want them to be.

Conferencing is a critical component of any writing or assessment program. It provides time to celebrate the progress that young writers have made, the opportunity to assess where children are in their writing development, and the ideal context in which to gently guide them toward the next step in their development.

It is vitally important for teachers to keep records of their assessment results. Record keeping enables teachers to plan and organize

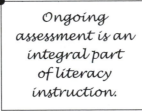

Ongoing assessment is an integral part of literacy instruction.

in a systematic way, as well as effectively track the progress of individuals over time. In this way, information on children's progress can be provided in a well-documented, clear, and precise way for teachers, children, parents, and administrators.

Along with the assessment ideas provided after each teaching strategy, the assessments in this section assist teachers in developing a richer view of children's overall progress. The conferencing strategy provides an outline for emergent and developing writers, including questions designed to help children begin to self-assess. This strategy also includes a form to record information obtained during each conference. The self-assessment form guides children in assessing their own writing. For emergent writers, this form can be completed for children during writing conferences. For developing writers, however, this assessment should be done only at the beginning of the year. Children should then be encouraged to assume the responsibility for completing the form as the year progresses. The writing profile provides a thumbnail sketch of emergent and early writing behaviors that can guide instruction for individuals, as well as larger groups. The writing rubrics provided were developed by the literacy coordinators of East Peoria, Illinois, School District #86. They were designed to assess children's independent writing in kindergarten, first, and second grades using specific descriptors on a four-point scale.

Conferencing is the core of the writing program. It provides one-on-one time to celebrate what the children have accomplished and gently nudge them along in their writing development. The conference is focused not so much on perfecting that day's writing as on developing strategies to improve the child's future writing. Conferencing is recursive in that it provides valuable information that guides future instruction, encourages children to attempt new skills and strategies, which are discussed in conferences, provides information for the teacher, and on and on. Conferencing is also important in encouraging children to self-assess their writing and assume increasing responsibility. Even emergent writers can assess their writing if provided with the modeling and guidance that conferencing affords.

Directions

1. Use conferences during your writing block. Engage each child in a conference that is designed specifically to address the needs of that particular child. The maximum time required is approximately five minutes per child. Children can be rotated throughout the week to be sure that you have the opportunity to conference with every child.

2. Conference with children before, during, and after writing. It is important to provide support throughout the entire writing process for emergent and developing writers to help them acquire strategies to better express themselves. This is not a time to work on correcting to perfection, but to focus on what each child can do and go on from there.

3. Discuss where the child is in the writing process. If he or she is in the planning stages, discuss the topic, the form that will be used, and the audience for which the writing is intended. You might comment as follows.

> *What are you planning to write about today? Your family vacation would be very interesting. Be sure to write about where you went, who you were with, and how you felt during your vacation. Who will be reading your story? Is it for other children to read or is this something that you will want to take home for your parents?*

This child will remember conferencing as a positive experience.

4. During the writing stage, be sure to have the children "read" what they have written for you. With emergent writers, this might be telling you what their pictures are about or what the markings on their paper mean. Therefore, you might say, "Tell me about your story." For the developing writers, ask them to reread their stories orally.

5. Make positive comments about the message first. Then comment on particulars like the illustration, the print (letter, sounds, words), or the effort that the child exhibited. For emergent writers, you might make the following remarks.

> *I like your story about your dog. You showed me in your picture what your dog looks like, as well as telling me about him in your story. I really like the way that you spelled dog. I know exactly what you meant because you listened to the word and wrote what you heard.*

6. For emergent writers, select one or two teaching points from their writing that will help them to move along in their development. An example follows.

> *I would like to look at the word dog, again. You listened very carefully to the word and wrote d. That was very good. Now I want you to listen as I stretch it out and see if you hear anything else in that word. Listen, d-o-g. Did you hear any other sounds that you know? Yes, there is a g at the end of the word dog. Would you like to add that letter to the end of the word dog? Well done!*

7. For developing writers, select one or two teaching points from their writing to discuss. In their writing, children show us what they know about writing and how print functions. Based on this information, we can provide support in areas that will help them along in their development. See the following example.

> *Michelle, you have really told me a lot about your vacation. I like the way you mentioned the names of all the people in your family. I think you are ready to learn how to use commas when you write a list of things, like names. This is what you do. . . .*

8. For developing writers, you might ask questions to provoke thinking (metacognition) about the writing process. If children have shared their writing with others, discuss the comments and questions that were raised and have the child decide if he or she wants to revise the writing. If not, you might ask the following questions.

   - *Do you think the reader will understand what you meant in this sentence?*
   - *What part do you like the best? Why?*
   - *What part was hard to write? Why?*
   - *Was there anything that you had a question about?*
   - *What words did you use to paint a picture in the reader's mind?*
   - *Can you think of any other words that would help the reader with that mental picture?*

9. Revising at this early stage of development should be accomplished during the writing conference. The child should decide if he or she wants to revise and the revisions should be done with the teacher. In this way, the teacher can provide support and tailor the instruction to meet the individual needs of each writer.

10. Most of the metacognitive talk is done by the teacher at the beginning of the year. As the year progresses, the children should take over more of this responsibility.

11. Use the reproducible on page 86 to record writing conference information.

Assessment

Because children demonstrate what they know about writing within their writing, teachers have a concrete record of what children understand and what they might be confused about. Keeping records of conferences in terms of what new strategies, forms, or skills the child is attempting, what he or she seems to have grasped, and noting the teaching points presented at each conference provides a powerful guide for future instruction. These records can help with individual children and instruction. They also provide information for whole group or small group instruction. By comparing notes taken on children throughout the week, the teacher may discover an overall need for particular strategies.

Conference Record

Child's Name _____ Date _____

Title of child's writing _____

Stage
Prewriting _____

Drafting _____

Revising/Editing _____

Strategies used consistently

Strategies attempted

Teaching points presented

Instructional Plan

SELF-ASSESSMENT •

To become lifelong learners, children need to be able to self-assess. Such assessment requires careful modeling and scaffolding for young writers. When children are taught to reflect on what they know about writing and what they have demonstrated in their own writing, they begin to view themselves as writers. They also begin to appreciate and understand their progress, which increases their confidence and self-esteem. By learning to self-assess, children begin to understand their role in their literacy development and are encouraged to set goals to improve their writing (Rhodes & Shanklin, 1993).

Directions

1. Use this strategy during individual writing conferences.

2. After a piece of writing has been discussed and the children have made any revisions that they feel are needed, use the Self-Assessment Form that follows to guide the children in assessing their writing.

3. Write the title of the piece, the name of the child, and the date of the conference on the Self-Assessment Form on page 89.

4. Ask children to describe what they liked about their pieces of writing. Have children explain why they liked them, and write their responses on the Self-Assessment Form.

   If it is necessary to prompt children, you might ask "What did you do really well?" or "What part do you like the best?"

5. Then ask children to tell you what they might have had trouble with. If children are hesitant to admit to having difficulty, you might tell them about problems you have had when writing, as in the following example.

   I often have trouble spelling big words when I write. So I just circle the ones that I don't know and keep writing. Sometimes I have trouble thinking of just the right words to use. Did you have trouble with anything while you were writing? Was something hard for you to do?

6. Always ask children to explain why they think something was difficult for them. This information allows the teacher to provide instruction at the point of need. When children see a need for a skill or strategy, instruction is more effective and learning takes place more readily.

7. Note any difficulties that children had with their writing on the Self-Assessment Form.

8. Remind children of any recent writing activities and the strategies or skills that were introduced or reinforced. Ask children if they tried something with this piece that they hadn't tried before. Have the children explain what was attempted and discuss how well it worked. Add the information to the form.

9. The Self-Assessment Form becomes a permanent record of how well children are assessing their own writing. What children notice about their writing is an indication of what they have learned, what they are learning, and what they still need to learn. Therefore, the Self-Assessment Form is a perfect companion to the Conference Form.

10. *Developing writers* should have the use of the Self-Assessment Form modeled for them for several months. When children are able to easily answer the three items on the form, provide support in their initial attempts to write their answers. Once children are able to complete the form without assistance, they should be expected to assume this responsibility.

11. Do not expect developing writers to independently complete this form for each piece of writing they do. Too much of a good thing is still too much. Have children complete the Self-Assessment Form periodically so you can check their progress.

Self-Assessment Form

Title of writing _____

I like  . . .

I had trouble  with . . .

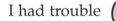

I tried  . . .

This Writing Profile provides teachers with an overview of emergent and developing writing behaviors. It includes a wide range of behaviors to cover the diversity found within most primary classrooms. Teachers can use the profile to check children's progress and provide information and direction for instruction. For individual children, the information can be used during writing conferences to provide instruction targeted for a particular child's needs. When children exhibit common needs, the Writing Profile can assist teachers in grouping children for small group instruction. The profile can also pinpoint common needs that can be addressed using whole group instruction.

Directions

1. Become familiar with the behaviors listed on the Writing Profile on page 91 so it can be used efficiently during observations.

2. Observe each child during independent writing activities.

3. Observe each child over several days. This provides a more accurate assessment of writing behaviors and accounts for those "bad days."

4. Determine if the child exhibits each behavior, and how often it is exhibited. Some of the behaviors are not developmentally appropriate for emergent writers.* Therefore, there is a column for behaviors "not yet" observed.

5. Observe children over several days to determine the frequency with which they exhibit writing behaviors. Children who attempt a behavior once, perhaps after it is modeled, may not incorporate it into their writing on a regular basis.

6. How often children exhibit certain writing behaviors can indicate their level of learning. Children who use a skill or strategy only occasionally are still "trying it on for size" and have not internalized that particular skill. However, children who exhibit behaviors on a regular basis have successfully incorporated them into their writing repertoire.

7. Emergent behaviors to look for by the end of kindergarten include writing left to right, selecting own topic, using consonant sounds in the initial and final positions, using capital letters and some end punctuation marks, relating oral/written story to illustration, and willing to attempt new strategies or skills.

8. Developing writers' behaviors that are beginning to appear by the end of first grade include sequencing ideas, expressing ideas effectively, writing confidently, circling words to correct, using commas and quotation marks, attempting to include details, and using good leads and endings.

---

* Behaviors not appropriate for emergent writers include expressing ideas effectively, writing using medial vowels, circling words to correct, using commas and quotation marks, and using good leads and good endings.

Child's Name _____ Date _____

Writing Profile

	Not yet	Occasionally	Often	Consistently
Selects own topic				
Sequences ideas logically				
Expresses ideas effectively				
Writes confidently				
Shares writing willingly				
Writes left to right				
Spaces correctly				
Uses developmental spelling				
Writes using initial consonant sounds				
Writes using initial and final consonant sounds				
Writes using medial vowels sounds				
Uses some high frequency words				
Circles words to check for spelling				
Uses classroom resources for spelling				
Uses capital letters appropriately				
Beginning of sentence				
Proper names				
Uses end punctuation appropriately				
Periods				
Question marks				
Exclamation marks				
Attempts other punctuation				
Commas				
Quotation marks				
Rereads to be sure writing makes sense				
Attempts to include detail				
Attempts to use good leads/endings				
Illustrations relate to oral and/or written story				
Willing to attempt new strategies and/or skills				

Writing Rubrics are assessments based on writing descriptors. These descriptors clearly define the desired standard of achievement. By clearly describing specific characteristics of writing, rubrics can reduce the chances of inaccurate and inconsistent scoring. The scoring system for most rubrics is easy to learn and use. When used throughout the year, rubrics can document a child's growth and progress. Sharing rubrics with developing writers can help them to determine how their writing measures up and how to improve it (Hart, 1994).

Directions for Kindergarten Writing Rubric

1. For kindergarten children early in the year, assessment is generally based on dictation given orally by the children. Later in the year, when children are able to write for themselves, assessment is based on their independent writing.

2. Provide a writing prompt or allow children to choose a topic to write about.

3. Ask children to draw and write about the topic. If children express their inability to write, tell them that "it doesn't have to be like grown up writing. Just write your own way" (Sulzby, Teale, & Kamberelis, 1989, p. 70).

4. Accept whatever form of writing children use. Some may draw a picture, some may make scribbles or use letter-like symbols; others may write with conventional letters using sound/symbol relationships; and still others may produce readable writing.

5. If the writing is unreadable, ask children to "read" what they have written. If they indicate that they cannot read, ask them to tell you about their story. Write what is dictated by the children somewhere other than on the front of their paper.

6. Use the Kindergarten Writing Rubric on page 93 to assess the child's writing. Descriptors are placed on a scale from zero to four. A score of four is reserved for those few children who demonstrate advanced levels of skill for kindergarten.

7. Begin with *sound/symbol relations* and decide which of the characteristics best describes the child's writing. If writing is not provided, even though a child may have drawn a picture and given an oral story relating to the picture, the piece receives a zero for sound/symbol relations.

8. Next, look at the *content* of the piece. If there was no response of any kind from the child, the score is a zero. However, if a child provides an oral response that relates to the picture, he or she receives a score of one. This allows for growth from the beginning of the year to the end of the year when most kindergarten children will be able to write to some extent.

9. Assess *conventions* using the last line of the rubric. This area has two sets of descriptors in each box, and a child's writing is assessed using both to receive a score.

10. If a child's writing falls between scores, determine which of the two scores is to be given by a more holistic assessment of the piece. If the majority of the child's work is scored as a three and the conventions score is between a two and a three, holistically the paper is more of a three and should be scored accordingly. (Remember that writing is not eas-

ily reduced to a quantitative score; therefore an assessment of this type will not always provide for every situation or give precise measurement.)

11. Add all three scores to determine a global score for the writing. Using the scoring guide at the bottom of the rubric, scores of 11 or 12 exceed the standard for kindergarten writing, scores of 8 to 10 meet the standard, and scores of less than 8 do not meet the standard. (You can change the numbers for the standards to fit your particular teaching situation.)

12. This rubric must be appropriate for your population if it is to be effective. The indicators in the Kindergarten Writing Rubric may be above or below the writing standard that you need to establish for your children. In this case, use whatever elements of the rubric are appropriate and change the others to reflect the abilities of your population.

			Kindergarten Writing Rubric		
Indicators	0	1	2	3	4
SOUND/SYMBOL RELATIONS	No written response	Uses random scribbles and/ or letter-like symbols	Uses conventional letters No sound/symbol relationships	Uses conventional letters with some sound/symbol relationships	Uses conventional letters with readable sound/symbol relationships
CONTENT	No oral or written response	Only an oral response relating to the picture	1 or 2 readable written words relating to the prompt	Writes a partial sentence (ex.—"in the barn")	Writes one or more sentences
CONVENTIONS	N/A	Random scribbles or letter-like symbols	Readable letters	Mixture of lowercase and uppercase letters	Appropriate use of lower and uppercase letters
	N/A	N/A	No attempt at spaces between words	Attempt at spaces between words	Spaces between words Attempts end marks

Courtesy of East Peoria School District #86

Scoring

11–12 Exceeds Standard
8–10   Meets Standard
< 8   Does Not Meet Standard

Directions for First-Grade Writing Rubric

1. Ask children to write using a specific prompt or one of their own choosing.

2. Assess only writing done independently, using the First-Grade Writing Rubric on page 95.

3. Descriptors are placed on a scale from zero to four. A score of four is reserved for those few children who demonstrate advanced writing skills for first grade.

4. When used to assess papers throughout the year, the writing rubric can show growth. A score of zero or one at the beginning of the year is not unusual. As children progress throughout the year, the scores they receive will usually move up into the meets or even the exceeds categories.

5. Most indicators have several descriptors for each score. If a child's writing falls between scores, determine which of the two scores is to be given by a more holistic assessment of the piece. For example, if a child's writing exhibits characteristics of both a two and a three under a specific indicator, and the majority of the child's work has scored a three, then, holistically, that indicator should also be scored as a three. (Remember that writing is not easily reduced to a quantitative score; therefore an assessment of this type will not always provide for every situation or give precise measurement.)

6. Using the descriptors for *content*, assess the child's writing. If the child wrote words or attempted to write words that have no meaning, the score is a zero. Sometimes when asked to write, beginning first-grade children resort to "safe" words. These are words that they know how to spell and may have no relation to the topic of the paper.

7. Next, assess the piece for *organization*. Determine if the topic is evident, if the paper stays on topic, and if it has a definite beginning, middle, and end. Beginning first-grade papers will not usually have all of these descriptors present. By the end of first grade, however, most of them will be present to some extent.

8. Assess *fluency* by looking for sentences that sound natural (like a child would talk). Stilted sentences do not flow and are difficult to read. Patterned sentences resemble the "I like . . ." sentence pattern and are used repeatedly throughout the paper.

9. *Conventions* are a courtesy to the reader and should be part of the overall assessment, not the majority of it. In the first-grade rubric, conventions consist of spelling accuracy, use of capital letters, end marks, subject/verb agreement, and spacing. A first grader who consistently demonstrates all of these descriptors shows an advanced level of development and scores a four.

10. Add all four indicator scores to determine a global score for the writing. Using the scoring guide at the bottom of the rubric, scores of 15 or 16 exceed the first-grade standard, scores of 11 to 14 meet the standard, and scores of 10 or less do not meet the standard.

11. This rubric must be appropriate for your population if it is to be effective. The indicators in the First-Grade Writing Rubric may be above or below the writing standard that you need to establish for your children. In this case, use whatever elements of the rubric are appropriate and change the others to reflect the abilities of your population.

First-Grade Writing Rubric

Indicators	0	1	2	3	4
CONTENT	Words used without meaning	Of little interest No details or examples	Interesting Attempts detail or example	Interesting Some details or examples	Interesting Several clear details or examples
ORGANIZATION	N/A	Topic is not clear No evident beginning, middle, or end	Topic is evident Beginning and middle are attempted	Paper stays on topic Beginning, middle, and end are evident but not clear	Stays on topic Paper has a clear beginning, middle, and end
FLUENCY	N/A	Unnatural language patterns	Patterned or stilted language	Some natural and some patterned language	Paper is written in natural, not patterned, language
CONVENTIONS	N/A	Little evidence of conventional spelling Little evidence of correct conventions • capital letters • end marks • spaces between words	Conventional spelling attempted Correct conventions evident but not used throughout the paper • capital letters • end marks • spaces between words	50% of the words are spelled with conventional spelling Conventions are generally correct with some errors • capital letters • end marks • spaces between words	Spelling is nearly conventional (80% of the words used) Convention use is consistent but not perfect • capital letters • end marks • spaces between words

Courtesy of East Peoria School District #86

Scoring

15–16 Exceeds Standard
11–14 Meets Standard
<10   Does Not Meet Standard

From Susan Davis Lenski and Jerry L. Johns, *Improving Writing K–8: Strategies, Assessments, and Resources* (2nd ed.). Copyright © 2004 by Kendall/Hunt Publishing Company (1-800-247-3458, ext. 4 or 5). May be reproduced for noncommercial educational purposes within the guidelines noted on the copyright page.

Directions for Second-Grade Writing Rubric

1. Ask children to write using a specific prompt or one of their own choosing.

2. Assess only writing done independently, using the Second-Grade Writing Rubric on page 97.

3. Descriptors are placed on a scale from zero to four. A score of four is reserved for those few children who demonstrate advanced writing skills for second grade.

4. When used to assess papers throughout the year, the writing rubric can show growth. A score of zero or one at the beginning of the year is not unusual. As children progress throughout the year, the scores they receive will usually move up into the meets or even the exceeds categories.

5. Most indicators have two or three descriptors for each score. If a child's writing falls between two scores, determine which of the two scores is to be given by a more holistic assessment of the piece. For example, if a child's writing exhibits characteristics of both a two and a three under a specific indicator, and the majority of the child's work has scored a three, then, holistically, that indicator should also be scored as a three.

6. If there are three descriptors for a given score, the paper should exhibit two of the three to receive that score. (Remember that writing is not easily reduced to a quantitative score. Therefore, an assessment of this type will not always provide for every situation or give precise measurement.)

7. Using the descriptors for *content*, assess the child's writing. The paper should be interesting and have examples or descriptions. If the piece is a narrative, it should also express feelings or emotions.

8. Next, assess the *organization* of the piece. Look for the paper to have a clear topic, to stay on topic, and have a clear beginning, middle, and end.

9. *Fluency* is determined by looking at how sentences flow from one to the other, the variety in sentence length, and how natural the sentences sound (like a child would talk). If sentences are choppy or run-on, they do not flow. Natural transitions also affect fluency. Forced or canned transitions interrupt rather than add to the flow. Second-grade children will begin to use more natural transitions by the end of the year, if they are allowed to experiment and are not forced to use prescribed transitions.

10. *Conventions* are a courtesy to the reader and should be part of the overall assessment, not the majority of it. In the Second-Grade Writing Rubric, conventions consist of spelling accuracy, use of capital letters, end marks, subject/verb agreement, and paragraph form. A second grader who consistently demonstrates all of these descriptors shows an advanced level of development and scores a four. (Percentages are merely estimates and scoring should not be reduced to counting. If the other benchmarks are met, look at spelling in terms of how it affects the reader's understanding.)

11. Add all four indicator scores to determine a global score for the writing. Using the scoring guide at the bottom of the rubric, scores of 15 or 16 exceed the second-grade standard, scores of 11 to 14 meet the standard, and scores of 10 or less do not meet the standard.

12. This rubric must be appropriate for your population if it is to be effective. The indicators in the Second-Grade Writing Rubric may be above or below the writing standard that you need to establish for your children. In this case, use whatever elements of the rubric are appropriate and change the others to reflect the abilities of your population.

Second-Grade Writing Rubric

Indicators	0	1	2	3	4
CONTENT	Consists of one sentence	Of little interest No specific descriptions or examples (NARRATIVE) Does not express emotions or feelings	Mildly interesting Few specific descriptions or examples (NARRATIVE) Some emotions or feelings expressed	Fairly interesting Some specific descriptions or examples (NARRATIVE) Expresses feelings or emotions	Captures reader's interest Several vivid descriptions or examples (NARRATIVE) Effectively expresses emotions or feelings
ORGANIZATION	Consists of one sentence	Topic is not clear No evident beginning, middle, or end	Topic is evident but not clear Beginning, middle, or end omitted	Stays on topic w/ 1 or 2 exceptions Beginning, middle, and end are evident but not clear	Stays on topic Has a clear beginning, middle, and end
FLUENCY	Consists of one sentence	Choppy/run-on sentences Sentences do not vary No transitions	More choppy/ run-on sentences than natural expression Little variation in sentence length Some transitions	Some sentences flow naturally, but not throughout the paper Some variation in sentence length Transitions throughout but may be stilted	Sentences flow naturally from one to another Sentences vary in length Transitions between sentences are natural
CONVENTIONS	Consists of one sentence	Little evidence of conventional spelling Little evidence of correct conventions • capital letters • ending marks	Conventional spelling evident (50%), but not used throughout Correct conventions evident, but not used throughout • capital letters • ending marks	Most words (75%) are spelled conventionally Conventions are generally correct with some errors • capital letters • ending marks	Spelling is conventional (90% of the words used) Convention use is consistent, but not perfect • capital letters • ending marks • subject/verb agreement • paragraph form

Courtesy of East Peoria School District #86

Scoring

15–16   Exceeds Standard
11–14   Meets Standard
<10   Does Not Meet Standard

Informal Writing: Building Fluency

"Just get it down on paper, and then we'll see what to do with it."

—Maxwell Perkins

OVERVIEW

You may have heard the saying that good writing is 10% inspiration and 90% perspiration. That's because writing is both an art and a craft. Writing can be highly creative and, at the same time, it can be highly conventional (Cooper & Odell, 1999). When writers write, words can flow so quickly that each sentence is a surprise and the writing activity is thoroughly satisfying. Or writers can deliberate, mulling over thoughts and organizing ideas into carefully crafted groups of words. Often writers have moments of inspiration and moments of deliberation during the same writing event. Writing, therefore, is both a group of skills to be taught and an expression of ideas (Britton, *et al.*, 1975). In

> *Good writing is 10% inspiration and 90% perspiration.*

this book, we call the expressive form of writing "informal writing."

INFORMAL WRITING IS SIMILAR TO SPEECH. This is the kind of writing that can be termed "talk written down." As you know, when we talk, we use all sorts of nonverbal cues to express our meaning. We may gesture with our hands, use facial expressions, and use the tone of our voices to get our meanings across to our listeners. Since readers cannot take advantage of verbal cues, writing is usually different from speech. Informal writing, however, is much closer to speech. Informal writing is the ability to let the mind wander through words. It is expressing what

Do your students write every day?

the mind is thinking without taking the time to conform that meaning to the conventions of language. It is the work of the mind that is important in informal writing, not the organization or correctness of the words.

INFORMAL WRITING ACTIVITIES ARE ESSENTIAL TO A BALANCED WRITING PROGRAM. Think for a moment about a skill you have learned or that you watched someone else learn. For example, think about learning to play the cello. Imagine for a moment taking the cello in your arms and lifting your bow to the strings. Then imagine a teacher explaining the fingerings for the notes, how to read music, and how to move the bow across the strings. After being taught each one of these skills, would you be ready for a cello performance? Of course not. You need to practice and practice and practice. The same principle holds true for writing. Students need to practice writing in order to build the kind of writing fluency that good writers need.

INFORMAL WRITING HELPS STUDENTS EXPLORE THEIR THOUGHTS AND IDEAS, MAKE TENTATIVE RESPONSES TO LITERATURE, AND INVESTIGATE THEIR LEARNING. When students write using informal writing activities, they use words and

> *Three Ways to Experience Writing*
> Journals
> Response to Literature
> Writing to Learn

language to discover the meaning of their experiences and of their learning (Murray, 1982).

In addition to giving students a deeper understanding when writing, informal writing activities also can help students learn the craft of writing. When students have the opportunity to experiment with language in risk-free environments, they build writing fluency.

There are three ways you can structure informal writing activities so that students can experience the range of possibilities in writing.

- One way to help students experience writing is to give them opportunities to write in journals. When students write in journals, they learn to reflect about themselves and their lives. They come to grips with their own thoughts and feelings. They discover who they are and what they think. They write to discover.
- A second type of informal writing activity is responding to literature. When students read, they construct meaning. By responding to literature in writing, students can deepen their construction of meaning and better understand what they are reading. In this type of informal writing activity, students write to give a personal response.

- The third type of informal writing activity is writing to learn. Through activities such as writing in response to content learning, students process, learn, and remember content material.

These three types of informal writing activities can help students deepen their thinking while they improve their writing fluency.

As students experience informal writing activities, they need to express themselves without fear of being judged for what they are writing. As in any type of learning, practice should not be evaluated. Therefore, when students engage in informal writing activities, your assessment of their writing should be encouraging yet minimal.

Your role as a teacher of writing is to encourage students to write, to reflect, and to learn in order to build their writing fluency (International Reading Association and National Council of Teachers of English, 1996). And, as students write, they will reap the benefits of developing the expressive side of writing as they discover their interpretations of events, clarify meanings of literature, and learn content materials through writing. This chapter contains resources, teaching strategies, ideas, and activities to help students develop the expressive side of writing so that writing can be inspiration as well as perspiration. Ideas for assessment also are included.

Journal Writing

Goal • *To promote students' self-discovery through writing in journals.*

BACKGROUND

Writing is not merely a process of recording thoughts, experiences, and ideas—writing can be a process of discovery. When you write, you can relive experiences from a different time and perspective, you can let your imagination redefine reality, you can explore new worlds, and you can become more aware of your own personal beliefs. Writing can take you places your mind doesn't know ahead of time.

Not all writing is this magical. When writers have the chance to write in a nonthreatening situation, however, their thoughts become clearer and they generate more ideas. Perhaps that's why many people keep journals (Mallon, 1984). A number of artists, scientists, engineers, dancers, and teachers write in journals to record events and to learn about their reactions to life. Journals are a spontaneous, unplanned means of understanding oneself (Giorgis, 2002).

Writing in journals helps clarify thoughts, but it also has another benefit for students learning to write. Journal writing helps writers develop fluency (Newman, 1983). When students put words on paper, they are experimenting with language and how words fit together to make sentences. Each time students

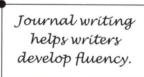

Journal writing helps writers develop fluency.

write in journals, they are practicing language. They are learning how to formulate ideas, how to put those ideas into words, how to make sentences readable, and how to string together sentences to make thoughts comprehensible. Journal writing, therefore, accomplishes two tasks:

- it helps students understand what they think, and
- it helps them learn ways to write those thoughts.

All students can increase their writing fluency when given the opportunity for journal writing—even students as young as those in kindergarten (Bouas, Thompson, & Farlow, 1997). They need time and the opportunities to write. However, just telling students to write in journals may not work. Some students will ask, "What do I write?" Therefore, we have included a variety of teaching strategies, activities, and ideas for you to use as you help students understand the value of writing in journals and to give them the chance to become more fluent writers by journal writing.

Teaching Strategy 1

PERSONAL JOURNALS

Personal Journals are journals where students can write what they think, see, or feel. These journals are notebooks where students can write whatever they want. They are a place where students can write about difficult issues that confront them (Frost, 2001). Personal Journals are places where students can keep entries of ideas and thoughts that can eventually be used in other types of writing. Such journals are not graded, and students decide whether or not something in the journal will be shared with another person.

Directions

1. Tell students that they will be writing in Personal Journals at least three times each week. Explain that Personal Journals are places to record thoughts, feelings, and ideas.

2. Provide students with blank notebooks or have them bring them from home. Tell students that these notebooks are their own personal places to write. Explain that, even though the Personal Journals will be students' own private possessions, you cannot guarantee that no one will read them. Tell students that they should not write anything that is so personal that it cannot be shared with their classmates.

3. Tell students to begin keeping lists of writing topics. Help students create lists by providing them with the list of Journal Topics that follows. Make copies of the list and distribute a copy to each student. Staple the list in the front of each student's Personal Journal.

4. Each week give students 10 minutes to create additional lists of writing topics. Divide the class into groups of three or four students. Have students brainstorm ideas for their Personal Journals. Encourage students to add to their lists at other times during the week.

5. Provide students with at least 15 minutes three times each week to write in their Personal Journals. During journal writing time, have students refer to their lists, decide on a topic, and write steadily for 15 minutes. Encourage students to write whatever comes to their minds.

6. Occasionally give students a topic for their journal writing rather than allowing them to choose their own topics. An example of a first-grade journal entry follows on page 106.

Students of all ages can write in journals.

Assessment

Tell students that you will not be grading their Personal Journals but that you will read their journals occasionally. Explain that writing in Personal Journals is something students do for themselves, not for a grade. Tell students that journal writing is practice writing and an idea bank for other writing. Then read their journals when you have time. Do not feel you need to read each student's journal every week.

Journal Writing Ideas

http://www.educationworld.com/a_curr/curr144.shtml

Journal writing ideas that can be used in any classroom are presented on this site.

Journal Topics

Things on my mind . . .

What I usually talk about . . .

What bothers me . . .

What pleases me . . .

How I spend my time . . .

What surprises me . . .

Books I have read . . .

People I admire . . .

My dreams . . .

Things I look forward to . . .

Things I enjoy . . .

Things that I dread . . .

What I have learned recently . . .

How I feel about my life and family . . .

Favorite places . . .

What I want to know . . .

What I would like to change . . .

My goals . . .

My biggest problems . . .

Dangerous things . . .

Valuable possessions . . .

Past experiences . . .

Places I'd like to go . . .

Things I wonder about . . .

When I grow up . . .

When I Grow Up

By
Mallorie
First Grade

When I grow up, I want to be a singer. A singer needs to practice her songs. I will go on stage to sing songs at night. Each night, I will wear different clothes. I want to be a singer because singing songs is my favorite thing to do. I'll sign autographs and have a microphone. If I'm really good, I could be on TV or on the radio. I might even have CD's or music videos. I have to write songs I sing. I'm famous and rich. I can't wait to grow up and be a singer.

Teaching Strategy 2

WRITER'S NOTEBOOK

A Writer's Notebook is a journal that writers use to record thoughts, feelings, and ideas that can later be turned into stories. Shelly Harwayne (2001) states, "We want children to notice, pay attention, marvel, and be fascinated with the world around them, both at school and outside of school. . . . Our main tool for encouraging children, in grades three through five, to always lead attentive and observant lives is the writer's notebook" (p. 43). Students of all ages can benefit from using a Writer's Notebook. These notebooks can help students learn to look at themselves as writers.

Directions

1. Provide students with bound books such as spiral notebooks. Encourage students to decorate their notebooks with pictures or stickers so that they are personalized and attractive.

2. Tell students that these new journals will be their Writer's Notebooks. Explain that a Writer's Notebook is a journal that writers use to record thoughts, feelings, and ideas that intrigue them. State that writers use notebooks such as these to list ideas that can later be turned into a story.

3. Duplicate and distribute the Writer's Notebook Ideas reproducible on page 108. Tell students that these ideas are just some of the things they can write in their Writer's Notebook. Model how writers think by saying something like the following.

   I was sitting in a coffee shop one morning with my Writer's Notebook just writing some of my thoughts. I was thinking about the flowers I wanted to plant this year so I began with a list of flowers to buy. Then I started thinking about our neighbor's flower garden so I started to describe the colors of the flowers. As I was creating sentences describing the brilliant flowers, I decided to think about the insects in the garden. That reminded me of a feeling I had when I was stung by several bees. I described the pain and the itching of the bee stings. Then I looked around the coffee shop and saw twin girls about three years old. They had curly black hair and chocolate colored eyes. I started writing some sentences describing the girls. Before I knew it, I had written five pages.

4. Have students read the Writer's Notebook Ideas list and think about some of the things that they could write. Have students discuss some of their ideas in small groups and then have students write about one idea.

5. Encourage students to take their Writer's Notebooks home with them to record ideas outside of school. Occasionally assign students to record in their Writer's Notebooks in school or for a homework assignment.

Writer's Notebook Ideas

- Lists
- Jokes and puns
- Descriptions of people
- Images that I like
- Feelings
- Opinions
- Dreams
- Responses to what I read
- Good sentences
- Memories
- Family stories
- Observations
- Questions I have
- Quotations
- Interviews
- Interesting words
- Schedules
- Quotes
- Ideas for stories
- Descriptions
- Free writing
- Conversations
- Notes about my learning
- Reaction to an experience
- Description of something I saw
- _____
- _____

FAMILY MESSAGE JOURNALS

"Family Message Journals are notebooks in which children write a message to their families each day about something they did or learned or thought about in school, and a family member (or other willing adult, aside from the classroom teacher) writes a message in reply" (Woolman-Bonilla, 2000, p. 2). In these journals, students think about one activity they did in school and write about it for their families. Their families, in turn, learn about school experiences and are offered the opportunity to reply to the children. Teachers can also learn from Family Message Journals, both how the students perceived the school activity and the reaction of the families.

Directions

1. Tell students that they will be starting a new type of journal: a Family Message Journal. Ask students what they think will be in a journal of that type and encourage students to provide a variety of responses.

2. Duplicate and distribute the Family Message Journal reproducible that follows. Show students the area for them to write their message and explain that they will be writing about one activity from the school day. Tell students that you will often suggest which activity to write about and that some days they will have a free choice. Give them an example similar to the following one.

    Teacher: Today we had a special treat. A group of middle school students came to our school to read with us. What could you write about that activity? Let's write a Family Message on the white board as an example.

    Student 1: They came on a bus from the middle school.

    Student 2: Enough students came to our class so that we each could read with one student.

    Student 3: They brought picture books, crayons, and paper.

    Teacher: Good. Now let's compose a journal entry that describes this activity.

Students enjoy sharing their learning experiences with their families.

3. Guide students through writing a class message so that students understand how much detail to use in their Family Message Journal entries as in the example that follows.

We had a fun time today when the students from the middle school came to read with us. They all brought books to read with us. Some of the books were new and some were our old favorites. The students also brought crayons and paper so we could draw pictures. We really enjoyed their visit.

4. Then determine which days you will send these journals home. You might decide to send them home every day or on selected days of the week. Inform the parents about the Family Message Journals by a parent meeting, a letter home, or individual phone calls. Make sure that each family is aware of their responsibility to respond to their child's journal.

5. Rotate the activities that you have students write about so that families learn about an array of school activities. Include content area activities, such as science, social studies, and math, and special subjects, such as physical education, music, and art.

Name _____ Date _____●

Family Message Journal

My Message _____

_____

_____

_____

_____

_____

_____

_____

_____

Family's Response _____

_____

_____

_____

_____

_____

_____

_____

_____

_____

Sometimes students balk at writing in journals. They say, "I don't know what to write," even after you've modeled journal writing, suggested ideas, and given them ample time. That is the time for Speedwriting (Luse, 2002). In Speedwriting, "students are instructed to write down all their ideas as quickly as they can" (p. 20). The teacher gives students a short amount of time to write and requires that all students write words, sentences, or paragraphs about a specific topic.

Directions

1. Tell students that they will be participating in a different form of writing called Speedwriting. Explain that students will be given two minutes to write as many words as they can about a specific topic.

2. Choose a topic that students have been studying for them to use for their Speedwriting activity and model the types of things students can write. An example adapted from Luse (2002) follows.

    Teacher: We've been learning about the Boston Tea Party in this class and you all know many things about the Boston Tea Party and the context in which Paul Revere made his famous ride. If the Boston Tea Party was your Speedwriting topic, what could you write?

    Student 1: The United States didn't exist yet. It was a group of colonies.

    Student 2: People in Boston didn't like the taxes from the king. They dumped the tea into the ocean. We call that the Boston Tea Party.

Students who dislike writing in journals often enjoy speedwriting.

Student 3: The Boston Tea Party was a revolt against the king.

Teacher: You know quite a bit about the Boston Tea Party. I'm going to give you two minutes to write as much as you can about that topic.

3.   Duplicate and distribute the Speedwriting sheet that follows. Have students practice Speedwriting with the topic that you modeled.

4.   After students have completed their writings, have them count the number of words that they wrote. After each Speedwriting activity, have students record the number of words as in the following example.

   Tea was thrown off a ship in Boston because tea was taxed. This made the British very angry and soon a war started. (23 words)

5.   Tell students not to share the number of words they wrote, but to use the information to try to increase how many words they write each time they participate in Speedwriting.

Assessment

Keep track of the number of words students write so that you can determine their progress. When students are able to write a sufficient number of words, scale back on the Speedwriting assignments.

Name _____ Date _____

Speedwriting

Topic _____

_____

_____

_____

_____

Number of words _____

Topic _____

_____

_____

_____

_____

Number of words _____

Topic _____

_____

_____

_____

_____

Number of words _____

Teaching 5 Strategy

FIVE-ALIVE

To help students develop writing fluency, Belk and Thompson (2001) suggest a strategy called Five-Alive. Five-Alive is an observational strategy that guides students in using their five senses as they write. When students use their five senses, they have more content to build into their writing, thus increasing writing fluency.

Directions

1. Tell students that they will be using their senses to write an observation for their journal. Explain that descriptive writing is one of the ways writers develop visual imagery.

2. Take students to a spot in the school or outside where they can observe something. For example, students might sit in the entryway of the school and observe the furniture, signs, rugs, and so on.

3. Tell students to choose something to observe. You might provide students with some ideas for observation.

4. After students have chosen a topic or object to observe, explain that they will be writing descriptions using their five senses. Duplicate and distribute the Five-Alive reproducible on the next page. Model the kinds of things students could observe using the Five-Alive reproducible with a sample topic or object as in the following explanation.

    I'm going to write about the box of unclaimed hats and mittens that sits by the office. First, I'll look at the Five-Alive sheet for directions. I need to think about what I see, what I smell, what I hear, what I feel, and relationships I observe. As I observe the box, I notice that two girls walk over to rummage through the mittens. They take out one bright pink mitten and begin to walk away. I ask them if I can touch the mitten. It's soft and warm. It smells pungent like wet wool. The mitten is pink, and the weaving of the mitten is loose with several pulled threads. I move the thumb and fingers of the mitten against each other and hear a faint scraping noise. One of the girls puts the mitten on her hand and runs out the door to recess.

5. Give students 10 minutes or more to write descriptions on their Five-Alive sheets. When they finish, encourage students to share their observations. Tell students that writers need to be observant so they can write more vividly.

6. Students may want to develop their Five-Alive journals into paragraphs. Hang the paragraphs on a bulletin board and give other students the opportunity to read them.

Assessment

Evaluate the students' descriptions by noting whether each of the five senses has been described fully. Since this is a journal assignment with the purpose of encouraging students to write observations, do not grade the journals on spelling or punctuation.

Name _____ Date _____

Five-Alive

Topic _____

Location _____

What do you see? _____

_____

_____

What do you smell? _____

_____

_____

What do you hear? _____

_____

_____

What can you touch? _____

_____

_____

How does it feel? _____

_____

_____

What relationships do you observe? _____

_____

_____

Teaching **Strategy**

MEMORY WRITING

Memory Writing is an excellent way for students to practice writing and to build their sense of identity (Van Sluys, 2003). When students write about their memories over time, they are able to notice themes that surface time and again during their writing. Occasionally, they write about issues and emotions that they didn't realize existed. Linda Ellerbee, a noted journalist, said about this type of writing: "Sometimes I don't know what I think until I see what I write. I would write my emotions in my journal, sometimes emotions I could tell no one else" (Anderson & Anderson, 2003, p. 94). Therefore, Memory Writing is a valuable activity to develop writing as well as for students to understand themselves.

Directions

1. Tell students that they will be engaging in Memory Writing, or writing about some of their memories. Explain that memories need to be jogged at times or they will be forgotten. Say that writing can help students remember their lives and understand their characters better.

2. Model Memory Writing by telling students about one of your memories that reveals your character. An example follows.

    I'm going to tell you about a time when I was your age. I was playing softball at school recess, and I was up to bat. I wasn't a very good baseball player and I was worried about striking out. There were already two outs, and I was desperate to hit the ball. When I came up to bat, all of the outfielders moved in because they knew I couldn't hit the ball very well. They embarrassed me, but I realized it was natural. I walked up to bat, very nervous. I swung at the first pitch. Crack! I hit the ball right in the sweet spot of the bat. The ball soared in the air above and behind all of the outfielders. I stood there a minute, amazed. My teammates started yelling at me to start running. I did. I ran around all the bases making a home run. Everyone clapped me on the back. I was thrilled, but most of all I was relieved that I hadn't let the team down.

3. Duplicate and distribute the Memory Prompts reproducible that follows. Tell students that they can use this idea sheet as they think about their memories.

4. Read over the list of ideas with students and then divide the class into groups of two or three students. Have students share some of their memories with their classmates.

5. After students have had a chance to discuss some of their memories, have them engage in Memory Writing.

6. After students have written about several memories, have them choose portions of their drafts to integrate into an autobiography. An example of an autobiography is on page 119.

Memory Prompts

I remember a time when . . .

- I made something.
- I played a game.
- I had the hiccups.
- I lost something.
- I learned something new.
- I met someone.
- I performed in front of an audience.
- I saw a great movie.
- I said good-bye to someone.
- I solved a problem.
- I started a hobby.
- I visited a relative.
- I had something on my mind.
- I told a story.
- I was upset.
- I was thrilled.
- I took a vacation.
- I was surprised.
- I had a dream.
- I was afraid.
- I set a goal.
- I changed something.

My Life

By Cindy
First Grade

I was born in Illinois in the year 1994. My birthday is November 21. I have one brother and three sisters. I had a mom and dad, except my mom died in a car accident. My sister was with my mom. She had to go to the hospital. She broke some ribs. Now I only have a dad. My dad, mom, and two of my sisters were born in Mexico. One of my sisters, named Nely, was born in California. My brother and I were born in Illinois. My favorite colors are red and pink. I have glasses. I got them in 2000. When I brought them to school, I was embarrassed. I like to play Candyland with my brother, Martin. My favorite sport is soccer. My family might move to Texas this summer. I can't wait to see what happens next.

Responding by Writing

Goal ● *To help students expand meanings of literature by responding in writing.*

BACKGROUND

As students read, they reach provisional understandings of text and often choose to move through the text, resulting in what Mackey (1997) terms "good-enough" reading. "Good-enough" reading is sufficient for some reading tasks. One legitimate purpose for recreational reading, for example, might be merely to finish a book. In this case, the reader might be satisfied with minimal comprehension. Reading, therefore, can be viewed as an act of compromise between the need for a deep comprehension of text and the desire for momentum—to find out what happened (Mackey, 1997). For much of the reading required in schools, however, "good-enough" reading is not good enough. Responding in writing to literature can help students move beyond "good-enough" reading to focus on what the reader is seeing, feeling, and thinking (Rosenblatt, 1985).

When students write in response to stories or books that they have heard or read, they begin to listen to their hearts as they read. Stories have the power to reach our emotions, to help us understand life. As students read, they begin to comprehend the story by understanding the plot, setting, theme, and characters. Then, as students respond to the stories in writing, they can pay attention to their feelings. As they identify their thoughts and feelings, students can reach deeper levels of comprehension about the text. Writing in response to literature, therefore, can help students construct meanings of texts while it promotes writing fluency.

> *Responding in writing to literature can help students move beyond "good-enough" reading.*

It's important that you give students a variety of response activities to pursue. When engaged in different response activities, students think in different ways (Ollmann, 1996). For example, if students write in Response Journals, they write primarily about their feelings. When students write a Two-Column Response, they identify a quotation from the book and use their background experiences to create meaning. Each strategy promotes student learning. Therefore, we encourage you to use a variety of the resources, teaching strategies, ideas, and activities presented in this section. If you do, your students will learn how to expand meanings of literature while writing, and they will become more fluent writers.

Would writing about this story help the student understand the content more clearly?

Teaching **1** *Strategy*

Section 3.2

RESPONSE JOURNALS

Response Journals encourage students to express their feelings about and reactions to books they have read (Barone & Lovell, 1990). Response Journals are usually spiral notebooks that students can use to record their thoughts, feelings, and reactions to stories as they read them. As students write in Response Journals, they take the time to move beyond their initial comprehension of the text to a richer understanding of the story.

Directions

1. Introduce Response Journals by modeling your own response to literature. Tell students about a book you are reading. Tell students the name of the book and the author and then give them a brief summary of the book. Then complete one of the Response Ideas on the following page and model it for the class.

2. After you have shown students a response to your own reading, tell students that they will be writing in Response Journals. Explain that writing in Response Journals helps students think about what they have read, perhaps in a new way.

3. Tell students that after they have read a book or a story they will engage in response activities. Duplicate the list of Response Ideas on the following page and distribute copies to students.

4. Explain to students that after they have read a book they should choose one of the activities to complete. Tell students that the activities have been designed to help them think about the story.

5. Provide students with adequate time to complete Response Journals after reading a story or a book.

Assessment

Read Response Journals to determine how well students understood their reading. Make sure students write enough so that their thoughts and ideas are clearly stated.

Response Ideas

1. Write a letter to a friend about the book.

2. Write several endings to the book.

3. Write a play about the main character.

4. Rewrite the story using students from the class as characters.

5. Write a calendar of story events.

6. Design a classified ad for something in the book.

7. Create a glossary of words from the story.

8. Write a horoscope for a book character.

9. Identify phrases from the book that could be used as quotations for a display.

10. Pretend you're a story character and write a letter to someone in the class.

11. Compose a song about the plot of the book.

12. Write a picture book about the events in the story.

13. Write a news report about the plot.

14. Create a budget for travel to the setting of the story.

15. Develop a website for the main character of the book.

16. Keep a journal from the point of view of one of the characters.

17. Write a newspaper article about one of the characters.

18. Write a fictional journal entry about a book character.

19. Create a political cartoon about a character in the book.

20. Write a radio show about the book.

Two-Column Response Charts (Ollmann, 1991/1992) are designed for students to think more deeply about specific things authors write in stories. Authors often include pearls of wisdom embedded within texts. Of course, any quotation from a story may be meaningful for one person and not significant to another. Two-Column Response Charts offer students an avenue for identifying quotations that interest them and a chance to write their reactions to the quotations. This activity can lead to lively discussions about the literature.

Directions

1. Tell students that different readers will construct different meanings from the same text. Tell students that they can identify and respond to sentences from texts using Two-Column Response Charts.

2. Introduce the Two-Column Response Charts by showing students a completed chart similar to the example from *Children of the Wild West* (Freedman, 1983) that follows. Point out the sentences that were chosen and the responses. Tell students that a different person completing the chart could have entirely different responses.

Quotes	Responses
"The growth of photography and the opening of the American West took place at the same time" (p. 9).	I didn't realize that photography was invented at that time. I thought there were photographs before the 1840s.
"They called themselves 'emigrants' because, as they started their journey, they were actually leaving America" (p. 17).	The West was not part of the United States at that time. The United States is really a young nation.
"It took a full acre of sod to build a typical one-room sod house, which measured 16 by 20 feet and weighed about 90 tons" (p. 29).	Sod houses are fascinating. They seem small and dirty. The size of this house is about the same size as our living room. Thinking about an entire family living in such a small place is mind-boggling.

3. Give students a two-column chart or have them divide a piece of paper in half. On the top of the left side of the paper have students write the word "Quotes" and on the right side have them write "Responses" as in the Two-Column Response Chart that follows.

4. Tell students that as they read they should identify quotes that interest them and write the quotes and the responses on the chart.

5. After students have written at least three quotes and responses, divide the class into groups of three or four students and have students share their Two-Column Response Charts.

Two-Column Response Chart

Quotes	Responses

Teaching Strategy 3

RESPONSE QUESTIONS

When students read on their own, they may miss important parts of the story and have minimal comprehension as a result. When students have to write responses as they read, they stop and reflect, thus increasing their understanding of the story (Berger, 1996). Students also should be encouraged to write responses to their self-selected reading. The following list of Response Questions can help guide students' comprehension as they read independently.

Directions

1. Provide students with a spiral notebook for their Response Questions. Tell students to use this notebook for their self-selected reading response notebook.

2. Duplicate and distribute copies of the Response Questions that follow. Tell students that they can use these questions to respond to their independent reading.

3. Ask students to write two or three times per week in response to their independent reading. Tell them to choose one of the questions from the list of Response Questions and answer it in their notebooks. Provide students with adequate time for writing.

Response Questions

AUTHOR

1. Why do you think the author wrote this book?
2. How does the author organize the book?
3. How does the author create suspense or humor?
4. Who do you think the author intended as the primary audience for this book?
5. What does the author have to know in order to write this book?
6. How does the author interest you in the book?
7. Why do you think the author wrote the ending this way?
8. How do you picture the author?
9. How does the author use setting in this book?
10. What would you ask the author if you could?

CHARACTERS

1. How would you describe the main characters?
2. Would you choose the main characters as friends? Why or why not?
3. How do the characters change in the story?
4. How does the author create an image of the main characters?
5. How does the author help the reader get to know the main characters?
6. How are some of the characters different from other characters?
7. How are the characters like your friends or family?
8. How are the characters like other characters in books you have read?
9. Which character was your favorite? Why?
10. How would you change one of the characters?

PLOT

1. What happened in the story?
2. What was the sequence of events?
3. What was the problem in the story?
4. How was the problem resolved?
5. What parts of the plot kept you interested in the story?
6. What part of the plot was the most exciting to you?
7. Did the ending surprise you? Why or why not?
8. Was the plot effective? Why or why not?
9. What other directions might the plot have taken?
10. What was the point of the story?

STYLE AND MOOD

1. How did you feel while you were reading this book?
2. What part of the book was your favorite?
3. Did you like the author's style of writing? Why or why not?
4. How did the mood of the story change during the book?
5. Why did the author select the mood of this story?
6. What picture has the author's writing left in your mind?
7. How is this book like something you have written?
8. How would you describe the author's style?
9. Did you like the first sentence of the book? Why or why not?
10. What sentences did you think were especially effective?

RESPONSE CARDS

Response Cards are a strategy to encourage students to respond to literature in a variety of ways. Response Cards' questions can be organized in many ways. Questions can be organized by Bloom's Taxonomy, or they can be priorities that the teacher and students have established. The purpose of using Response Cards is to guide students' responses to literature in the areas that are important in the curriculum.

Directions

1. Duplicate and distribute the Response Cards that follow or create some with categories that you feel are important.

2. Tell students that each category has different questions. Point out the names of the six categories.

    - knowledge
    - comprehension
    - application
    - analysis
    - creative thinking
    - critical thinking

    If necessary, discuss and explain the categories.

3. Have students read the questions under each category. Tell students that they can answer any of the questions when their category is selected.

4. When you want students to write responses to literature, select a category. Have students write a response to any question in that category on that day. Provide ample time for students to write.

5. After students have learned how to use the Response Cards, allow students to select their own categories during writing time. Tell students that they need to alternate categories each time they write.

6. Create new Response Cards periodically. Have students suggest categories and questions for the new cards.

Response Cards

Knowledge	**Comprehension**
1. Who are the main characters?	1. Retell the story in your own words.
2. What is the story about?	2. Describe the main characters.
3. List the sequence of events.	3. Explain the problem and resolution.
Application	**Analysis**
1. What does the author do to "paint a picture" of the setting?	1. What happened at the beginning, middle, and end of the story?
2. Choose a new title for the section you have just read.	2. How did the author draw you into the story?
3. If you could interview a character from the book, what questions would you ask?	3. What are some of your favorite words, phrases, or sentences from the story?
Creative Thinking	**Critical Thinking**
1. If you could change a character in the story, who would it be?	1. What character would make a good friend?
2. What would happen if the story took place in a different time?	2. Would you recommend this book to someone else? Why or why not?
3. How would the story change if it were written from a different point of view?	3. What is the most memorable part of this book? Why?

E-MAIL DIALOGUE JOURNALS

E-mail is a familiar communication tool for many students today. Therefore, e-mail can be a good method for students to write dialogue journals, especially if they are writing to their teacher. When some students write e-mail, they do not use punctuation or capitalization but solely concentrate on their message. This makes e-mail a good illustration of informal writing. Using e-mail in school can present some problems since teachers cannot monitor all communications. However, if students are using e-mail to write to their teacher, they are able to use writing to express themselves and they often develop a more positive relationship toward their teacher (Doherty & Mayer, 2003). E-mail exchanges can take the form of personal sharing, or they can be a way for students to share responses to literature.

 ## Directions

1. Contact a technology leader or a media specialist and request e-mail addresses for each student in your class. Write the students' e-mail addresses on individual cards so that the addresses are not shared with other students.

2. Set up an e-mail system on a classroom computer so that students can only send messages to you and receive messages from you.

3. Tell students that they will have the opportunity to use e-mail in the classroom in order to communicate with you. Emphasize that they will not be able to use the computer to send messages to anyone else.

4. Distribute the individual e-mail addresses. Remind students to keep their addresses private and tell students that their e-mail addresss will only work to send messages to you.

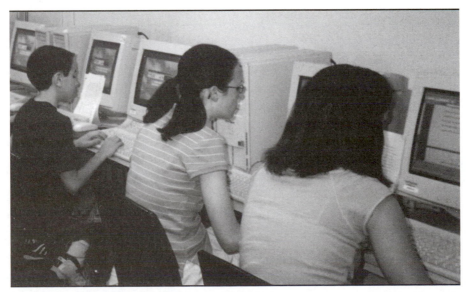

Many students prefer to write e-mail messages.

5. Explain to students that you will be sending them messages every week and that they should check the classroom computer for messages occasionally. Tell students that your e-mails will be personalized to them by saying the following.

   I will be sending each of you one or more e-mails each week. Please check your e-mail every few days so that you can respond to my messages. You can also send me messages any time you want. When you send me messages, though, please write a question or explain something that deals with your life or this class. As in all of your writing, make sure that your e-mail messages are appropriate for school.

6. Tell students that they can ask you about the literature they are reading in class. Explain to students that you will be eager to discuss literature with them. Tell students that they can use the Questioning Ideas sheet as a basis for designing questions for you (Christian, 1997).

7. Duplicate and distribute the Questioning Ideas reproducible that follows. Tell students that they should keep this sheet in their journals.

Questioning Ideas

1. Emotional Questions
   - Evoke happy, sad, or angry emotions

2. Structural Questions
   - Question the plot, setting, characters, theme, and so on

3. Interpretive Questions
   - Ask for inferences on character motivation, symbolism, patterns, and so on

4. Evaluative Questions
   - Query about the author's style and use of literary devices

5. Generative Questions
   - Ask for a personal response

Based on Christian, S. (1997). *Exchanging lives: Middle school writers online*. Urbana, IL: National Council of Teachers of English.

Learning Through Writing

Goal • *To help students learn content material through writing activities.*

BACKGROUND

There are a number of ways that students can process information in order to learn. One of them is through writing (Elbow, 1981). When students engage in a writing activity about a specific topic, they need to think about the topic and form ideas and opinions. As they form ideas and opinions, students make decisions about what they believe, and they make a commitment to those decisions. Students form their ideas in language, that is, words and sentences. As they choose words to express ideas, they revise and clarify their thinking. Students learn content material through the mental processes they experience as they write (Forman & Dahl, 2003).

> No student is too young or too old to use writing as a learning tool.

Asking students to record what they have learned helps them understand what they know (Fulwiler, 1987). For this reason, having students write in order to learn is a powerful learning tool, both in content area learning and for writing instruction. When students write in order to learn, they wrestle with new terms and concepts and learn how to write them in sentences. Students learn to become fluent not only by writing but also in the contexts for their writing. Therefore, writing in order to learn is not merely a language arts strategy; it also is a way to help students process information.

Students of all ages should engage in writing to learn strategies. No student is too young or too old to use writing as a learning tool. Sometimes we think that young students cannot participate in writing to learn. However, a number of strategies are especially appropriate for young students. For example, young students can "write the room," or write about the displays and bulletin boards in the classroom. They can write sentences about the classroom and about content subjects while building their writing fluency. Older students can engage in a number of writing to learn activities such as Learning Logs and Writing Format Fiesta. These strategies are a fun way to encourage students to learn and to help them build writing fluency.

The resources, teaching strategies, ideas, and activities in this section are designed to help students use writing as a learning tool. Each strategy should be adapted for your grade level and the content you want to teach. All of the strategies have been tried in classrooms and have been effective in helping students learn content material through writing.

Writing is a good way to learn content.

Learning Journals (Hughey & Slack, 2001) provide students with an opportunity to think about, react to, respond to, synthesize, connect, and question information they are learning. Learning journals have three main purposes:

1. They give students the opportunity to process and reinforce concepts learned in school.

2. They provide students and teachers with documentation of students' learning.

3. They give students the opportunity to review content information before they are tested.

A Learning Journal is a powerful strategy for students to learn through writing.

Directions

1. Tell students that they will be writing in journals about the content area you are teaching. Explain that writing can be a tool for learning and that their Learning Journals will be similar to other types of journals they have completed in school, except these journals will be used when you teach science, social studies, math, and so on.

2. Provide students with spiral notebooks to use as Learning Journals. Tell students that periodically you will be giving them writing assignments to complete in these notebooks. Explain that these pieces of writing will be assessed only for completion, not for their content. Emphasize that writing in a Learning Journal is a tool for students to learn rather than an evaluation of learning.

3. Duplicate and distribute the Learning Journal Prompts that follow. Have students staple a copy of these prompts in the front of their spiral notebooks. Tell students that they can add their own ideas on the blank lines.

4. Give students directions for writing in Learning Journals as follows.

   Some days I will give you time to write in your Learning Journals after a science, social studies, or math lesson. At these times, you should choose one of the prompts in your Learning Journals to use for your writing. You should write one or more paragraphs in your journals. You should use your knowledge about spelling and punctuation as you write, but since a public audience won't read these writings, you will not be expected to revise them. I will be reading your journal entries occasionally to get a glimpse of your views, feelings, and knowledge about the subject. However, I won't grade your journals for accuracy.

5. Give students at least 10 minutes to write their responses in their Learning Journals.

Assessment

Use Learning Journals as a window into your students' minds about the content you are teaching. You can learn about the students' feelings and understandings about lessons you are teaching. Evaluate the entries only on completeness and do not grade them. You could discourage students from honestly discussing the topic if you assign a grade.

Name _____ Date _____•

Learning Journal Prompts

Directions: Choose one of these ideas to write in your Learning Journal. Write at least a paragraph during your writing time. Write on a different prompt each day until you have written about each of them at least once. Use the lines at the bottom of the page to create your own Learning Journal Prompts.

- Write what you learned from today's lesson.

- Record your feelings about the subject you are learning.

- Explain why you think your teacher chose this lesson.

- Explain how this lesson relates to your life.

- Select an idea from the lesson and explain your understanding of it.

- Compare what you learned in this lesson to a previous lesson.

- Explain how you would teach this lesson to a friend.

- Discuss other things you know about this topic.

- Connect this lesson to other subjects you have learned.

- _____

- _____

- _____

Teaching 2 Strategy

QUESTION ALL-WRITE

The purpose of the Question All-Write strategy (Yell, 2002) is for students to use writing to think about what they have learned during a lecture or a video. Writing can be a useful tool for students to use as they develop metacognition, or awareness of their comprehension. Often students do not stop and think about what they have learned until the end of a lecture or video, which is too late to employ the fix-up strategies necessary for students to learn. When students use Question All-Write, they not only learn that writing can facilitate learning, but they also learn to become more strategic listeners and viewers.

Directions

1. Tell students at the beginning of a lecture or video that you will be stopping halfway through the time to ask students questions. Tell students that they will be responding to the questions through writing.

2. Begin your lecture or video. For example, let's say you are teaching about ancient civilizations. After you have talked for 10 minutes or so, ask students two or three open-ended questions that they could answer in a few sentences. Open-ended questions should begin with the words In what *ways* . . . or *How*. An example follows.

    • In what ways did the ancient Egyptians honor their dead?

    • How did the Mayan civilization promote learning?

3. Duplicate and distribute copies of the Question All-Write sheet that follows.

4. Tell students that they should answer one of the questions using several sentences. Give students ample time to think and write.

5. After students have finished writing, encourage them to use this strategy to improve their listening and viewing abilities. Conduct a class discussion about ways students could improve their comprehension during lectures and videos. Have students write some strategies that they could use to improve their comprehension.

Assessment

Evaluate students' work by determining whether or not their writings answered your questions accurately. If students were unable to answer your questions, consider whether you have been introducing too much information or whether students were not attentive. Use the Question All-Write to revise your teaching if necessary as well as to help students become more aware of their comprehension.

Question All-Write

1. Write the question that you will respond to.

_____

2. Write your response.

_____

_____

_____

_____

_____

_____

_____

_____

_____

_____

3. What strategies could you use to improve your comprehension as you listen or view?

_____

_____

_____

_____

Teaching Strategy 3

One of the best ways for students to learn from their writing is to prepare a summary of something they have read (Armbruster, 2000). Summary writing is a complex skill that has students think about the main point of the text and the important details. A variety of strategies have been used to teach students how to write summaries, one of which is an Exit Card. Exit Cards are not traditional summaries; rather, they encourage students to use the mental processes necessary to create a summary. An Exit Card helps students think about what they learned—from a text, lecture, or video—and to consider what they would like to add to that knowledge.

Directions

1. After students have read a text, listened to a lecture, or watched a video, explain that you will be asking them to summarize what they have learned on Exit Cards. Tell students that Exit Cards are required for them to leave the room, hence the name.

2. Duplicate and distribute the Exit Cards that follow. You might also make a transparency of one card to demonstrate its use for students.

3. Remind students about the text they have read. For example, if students just finished reading *The Orphans of Normandy* (Amis, 2003), you might make the following remarks.

    The Orphans of Normandy was about a group of 100 orphaned girls who were forced to leave their home when the Allies invaded Normandy on June 6, 1944. They began walking to a new location over 150 miles away. You noticed that this true story was told through the children's drawings and writings. What did you learn from your reading?

4. Divide the class into groups of two or three students to discuss what they learned. Give students ample time to respond to your question. Then ask students to share their responses. An example follows.

    I learned more about World War II. I learned that the Germans occupied France from 1940 to the end of the war and that it was a hard time for the French. I also learned that the girls took a white flag and they walked to symbolize surrender in case they were caught.

5. Provide praise for students who were able to give examples of ideas or events that occurred in the book. If students have strayed too far from the text, gently guide them back as in the following example.

    Student: I learned that the orphans ate lunch with the Germans after they walked for a while.

    Teacher: Where in the book did you find this information?

    Student: It says on the entry for July 15 that the girls "finished our lunch with hearty appetites under the terrified eyes of the Germans."

    Teacher: Why do you think the Germans were terrified?

    Student: I don't know.

    Teacher: Do you know why the girls left their orphanage?

    Student: The Allies were bombing Normandy.

Teacher: Yes, and the Allies were bombing Normandy to defeat the Germans and help the French. As the girls left the orphanage, the Germans were also running from the area to escape the bombings. So, how could you revise your summary?

Student: Oh, now I see. The orphans left their home to escape the bombs and so did the Germans.

6.   After students have finished writing something they learned, ask them to write what they would like to learn more about. For example, some students might want to learn more about France during World War II, D-Day, orphanages, and so on. If you are not planning to teach these topics, encourage students to investigate them on their own.

7.   Have students write Exit Cards independently when you want them to summarize what they have learned.

Assessment

As students write their Exit Cards, walk around the room, reading students' work. Evaluate whether students were able to pinpoint and summarize information. For those students who are experiencing difficulty, help them understand where their summaries have diverged from the text. Guide them into more accurate summaries. Give students a plus (+) if their Exit Card shows accuracy, creativity, and thought; a check (✓) if their Exit Card is accurate; and a minus (–) if their Exit Card is not accurate.

Exit Card

Name _____ Date _____

Today I learned

Tomorrow I want to learn more about

Exit Card

Name _____ Date _____

Today I learned

Tomorrow I want to learn more about

Students rarely pay attention to all of the types of writing that they use in their daily lives until you draw their attention to them. The Writing Format Fiesta strategy helps students notice the writing in their lives and helps them connect that writing to learning in content areas. Writing Format Fiesta is an explosion of writing formats that typically are not found in a particular area of learning. You can use this strategy to have students create new Writing Format Fiesta ideas or write using the ideas that are presented in the strategy.

Directions

1. Tell students that they will be using writing in new ways using the strategy Writing Format Fiesta. Explain to students that there are hundreds of writing formats that can be fun to use when writing. (See the chart that follows for examples.) Tell students that Writing Format Fiesta is a new way to think about writing to learn.

2. Explain to students that all pieces of writing have a format. That format can be books, magazine articles, newspaper articles, poems, and essays. Tell students that there are many other formats they could use when writing to learn.

3. Print the list of writing formats on posters and hang them around the room for students to use for inspiration.

4. Model an example of ways to connect writing formats with content learning by writing an example on the chalkboard or on an overhead transparency. For example, tell students that an agreement is a writing format. For students who have been studying the cutting of old growth forests, tell them that the following statement would be an example of a writing assignment that merges the format "agreement" and the content that is being learned in science class.

Writing Format Fiesta Assignment

Craft an agreement between loggers and environmentalists about how much timber to cut in a given year.

5. Divide the class into groups of three or four students. In the groups, have students create writing ideas that fit the formats using all of the content areas that you teach in your grade. Tell students that if they are unsure of the meanings of some of the writing format terms to look for the definitions of the terms in a dictionary.

6. After students have developed a list of ideas, have them choose three of them to write about within the next week. Provide adequate time for students to write in class.

Writing Format Fiesta Examples

Abridgment: Write an abridgment of a story you have read recently.
Address: Provide the address for the vertex angle in an isosceles triangle.
Advice column: Write an advice column for a new athlete in your sport.
Analogy: Write an analogy to describe the differences between WWI and WWII.
Anecdote: Write an anecdote about a molecule.
Announcement: Create an announcement for a musical event featuring a favorite band.
Anthem: Create words for an anthem about eating healthy foods.
Bedtime story: Write a bedtime story beginning: Once upon a time there was a square.
Biographical sketch: Write a biographical sketch about a political leader.
Boast: Write a boast about your knowledge about science.
Bumper sticker: Write a bumper sticker about an event in history.
Calendar quip: Make up a health saying, or quip, for every day in one month.
Catalog description: Create a catalog description for sports equipment.
Complaint: Write a letter of complaint about pollution to a member of Congress.
Diet: Develop a diet for a sumo wrestler.
Epilogue: Write the epilogue for your career as a geographer.
Explanation: Explain the associative property of addition.
Habit: Describe your reading habits.
Hagiography: Create a patron saint of algebra.
Hyperbole: Describe an athletic event using hyperbole.
Index: Create an index for the historical events of the past decade.
Insult: Create an insult for a character in a book you are reading.
Interview: Write interview questions for a biologist.
Justification: Write a justification for your favorite subject.
Letter: Write a letter to your favorite person in history.
Lie: Write a mathematical lie.
List: List famous paintings for sale at an auction.
Memory: Write your memory of learning to read.
Myth: List the misconceptions, or myths, you had about musicians.
Palindrome: Write a mathematical palindrome.
Pedigree: Write the pedigree for your favorite bird.
Poster: Make a poster of the highest mountain peak on each continent.
Prescription: Write a prescription for becoming a successful scientist.
Rules of etiquette: Create a list of rules of etiquette for zoo animals.
Sale notice: Design a sale notice for a clipper ship.
Self-description: Describe yourself in terms of the colors of the spectrum.
Speech: Write a speech for a group of astronauts before they leave for space.
Survival guide: Write a survival guide for living under the sea.
T-shirt: Create a T-shirt slogan about the earth.
Wanted poster: Develop a wanted poster about a war criminal.
Wise saying: Collect wise sayings about economics.
Wish: Write your wishes for the next generation.
Yearbook inscription: Write a yearbook inscription to you from a character in a book.
Yellow pages ad: Create a yellow pages ad for a new business.

Based on McIntosh, M. (1997). 500 writing formats. *Mathematics Teaching in the Middle School, 2*, 354–357.

Teaching Strategy 5

K-W-L (Ogle, 1986) is a popular strategy to use before and during the teaching of thematic units. Teachers have students list what they know, what they want to know, and what they've learned. Often teachers use the K-W-L as a whole-class lesson and write the students' responses on a chart. Another way to use the K-W-L strategy, however, is through the use of journals. Cantrell, Fusaro, and Dougherty (2000) found that students using a K-W-L journal in social studies learned more content than did students who wrote summaries in journals. The K-W-L Journal, therefore, is a good way for students to use writing to learn from their content areas.

Directions

1. Tell students that they will be writing in their journals using a new format, the K-W-L Journal. Explain that K stands for what they already know, the W stands for what they want to know, and the L stands for what they've learned.

2. Select a content area text to use to demonstrate the K-W-L Journal. Have students scan the title, the headings, and the illustrations. Then say something like the following comment.

   As you preview the text, you can access your background knowledge about the topic by thinking about what you already know about the subject. Accessing your background knowledge will help you understand what you read because you are bringing the knowledge that you have to your conscious mind. As you read, then, you'll be able to make connections between what you already know and what you're reading.

3. Duplicate and distribute the K-W-L Journal sheet on page 144. Have students write what they already know about the topic in the Know section.

4. Then explain to students that readers typically think about a text before reading, asking questions and wondering about the topic. Model this thinking process for students as in the example that follows.

   I previewed the science chapter on the rain forest and noticed that I already knew about some of the plants and animals found in most rain forests. I've been wondering, though, what kinds of birds are found in rain forests. I also am curious about the kinds of medicines that can be made from the rain forest plants.

   Since I want to know about the rain forest birds, I'll write what I want to know and why in my K-W-L Journal. Then I'll write a question and rationale for my second question: the kinds of medicines that can be made from rain forest plants.

5. Give students time to write entries in the K portion and W portion of the K-W-L Journals. Then have students read the text. You could have students read independently, in pairs, or in groups.

6. After students read, tell them that you'd like them to complete the L portion of their K-W-L Journal with what they've learned from their reading. Provide students with ample time to record what they learned. Remind students to use their knowledge of spelling and punctuation as they write.

7. Explain to students that they can use this thinking process whenever they read to help them comprehend texts. Use the K-W-L Journal occasionally in order for students to learn through writing.

Assessment

Reading the K portion of students' K-W-L Journals can help you know the type of background knowledge students have about a topic you are teaching. Use this information to guide your instruction. You can use the W portion of the journals to understand how well students are questioning before reading, and the L portion to determine what students have learned. These journal entries should be used for your own information and for students to learn through writing rather than as a grade.

Name _____ Date _____

K-W-L Journal

Subject _____ Topic _____

What I Know

_____

_____

_____

_____

_____

What I Want to Know

_____

_____

_____

_____

_____

What I Learned

_____

_____

_____

_____

_____

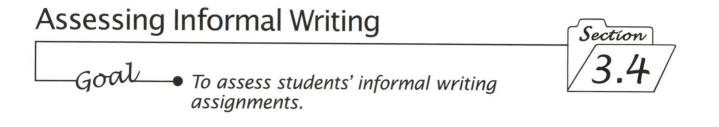

Assessing Informal Writing

Goal ● *To assess students' informal writing assignments.*

BACKGROUND

Informal writing is a different kind of writing; it is practice with language so that students can build writing fluency. When you think about assessing informal writing, you need to define the purpose of the writing and the purpose of the assessment (Spandel & Stiggins, 1997). The purpose of informal writing is to have students become fluent writers by promoting self-discovery, by constructing meaning through responding, and by learning content material through writing. The assessments used for informal writing should reflect these goals.

Frank Smith (1988) wrote that assessment is the greatest danger in education. Nowhere is this more true than in the assessment of informal writing. If the purpose of informal writing is to encourage fluency, risk-taking, and creative language, then checking to see if students remembered to capitalize proper nouns is counterproductive to the purpose of the assignment. However, many teachers are uncomfortable leaving writings ungraded. Therefore, we have provided two ways to assess informal writing for you to use or adapt. When assessing students' informal writings, however, remember that it's more important for students to write than it is for you to assess. Save the rigorous assessment for other types of writing.

> *It's more important for students to write than it is for you to assess.*

Is it difficult for you to leave a paper ungraded?

KidBibs

http://kidbibs.com/home.htm

This site identifies strategies and resources to help children of all ages to become better readers, writers, and learners.

You can develop an Informal Writing Scale to fit your writing purposes. If you use this type of assessment, you will need to collect students' writing periodically and apply the assessment to their work. Some teachers find that occasionally using an Informal Writing Scale keeps students on their toes.

 ## Directions

1. Duplicate and distribute the Informal Writing Scale that follows. Tell students that occasionally you will be assessing their informal writing with that scale.

2. Collect students' informal writing once every two weeks and assess it using the Informal Writing Scale.

Will use of the Informal Writing Scale keep these students on their toes?

Name _____ Date _____

Informal Writing Scale

1. Student has written the required amount.

3	2	1
Definitely	Partially	Minimally

2. Student has written about the topic.

3	2	1
Definitely	Partially	Minimally

3. Student has used interesting language.

3	2	1
Definitely	Partially	Minimally

4. Student was personally engaged in the writing.

3	2	1
Definitely	Partially	Minimally

JOURNAL SELF-ASSESSMENT ●

"The goal of all evaluation is the development of self-evaluation" (Parsons, 2001, p. 100). This is especially true for informal writing. When students are writing in journals, in response to reading, and when reading to learn, they are the best judges of their writing. Therefore, students should be given the opportunity to evaluate their informal writing periodically.

Directions

1. Remind students about the different types of writing that you do in class. Explain that some of their writings are graded by you, some writings are given to an audience, and some writings are not graded. Tell students that you don't grade all of their writings because you want them to evaluate their own progress.

2. Discuss the types of informal writing you do in your class. Perhaps you have students write Family Message Journals, Speedwriting, Personal Journals, Response Cards, and Learning Journals. List these types of informal writings on the chalkboard or on an overhead transparency.

3. Tell students that they will be evaluating themselves on these types of informal writings. Explain that the purpose of their evaluations is for them to make progress rather than to receive a grade.

4. Duplicate and distribute the Journal Self-Assessment sheet that follows. Read and explain each of the categories, modeling how students should think about their work as in the example that follows.

   The first statement states, "I like to write in my journal." That statement refers to all of the ways we do journal writing in this class that I've listed on the chalkboard. Think about this statement. Can you say you like to write in your journal? That doesn't mean you like it every time or that you like every journal assignment. Instead it means that you generally like writing in your journal as opposed to disliking it.

5. Give students time to complete the Journal Self-Assessment, checking the items they think characterize their informal writings. Then have students place a star next to one or two items that they want to emphasize in the coming weeks.

6. Remind students that they can use the Journal Self-Assessment to help them improve as writers if they honestly reflect on their writings.

Name _____ Date _____•

Journal Self-Assessment

Check each of the statements that sound like you when you write in your journal.
Place a star by the items that you want to emphasize for the next few weeks.

_____ I like to write in my journal.

_____ I really think about what I write.

_____ I try to write during the entire time period.

_____ I write in my journal outside of school.

_____ I tell my friends and family about my journal.

_____ I use my journal for ideas for stories.

_____ I try to write a paragraph or more each time I write in my journal.

_____ I try to use what I know about spelling and punctuation whenever I write.

_____ I use the Word Wall or other resources as I write.

_____ I try to use imaginative language when I write.

_____ I experiment with figurative language when I write.

_____ I try to be creative when I write.

Process Writing: Identifying Topics, Purposes, and Audiences

"I know what I know and I write it."

—Octavio Paz

OVERVIEW

"Writers don't improve their craft unless they have a real purpose, a real audience, and a real investment in their writing" (Fox, 1990, p. 471). Writing is, after all, a way for writers to express their thoughts and ideas. These thoughts and ideas are the content of writing. The content of writing depends on the writer's reasons for writing, the topic of the piece, and the audience for whom the piece is written.

The process that writers move through has been documented and refined by a variety of educators, most notably Donald Graves (2003). This process is often called "process writing," the "writing process," or "writing workshop." All of these terms imply that writ-

ers prewrite or plan before writing, that they draft a version of the piece, and then they revise and edit it before sharing it with an audience. The process that writers use, however, is not a series of steps. Writers move through the stages of writing recursively; in other words, writers can move directly through the stages, or they can move back through any one of them.

In order to teach students how to use the writing process, students must first want to write. Therefore, the first step for teachers is to encourage students to write. Some of the ways teachers can encourage students to write are to build writing suggestions based on students' interests and to tailor writing assignments to students' strengths. Another way to encourage students' writing is to help them develop the skills to tell stories about their lives. Writing about their lives is central to process writing: "It is a maxim of writing workshop that all adolescent writers—indeed all writers of any age—have a story to tell. One task of the teacher is to help the student discover that story and write it meaningfully" (Furr, 2003, p. 520).

Process writing has been translated by teachers into many different types of writing programs (Lipson, Mosenthal, Daniels, & Woodside-Jiron, 2000). Some teachers use a more structured approach and others allow students free reign. The details of process writing are not as important as the basic principles. Process writing is defined by the principles that follow.

> "Writers don't improve their craft unless they have a real purpose, a real audience, and a real investment in their writing."

volve a writing plan. The process of planning has two steps:

1. The writer must understand the writing task. This task includes the outcome of the writing.
2. The writer must carry out the task by making decisions about topics, purposes, and audiences.

The time needed for each of these steps varies from writer to writer. Writers, therefore, first think about what they want to do and then try different ideas to make it happen (Hayes & Nash, 1996).

An example of a writer making decisions is a veterinarian's technician preparing a report on the status of the health of a dog. The outcome is the report, and the technician then needs to address the following questions:

Basic Principles of Process Writing

- Emphasis is on the process, not the product, of writing.
- Students learn to write by writing.
- Students select topics and find audiences for their writing.
- Students write at their own pace.
- Instruction is delivered through mini-lessons.
- Instructional groups are flexible.
- Writing is shared with a variety of audiences.

Writer's workshop is one way to teach process writing.

When teachers use process writing as the framework for their writing instruction, students become writers with decisions to make. Some of the first decisions students make in-

- Why am I writing this (purpose)?
- What shall I write (topic)?
- What do I know? What do I need to find out (ideas)?
- Who will read this (audience)?

In the example of a technician reporting on the health of a dog, the technician is writing about the dog's health—with information coming from the dog's file, to be read by the veterinarian and the dog's owners—with the purpose of writing to inform. Similar decisions are made by all writers.

Students need to have opportunities to make writing decisions and develop personal responsibility for their writing. When asked, students responded that they would rather make writing decisions than have teachers make all of their decisions for them (Zaragoza & Vaughn, 1995). Students said that they liked to choose their own topics, decide on their audiences, and sign up to conference with their teachers. Students who are given ownership over writing decisions feel in control of their writing. These students are more motivated to write and they learn to act like writers.

When students have the chance to write for their own purposes about topics they choose for selected audiences, they perform at their best. It is the teacher's role to provide students with instruction on ways to generate topics, discover purposes, and identify audiences. This chapter provides resources, teaching strategies, ideas, and activities to help teachers instruct students on how to make decisions about the content of their writing. Some ways to assess content also are included.

Creative Writing

http://eric.indiana.edu/ieo/digests/d109.html

Teaching creative writing in the elementary school can be easy if you use ideas from this site.

Encouraging Students to Write

Goal • *To encourage students to write.*

BACKGROUND

Words have power. They have the power to persuade, to soothe, to hurt, to encourage, and to make us laugh. Why, then, do so many students dread writing? Lucy Calkins (1994) suggests that many students fear writing because of the ways in which teachers teach writing in schools. Too frequently, teachers assign meaningless writing assignments, try to motivate students to complete the assignments, and then point out students' errors. It's no wonder many students don't like to write.

> *Words have power.*

WRITING IS PERSONAL—ONE OF THE INTIMACIES OF LIFE. When you write, you share your heart, mind, and soul in fixed symbols with another person. Since writing is intrinsically personal, one of the most important things that teachers can do to encourage students to write is to learn about their students' interests. When teachers know their students' interests and their attitudes toward writing, teachers can provide motivating writing instruction that takes into account students' personal lives. Choice, challenge, and control are motivational factors that encourage student learning (Gambrell, 1996).

STUDENTS HAVE INDIVIDUAL TALENTS. Encouraging students to write should take many forms. Linda Rief (1999) suggests that teachers need to expand their notions of literacy and to take into account not only words but also the visual, the physical, the mathematical, and the sensual. As writers write, they use their many talents to put words on paper. Since students are individuals with unique gifts, teachers can encourage writing by customizing some writing assignments to students' various talents. Gardner (1993) posits that eight intelligences define human talent. Teachers can encourage students to write by varying writing assignments using multiple intelligences as a guide.

WRITING IS FUN. Encouraging students to write by learning about their interests and tailoring assignments to individual strengths is one step toward promoting positive attitudes toward writing. Writing, how-

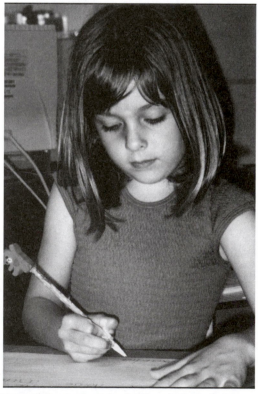

Does this student look like she's enjoying writing?

ever, is not only personal; writing can be fun for other reasons. Words have the power to make us laugh. Think about the jokes you know, the plays on words, the books in your class that use idioms in strange ways. Words that are used in unique ways are humorous. Word play is part of what can make writing fun, and helping students look for ways in which words make us laugh can also encourage students to write.

Writing instruction doesn't have to be a joyless affair.

8 Intelligences
Bodily/Kinesthetic
Logical/Mathematical
Interpersonal
Intrapersonal
Musical/Rhythmical
Naturalistic
Verbal/Linguistic
Visual/Spacial

- When teachers learn about their students and allow students choices in writing, teachers encourage writing.
- When teachers address the multiple intelligences of students in their classes, teachers encourage writing.
- When teachers help students see how much fun words can be, teachers encourage writing.

This section provides teaching strategies for encouraging students to write.

Teaching 1 Strategy

Section 4.1
INTEREST CHARTS

One of the primary ways to encourage students to write is to tailor writing assignments to students' interests. When students have writing projects that are of interest to them, they are more likely to have an intrinsic desire to write. You can use an Interest Chart to learn more about your students in order to tailor writing assignments to their interests. Certainly, you know many of your students' interests already. However, using an Interest Chart can provide you with many more insights about your students and their lives.

 Directions

1. Tell students that you want to learn more about their lives. Explain to students that you will be asking them to share their interests, feelings, and hobbies with you. Tell students that they should be honest; however, they should not include things that are overly private. Give students time to think about their interests, feelings, and hobbies.

2. Duplicate and distribute the Interest Chart that follows. Have students put their names and the date on their Interest Charts. Tell students to place one or more items in each of the sections of the chart. Give them at least 10 minutes to complete their Interest Charts. Provide students with extra charts if they write more than can fit in a section.

3. Collect the Interest Charts and read them carefully. Look for patterns of interest among the students. Where you see patterns of interest, adjust your instruction to take students' interests into account.

4. Return the Interest Charts to students. Have students place the Interest Charts in their writing folders to use as they select topics for writing.

5. Have students complete new Interest Charts every two or three months. Explain that many of their interests may change over time and that you want to stay current with their interests. Use the Interest Charts to plan your instruction and encourage students to use their Interest Charts to select topics for writing.

Interest Chart

My Hobbies	Sports I Like to Play	Other Interests I Have
My Likes	**My Dislikes**	**Books I Have Read**
Things I Love to Do	**Some Good Things about Me**	**Some Things about Me That Aren't So Good**

WRITING AUTOBIOGRAPHIES

Students can share their writing histories and their opinions about writing instruction through a Writing Autobiography. As students think about their writing experiences and share those experiences in a Writing Autobiography, they provide teachers with information about their writing lives. When teachers read students' Writing Autobiographies, they learn about students in a personal way, which can help promote a positive attitude toward writing (Lenski, Wham, & Johns, 2003).

📑 *Directions*

1. Introduce and discuss the idea of Writing Autobiographies. Tell students that an autobiography is an author's account of his or her life.

2. Tell students that you are interested in their writing histories and in their opinions about writing. Explain that you will use students' Writing Autobiographies as you develop writing assignments.

3. Duplicate and distribute the Writing Autobiography Thought Probes sheet that follows. Read the thought probes with students. Remind students that writing in this case does not mean handwriting but writing sentences or stories. Tell students to consider these questions as they complete their Writing Autobiographies.

4. Provide students with ample time to complete their Writing Autobiographies. After students have finished, collect the papers and read them, looking for insights into students' writing histories. For example, if students complain about spending most of their writing time learning grammar, organize your writing instruction so that more time is devoted to teaching writing fluency.

5. Return the Writing Autobiographies to students. Ask students to share their Writing Autobiographies with their classmates either by reading them aloud or by displaying them on a bulletin board.

Assessment

Assess Writing Autobiographies by a rubric that emphasizes writing content. It is important that students feel successful as they write about their lives.

Writing Autobiography Thought Probes

1. Do you consider yourself to be a writer? Why or why not?

   _____

2. How did you learn to become the writer that you are?

   _____

3. What kind of writing do you like best?

   _____

4. What piece of writing are you most proud of? Why?

   _____

5. What do you like least about writing?

   _____

6. What is your favorite memory of writing?

   _____

7. What is your least favorite memory of writing?

   _____

8. What makes a person a writer?

   _____

9. How can your teacher make writing more enjoyable for you?

   _____

10. How can your teacher help you become a better writer?

    _____

Teaching 3 Strategy

MULTIPLE INTELLIGENCES

Different students have different talents, identified by Gardner (1993) as eight aspects of intelligence, or multiple intelligences. Multiple Intelligences are an individual's learning strengths. Each student learns in preferred ways. Some students learn best through physical movement while others learn using shapes and colors. Some students may have obvious strengths in learning, such as the student who exhibits musical talent, but all students have capacities in all eight intelligences (Armstrong, 2003). To encourage students to write, you should vary your writing assignments and expectations and tailor writing assignments to students' strengths.

Directions

1. Become aware of the various strengths students bring to writing situations by carefully reading the Multiple Intelligences and Writing Chart that follows. Try to match the talents of students in your classroom with the eight intelligences.

2. Tell students that each person learns in his or her own way. Tell students that generally there are eight ways that people learn. Explain that, although these eight intelligences describe the most common ways people learn, students might identify their own unique learning strengths.

3. Have students write their learning strengths, along with their name, on a piece of paper. Read what students have described as their own learning strengths.

4. Because some students may be unaware of their own talents, guide students to understand what you perceive as additional areas of strength. Discuss students' learning strengths with them.

5. Celebrate multiple intelligences by congratulating students on their unique capabilities. Explain that all intelligences are valued in your classroom.

6. Vary your writing lessons based on the different aspects of intelligence. When you assign a writing project that is geared to the strength of only a few students, encourage other students to develop this area of learning.

7. Allow students as often as possible to choose writing projects that reflect their learning strengths.

8. Identify students who feel they have strengths in particular areas and who can be consulted as "experts" by other students.

All students have strengths and talents.

Multiple Intelligences and Writing Chart

Bodily/Kinesthetic Intelligence (body smart)

Refers to the ability to use movement of the body to perform tasks and to solve problems.	• Help students enjoy the physical movements of writing and typing. • Let students choose where they write, such as sitting on a bean bag chair or lying on the carpet. • Encourage students to dramatize their writing and put physical movements in the scenes. • Help students connect writing to physical activities such as writing rules of games or writing letters to sports' heroes.

Logical/Mathematical Intelligence (number smart)

Refers to the ability to use numbers and logic. It also refers to the ability to recognize patterns, to categorize, to calculate, to classify, and to hypothesize.	• Help students recognize and use organizational patterns of writing, such as the main idea-detail paragraph pattern. • Emphasize writing genres such as fairy tales and folktales. • Teach students to use logical progression of ideas in writing. • Incorporate writing in mathematics lessons.

Interpersonal Intelligence (people smart)

Refers to the ability to understand personal relationships and to act on that knowledge. It also refers to the ability to be sensitive to the needs of others and to work with other people.	• Provide students the opportunity to write with other students. • Emphasize audiences in writing. Tell students to visualize their audiences as they write. • Encourage students to write about situations that involve other students and about personal conflicts in the classroom. • Teach students to observe others and to write dialogue.

Intrapersonal Intelligence (self smart)

Refers to knowledge about the self. It refers to the ability to engage in self-reflection about emotions and thinking and to understand behavior.	• Provide students with opportunities to write independently. • Encourage students to write about their feelings. • Let students complete longer writing projects at their own pace. • Provide students with the opportunity to write personal narratives.

(continued)

Musical/Rhythmical Intelligence (music smart)

Refers to the capacity to identify, express, and appreciate musical forms. It also refers to the ability to think in musical terms and to identify rhythms.	• Emphasize the rhythmic quality of language. • Give students the opportunity to write poems and songs. • Emphasize writing genres such as parody, satire, and caricature. • Encourage students to write about musical patterns and themes.

Naturalistic Intelligence (nature smart)

Refers to a responsiveness to the environment and a love of the outdoors. It also refers to curiosity about and understanding of the natural sciences.	• Allow students to write outside, perhaps as an extension of outdoor recess or physical education class. • Encourage students to write about environmental issues. • Encourage students to make entries in writers' notebooks on field trips and on hikes. • Provide students with opportunities to write to naturalists such as birders, forest rangers, and deep sea divers.

Verbal/Linguistic Intelligence (word smart)

Refers to the ability to use words in writing and speaking. It also refers to the ability to use language in creative ways.	• Emphasize unusual word forms and meanings such as puns, jokes, and etymologies. • Encourage students to create word images and to write with descriptive language. • Encourage students to recognize and experiment with creative writing styles. • Provide students with the opportunity to edit class newspapers and books.

Visual/Spacial Intelligence (picture smart)

Refers to the ability to create mental images and to manipulate spacial configurations. It also refers to the ability to use shapes, forms, and space to create new ideas.	• Provide students with graphic organizers for planning their writing. • Provide mind maps of writing genres such as narrative, persuasive, and expository writing. • Provide students with the opportunity to create maps, graphs, and tables. • Encourage students to read about illustrators and to illustrate their own writing.

RAFT

RAFT is a writing strategy that encourages writing because it helps students organize their thoughts before writing (Santa, Havens, & Harrison, 1989). RAFT is an acronym for Role, Audience, Format, and Topic, all of the major components of writing. RAFT can also be used to design creative writing lessons in content areas such as social studies, science, and so on.

 ## Directions

1. Tell students that they will be deciding on a writing piece using the RAFT strategy. Explain that RAFT stands for Role, Audience, Format, and Topic as follows.

   - Role refers to the perspective of the writer.

   - Audience refers to the reader's perspective.

   - Format refers to the form of the writing product.

   - Topic refers to the specific content of the writing.

2. Duplicate the RAFT chart that follows or draw one on the chalkboard. Explain each category using examples from your curriculum such as the following ideas.

   Today, you're going to write a piece using RAFT as the organizing principle for your writing. I'll give you some examples. I've been thinking about the book I read to you by Pete Nelson (2002) Left for Dead. *I'm going to choose the role of a newspaper reporter. My audience will be people who read newspapers in 1945. The format will be a news feature, and the topic will be the sinking of the Indianapolis.*

   Now, I'd like you to think of some writing ideas using RAFT. You can think about stories you've read, or you can think about content area subjects. For example, using science as an idea, your role would be a planet, the audience would be the earth, the format a brochure, and the topic a description of your landforms.

3. Tell students that as they write you'll record their ideas on the RAFT chart. Divide students into groups of three or four to develop their RAFT frameworks.

4. Remind students that writing can take a variety of formats. There are many different types of writing other than books, magazines, and newspapers. Provide students with some ideas about formats for writing by duplicating and distributing the Writing Format sheet on page 164. Have students choose one of the writing formats on the list as an alternate to the one already chosen.

5. Explain to students that RAFT can be an organizing framework they can use as they write during process writing or writing workshops. Tell students that all writing will have a Role, Audience, Format, and Topic. Encourage students to use RAFT as they think about writing projects.

RAFT

Role	Audience	Format	Topic
Newspaper reporter	Readers in 1945	News feature	Sinking of the Indianapolis
Planet	Earth	Brochure	Description of landforms

Writing Formats

Advertisements
Advice columns
Allegories
Alphabet books
Anecdotes
Announcements
Apologies
Applications
Appointment books
Autobiographies
Autograph books

Ballots
Banners
Beauty tips
Billboards
Book jackets
Brochures
Bulletins
Bumper stickers

Captions
Cartoons
Catalogs
Certificates
Character sketches
Charts
Comics
Commentaries
Commercials
Computer programs
Contracts
Coupons

Debates
Definitions
Deposit slips
Diagrams
Diaries
Dictionaries
Directories

Editorials
Envelopes
Essays

Fables
Flyers
Folktales
Fortune cookies

Graphs
Greeting cards
Guidebooks

Horoscopes

Indexes
Interviews
Invitations
Itineraries

Jingles
Jokes
Jump rope rhymes
Junk mail

Lab reports
Letters
Lists
Lyrics

Maps
Memoirs
Memos
Menus
Messages
Minutes of meetings
Myths

Newsletters
Notes

Opinions

Paragraphs
Petitions
Plays
Poetry
Postcards
Posters
Prescriptions
Puzzles

Questionnaires

Recipes
Record albums
Requests
Reviews
Riddles
Rules

Scripts
Signs
Slogans
Songs
Speeches
Summaries
Surveys

Tables
Telegraphs
Telephone directories
Tickets
Tongue twisters
Travelogues

Valentines

Want ads
Weather reports

Yearbooks
You Are There stories

From Susan Davis Lenski and Jerry L. Johns, *Improving Writing K–8: Strategies, Assessments, and Resources* (2nd ed.). Copyright © 2004 by Kendall/Hunt Publishing Company (1-800-247-3458, ext. 4 or 5). May be reproduced for noncommercial educational purposes within the guidelines noted on the copyright page.

Creative Writing

www.lessontutor.com

This site offers samples of writing, suggestions on how to improve writing, and practice assignments for students in middle school.

Generating Topics

Goal ● *To help students generate topics for writing.*

BACKGROUND

"I don't know what to write about." This statement, echoed by many students, actually emphasizes a very important point. Content is the essence of writing. Every other part of writing—the organization, the mechanics, the style—takes a distant second place compared with the meat of writing, the content. Helping students generate topics for writing, therefore, is one of the key parts of writing instruction.

> *Content is the essence of writing.*

There are three areas from which students can choose topics for writing: personal experiences, imagination, and outside knowledge.

PERSONAL EXPERIENCES. Some writing educators suggest that students should write primarily from their personal experiences (Graves, 1994). When writing from personal experiences, students are encouraged to look at their lives from a writer's point of view. What have they done? What do they want? What do they think? Students writing about personal experiences "read their worlds" (Freire & Macedo, 1987). They take situations, events, memories, and opinions and form them into stories and essays.

Writing about their personal lives is an important outlet for students. When students are given free reign in their choice of writing topics, some of them turn to controversial issues such as family issues, feelings, and emotions. Some teachers feel uncomfortable reading such personal writings (Schneider, 2001), but Anderson and Anderson (2003) remind us that when students write about issues close to their hearts, teachers are able to connect with students in ways that are not usually possible in the classroom.

Writing about their lives is a good outlet for students.

IMAGINATION. Writers can find topics in their imaginations. Where creative ideas originate is still somewhat of a mystery (Sharples, 1996). Some people are able to take their background experiences and knowledge and organize them in unique ways. Having students imagine topics, therefore, is not an easy instructional goal to achieve. However, students need to let their imaginations take them to new places. They need to dream new dreams. They need to invent new ideas. Students also need the freedom to find topics in their imaginations.

OUTSIDE KNOWLEDGE. Writers need to write about topics outside of themselves in addition to writing about their personal experiences and from their imaginations (Stotsky, 1995). To gather information for writing topics, students can read, write, listen, and learn about new subjects. They can question other people, interview them, and discuss new things. In short, students can learn new information. Then students can write about topics using this new knowledge.

In schools, teachers frequently assign topics for writing. However, best practice suggests that teachers should allow students to choose their own topics from time to time (Bromley, 1999). This section provides resources, teaching strategies, ideas, and activities you can use to help students think of their own writing topics and you can use to assign students topics to write about.

Teaching **1** *Strategy* _____ *Section* 4.2

EXAMINE THE POSSIBILITIES

There is a wealth of topics that students can write about. Some of these topics can be found in students' own personal experiences. Others will be part of students' imaginations or learning. Sometimes students should have the chance to write whatever they want. To select a topic, however, students need to Examine the Possibilities.

Directions

1. Tell students that they will be writing about any topic they choose. Remind them that writers often choose their own writing topics.

2. Before students select a topic, have them examine the possible topics in their lives by using the strategy Examine the Possibilities.

3. Duplicate and distribute the list that follows. Tell students that in order to think of topics for writing they should try some of the items from the list. Inform students that they will have three days to think of topics for writing. Remind students each day to try one or two of the items on the list. Give students class time if necessary.

4. After three days, ask students to write down their topics for writing. Then discuss the ways they generated their topics. If students used another activity to think of a topic, add that activity to the list.

Examine the Possibilities:
Ways to Think of Writing Topics

- ▲ Read journals
- ▲ Talk with others
- ▲ Interview others
- ▲ Visualize stories and events
- ▲ Think about experiences
- ▲ Read books or magazines
- ▲ Free write
- ▲ Write five or more beginning sentences
- ▲ Doodle
- ▲ Outline
- ▲ Create lists
- ▲ Record dreams
- ▲ Attend plays
- ▲ Watch movies or television
- ▲ Look at pictures
- ▲ Explore the Internet

Teaching 2 Strategy _____ *Section 4.2*

LET ME TELL YOU ABOUT . . .

Sometimes writers find their own writing topics by talking with others. Writers often have stories in their lives that they could tell, if they had someone to listen to them. Students can generate topics by talking with classmates. The strategy Let Me Tell You About . . . gives students the opportunity to talk about topics of interest. Through discussion, students can explore and expand topics for writing.

Directions

1. Tell students that they will be writing about topics of their own choosing. Ask students if they have topics that they would like to write about. For those students who already have topics, ask them to begin writing. Those students who need to generate topics can participate in Let Me Tell You About . . . .

2. Duplicate and distribute the list that follows. Ask students to check three items on the list. Explain that they will be discussing their checked items with their classmates as one way to explore ideas for writing.

3. Divide the class into groups of two or three students. Ask students to bring their Let Me Tell You About . . . lists to the group.

4. Ask one student to volunteer to begin sharing. Tell the student volunteer to give the list to the other members of the group. Direct the members of the group to choose an item on the list. Give the student volunteer time to talk about the subject or to tell a story. Have the group members discuss whether there is a topic for writing in that discussion. After the first student has found a topic, provide time for the other group members to discuss their lists.

Name _____ Date _____●

Let Me Tell You About . . .

Please ask me about one of these ideas that I've checked:

_____ my family   _____ things I collect

_____ my pet   _____ a time I was afraid

_____ something I like to do   _____ a good story

_____ a special friend   _____ my favorite food

_____ an exciting event   _____ a special place

_____ a fun party   _____ a vacation or trip

_____ things I don't like   _____ a time I helped someone

_____ a TV show   _____ ways I've changed

_____ being lost   _____ when I was little

_____ my neighborhood   _____ places I've lived

_____ my lessons   _____ my favorite sport

_____ a hero   _____ a computer game

_____ things I like a lot   _____ a favorite book

_____ my town   _____ a special toy or game

_____

Teaching Strategy

PARENT RECOMMENDED TOPICS

Parents are a natural source of ideas for their children's writings. After all, most parents have known their children from birth. Parents have observed their children doing funny things, having adventures, learning, and growing. When asked, parents may be able to share many ideas for students' writings.

 ## Directions

1. Tell students that you will be sending a letter to their parents asking them for some of their favorite memories to use as writing topics. Ask students to alert their parents in advance that a letter will be sent home.

2. Duplicate or adapt the following letter and send it home with students. Give parents at least three days to think of topics before returning the letter to school. After three or four days, ask students to place their parents' letters in students' writing folders.

3. For parents who cannot read English or do not want to complete the letter, tell students they can give the letter to a friend or to a relative. Or students may be able to translate the letter for their parents. Tell students that a third option is to complete the list of topics themselves.

4. When students are asked to select topics for writing, have them refer to their Parent Recommended Topics list.

Parent Recommended Topics

Dear Parent,

In school, students often have the opportunity to choose their own topics for writing. Because you have more knowledge about your child than just about anyone else, I would like you to list 10 possible writing topics for your child. To identify writing topics, think for a moment about your child. Think of a funny story, a trip, or a learning experience your child will remember. Or think of the times your child got into trouble. Any of these ideas could make good topics for writing. You will love the stories your child will write about these topics.

Please list 10 writing topics and return this letter to school with your child in three days. If you have any questions, don't hesitate to ask your child or to call me at school.

Sincerely,

Potential Writing Topics

1. _____

2. _____

3. _____

4. _____

5. _____

6. _____

7. _____

8. _____

9. _____

10. _____

One of students' most valuable resources for generating topics for writing is their own hearts. Nancy Atwell (2002) suggests that students draw Heart Maps to tap into students' desires and interests as topics for writing. A Heart Map is simply a heart with a list of the experiences, memories, and ideas that are near and dear to the writer's heart. Students enjoy making Heart Maps and find them useful as they choose topics for writing.

Directions

1. Inform students that they will be drawing a Heart Map as a resource for writing topics. Explain that a Heart Map is a brainstormed list of things that students care about.

2. Duplicate and distribute the Heart Map on page 174. In the center have students write their names. Around their names ask students to think about things that are important to them. Model a Heart Map by placing your name in the center of a heart and listing things important to you. An example follows.

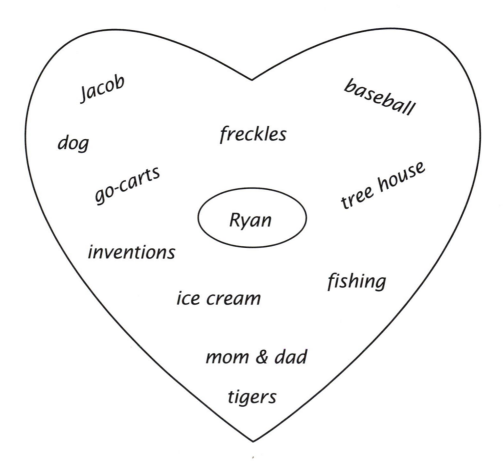

3. Have students begin thinking of their own lives. You can prompt them by making the following statements.

> *We all have different things that are important to us. I'm going to ask you some questions as you write in your Heart Maps to help you think about those things.*
> - *Think about your family members. Who is very important to you at this time?*
> - *Do you have pets? Are they important to you?*
> - *What memories from the past are important to you?*
> - *What do you really care about?*
> - *What do you like to eat? Watch on TV? Play on the computer? Listen to? Are any of these important to you?*
> - *What important sports or games do you play?*
> - *Do you have any important goals?*
> - *What else comes to your mind that's important to you?*

4. After students have developed their own Heart Maps, have them share their maps with a friend, discussing why each item is important. Tell students that sometimes listening to a classmate triggers additional ideas in their own minds. Give students a few minutes to revise their Heart Maps.

5. Ask students to place their Heart Maps in their writing folders. Encourage students to use these maps when they are thinking of topics for writing.

Heart Map

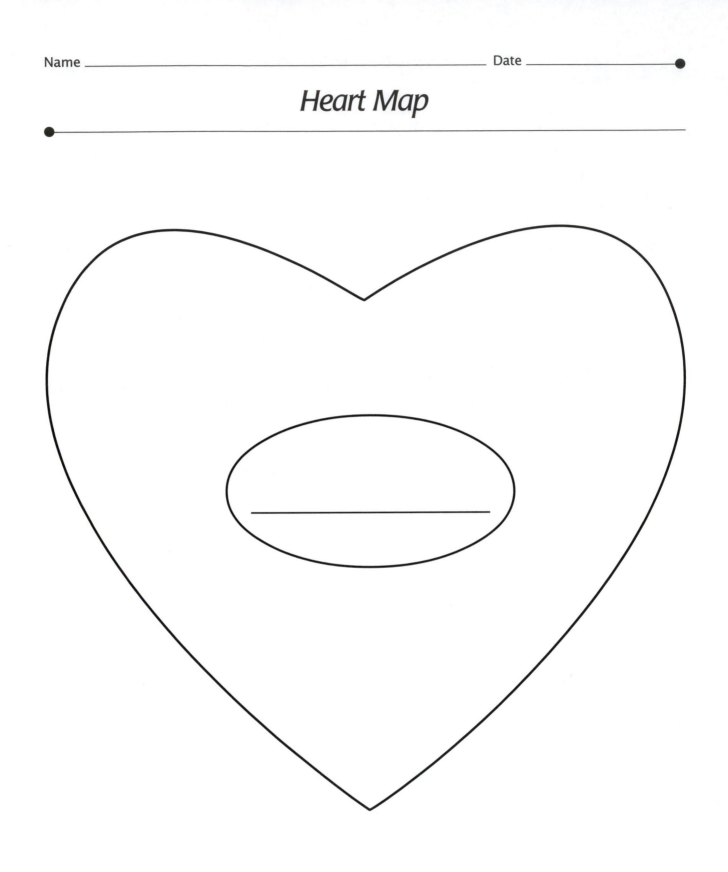

Adapted from N. Atwell. (2002). *Lessons that change writers*. Portsmouth, NH: Heinemann.

CIRCLES OF WRITING

One of the resources students can use for selection of topics is their journals. (See Chapter 3 for journal writing ideas.) Journals are a way for students to do prewriting of ideas that enter their minds. Students also use journals to express their feelings, which are a good source of ideas for both personal narratives and fictional writing. To help students capitalize on the many ideas they have written in their journals, Hughey and Slack (2001) suggest students develop Circles of Writing. Circles of Writing is a graphic that shows how journal ideas can be moved to topics for personal narratives and story narratives.

Directions

1. Have students take out their writing folders and the journal entries that they've saved throughout the year. Students should have a wide variety of journal entries that may be written in different journals. Have students locate as many journals as they can.

2. Tell students that they will be using their journal entries to think about topics for other pieces of writing. Explain to students that entries can be a form of prewriting and even drafting, two stages of the writing process. Inform students that they can use these journal entries as idea drafts for their next piece of process writing.

3. Illustrate the Circles of Writing graphic by duplicating the sheet on page 177 or by drawing it on the chalkboard. Point out the three levels of writing: journals, personal narratives, and story narratives.

4. Tell students that you will be modeling how to use journals as a springboard for personal narratives and story narratives. Use some of your own journals for the demonstration or the example that follows.

> *In one of my journal entries I wrote about how much fun I had one weekend when my nephews slept overnight in our tree house. So I'll write a few key words about that entry in the journal circle. I could easily use that idea to write a personal narrative that illustrates how I got to know my nephews better and how that made me feel. I think I'll give that piece the working title* Tree House Magic. *I could use some parts of the journal entry in that piece because I wrote in detail about what we did and how amazed I was at the complexity of my nephews' personalities. That information can get me started writing.*
>
> *I can also use this journal entry as the basis for a story narrative. I'm intrigued with mysteries right now, so I think I'll title my story* The Tree House Mystery. *I'll change the characters to Brenda and Brianna, the twins I've written about in other stories. I've never written a mystery about them, though. The tree house will be the setting, and I'll have to think about what mystery the girls will solve.*

5. Illustrate how your journal entries would look in the Circles of Writing graphic as in the following example.

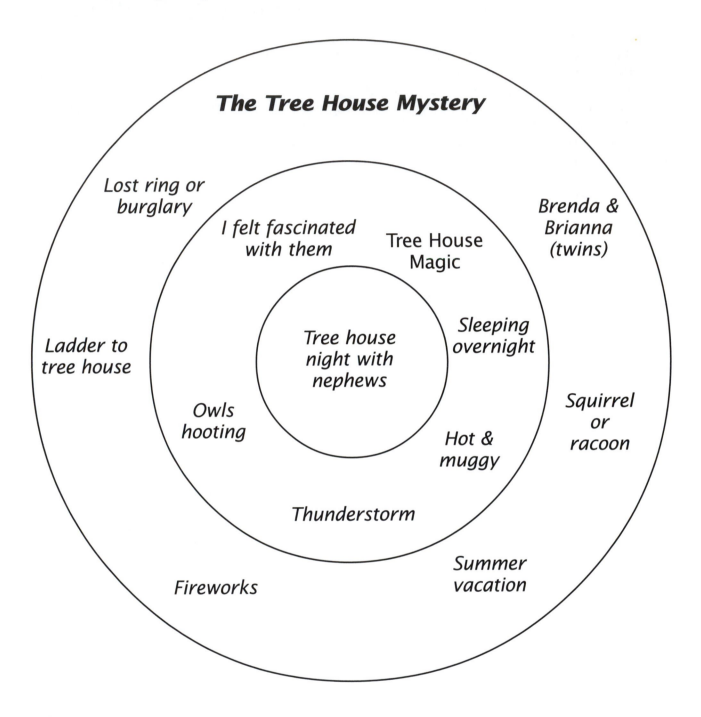

The Tree House Mystery

Lost ring or burglary

Brenda & Brianna (twins)

I felt fascinated with them

Tree House Magic

Ladder to tree house

Tree house night with nephews

Sleeping overnight

Owls hooting

Hot & muggy

Squirrel or racoon

Thunderstorm

Fireworks

Summer vacation

6. Ask students if they understand how to use their journals to develop topics of writing. Have students read through their journals and write some ideas in their Circles of Writing.

7. Provide students with additional Circles of Writing sheets to use with their writing folders. Tell students to use their journals to think of topics whenever they want.

Name _____ Date _____•

Circles of Writing

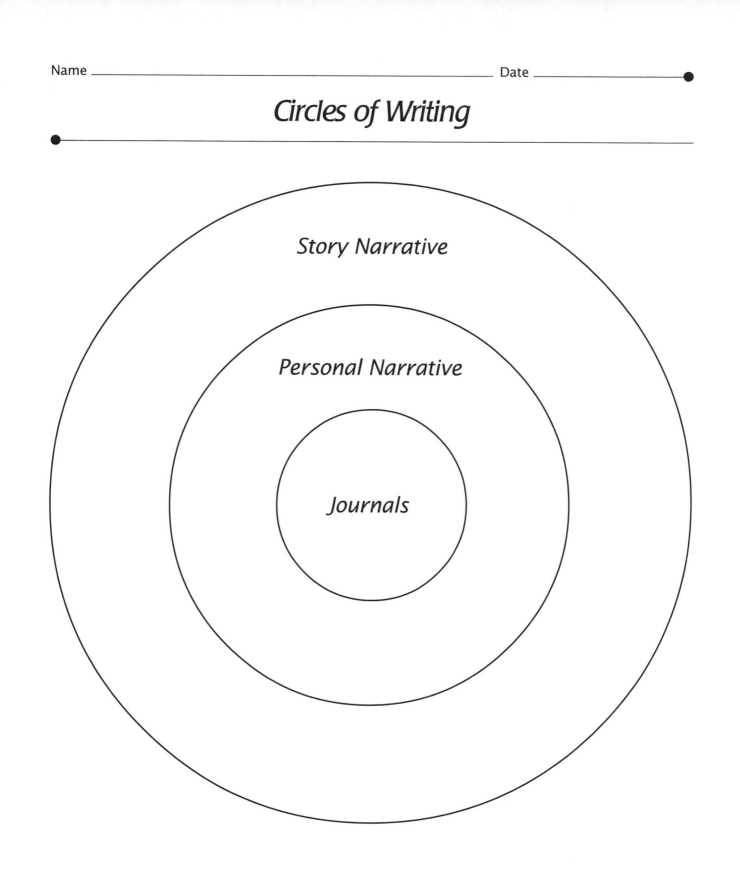

Story Narrative

Personal Narrative

Journals

Teaching Strategy **6**

Section **4.2**

PROCESS DRAMA

"Process drama is a method of teaching and learning that involves students in imaginary, unscripted, and spontaneous scenes" (Schneider & Jackson, 2000, p. 38). When used as a prewriting activity, Process Drama can help students imagine stories and plots that they can use in their writing. Students can record ideas on a Drama Frame that they generate while participating or watching.

Directions

1. Inform students that they will be engaging in Process Drama as a prewriting activity. Tell students that you want them to be thinking about writing ideas as they participate in Process Drama themselves or watch their classmates act out stories.

2. Explain to students that they will not need a script while participating in Process Drama. Tell them that they will be given roles, scenes, and action but that they will have to invent the dialogue as they go.

3. Select a theme, unit of study, or a book students have read as the centerpiece for the drama. Provide instructions for students about how to orchestrate Process Drama. An example follows.

   Last week I read the book Hana's Suitcase *(Levine, 2003) to the class. The book is about a suitcase that arrived at a Holocaust education center in Tokyo with the following words painted on the side, Hana Brady, May 16, 1931, orphan. Let's begin by pretending we've received this suitcase in our school. I have a pretend suitcase here. Joey, Adam, Tina, and Lisa, I'd like you to begin. You'll each be teachers in this school who are given the suitcase for a project you're doing. I'll give you some time to think about it before you begin acting out the scene.*

4. Instruct students to make up their dialogue as they go. You might have to intervene with ideas at times, but, as students become adept at Process Drama, your intervention will decrease.

5. Duplicate and distribute the Drama Frame that follows. As students are acting, have the remaining students use the Drama Frame to record writing ideas.

6. Demonstrate how to use the Drama Frame by saying the following.

   As you were acting out that scene, I thought of some other characters that I could try in my next piece of writing. Adam was playing a scatterbrained science teacher named Mr. Schmidt. I could use that character in the story I'm writing about a student who invents a time machine.

7. Have students record ideas on the Drama Frame. After they have finished, ask students to share ideas with each other. Give students the option of refusing if they want to keep their ideas to themselves, but encourage students to share as many of their ideas as possible.

Name _____ Date _____●

Drama Frame

Characters	Setting	Plot ideas	Dialogue

Discovering Purposes

Goal • *To help students discover purposes for writing.*

BACKGROUND

Why do people write? They write for as many different reasons as there are pieces of writing. Writers usually begin composing texts by having one or more purposes for writing. Their purpose may be to inform a relative about a wedding shower, to explain to the public the reasons why a school bond needs to be passed, or to entertain readers with a story. Writers' purposes should be a guideline that helps writers know what to say and to keep them on target (Graves, 2003).

The nature of writing, however, resists attempts to clarify purposes (Smith, 1990). Writers can set out intending to write with the primary purpose of informing and have their writing change in midstream to that of explaining. The process of writing creates its own realities as writers use initial purposes to direct the stream of words. As writers compose words, purposes may change.

All writing activities, however, should begin with some sort of real purpose, even if that purpose changes during writing. Writers need to have some reason to write, as fuzzy as it is, before they can proceed with the process of writing. In schools, however, the purposes for writing often do not go beyond completing an assigned task (Bright, 1995). Writing for an assignment rarely promotes the kinds of purposes writers should bring to writing situations.

Students in schools should have the opportunity to write for their own purposes. When writing for individual reasons, students can learn how real writers discover and refine their purposes while writing. That doesn't mean that teachers should never assign writing projects. However, when teachers assign writing projects, they should help students understand the purposes for the project. This section provides resources, teaching strategies, ideas, and activities to help students discover purposes for writing.

Students need a reason to write.

Youth Poetry

http://thegalleriesatmoore.org/poetry/

This site allows writers of all ages to see their poetry published online. It also allows students to view and read many other poems written by their peers.

FINDING REASONS TO WRITE

There are a multitude of writing purposes and reasons to write. We live immersed in so much print that we often take for granted the amount of writing that is in our environment. We live in a world that is filled with writing. Each piece of writing was created for a specific purpose. The strategy Finding Reasons to Write can help students become more aware of the writing in their worlds and the purposes behind that writing.

Directions

1. Tell students that there are many reasons to write. Explain to students that when they begin using Finding Reasons to Write they can discover many purposes for writing.

2. Duplicate and distribute the Finding Reasons to Write list that follows. Fold or cut the list in half so that students see only the left-hand side. Give a copy of the list to each student.

3. Read the Finding Reasons to Write list with students. For each reason to write, have students generate ideas about the types of writings that match the purposes. After students have shared a number of ideas, copy the types of writings on the chalkboard or on an overhead transparency and have students read the types of writings suggested on the right-hand side of the list. Tell students this list contains examples of types of writings. Explain to students that there are many more types of writings. Have students add additional ideas to the list.

4. Tell students to keep their own lists of Finding Reasons to Write and place them in their writing folders. Remind students to read their lists when they are searching for purposes to write.

Sean seems intent on his reason for writing.

FINDING REASONS TO WRITE*			
Purposes	Types of Writings	Purposes	Types of Writings
To record events	Lists Diaries Autobiographies Commentaries Letters Minutes of meetings Family histories	To entertain or amuse	Quizzes Jokes Bumper stickers
		To narrate	Fables Stories Myths
To explain	Charts Recipes Brochures Invitations Textbooks Rules	To invent	Plays Poems Song lyrics Slogans
		To inform	Announcements Book jackets News broadcasts Labels Catalogues Weather reports
To analyze	Theories Arguments Essays		
To persuade	Applications Instructions Advertisements Signs Warnings CD covers	To find out	Surveys Interviews Questionnaires
		To invite reflection	Questions Quizzes Quotations
To invite a response	Complaints Invitations Notices Notes	To summarize	Postcards Verdicts Signs
To predict	Graphs Forecasts Timetables	To give an opinion	Editorials Viewpoints Graffiti
To command or request	Directions Rules Warnings	To express gratitude	Thank you notes

*Adapted from Learning Media. (1992). *Dancing with the pen: The learner as writer*. Wellington, New Zealand: Ministry of Education.

Teaching Strategy

TAXONOMY OF WRITING PURPOSES

There are many reasons to write, but students don't always think of them. When students believe that the purpose for writing is to earn a grade, they can have a difficult time trying to move beyond that vision to authentic writing purposes. These students may need you to help them think of purposes to write. Rothstein and Lauber (2000) suggest using a taxonomy to help students remember writing purposes as they work in their writing workshop. A taxonomy is simply a way to organize ideas, in this case writing purposes.

Directions

1. Tell students that they need to think of purposes for writing and that you will help them. Inform students that one way to organize ideas is through a Taxonomy of Writing Purposes, better known to students as an alphabet chart. Have students say and spell the word "taxonomy" aloud. The word "taxonomy" will be new to most students.

2. Duplicate and distribute the Taxonomy of Writing Purposes sheet on page 185. Tell students that you will give them some ideas for writing purposes but that they will need to fill out their own sheets throughout the year.

3. Model how to use the Taxonomy of Writing Purposes sheet. For example, you might make the following remarks.

   Teacher: Let's look at the Taxonomy of Writing Purposes sheet. We're going to write as many purposes for writing as we can and list them by their beginning letter. Who can think of a reason to write?

   Student: I write to entertain.

   Teacher: Yes, I know you do. Let's write the word entertain next to the E. Who has another idea?

   Student: We write letters to give advice.

   Teacher: Yes, we write to advise others. Let's write that one next to the letter A. Any others?

   Student: I wrote an essay in defense of having recess.

   Teacher: Correct. We also write to defend our positions. That one goes next to the D. So far our Taxonomy of Writing Purposes sheet looks like this.

A	Advise others
B	
C	
D	Defend our position
E	Entertain

4. Divide the class into groups of three or four students. Have students think of more writing purposes to write on the class taxonomy. Encourage students to list several purposes for each letter.

5. After students have thought of several writing purposes, add them to the class taxonomy. Then have students use the class work as the basis for their individual taxonomy. Say something like the following.

    We have developed a Taxonomy of Writing Purposes for the class. Now I'd like you to prepare your own taxonomy. You can use any ideas you like from the class list to put on your own taxonomy.

6. Encourage students to keep their Taxonomy of Writing Purposes sheets in their writing folders to use as they think of writing projects. From time to time, have students add more ideas to their lists as well as to the class taxonomy.

Taxonomy of Writing Purposes

A _____

B _____

C _____

D _____

E _____

F _____

G _____

H _____

I _____

J _____

K _____

L _____

M _____

N _____

O _____

P _____

Q _____

R _____

S _____

T _____

U _____

V _____

W _____

X _____

Y _____

Z _____

Teaching **3** *Strategy*_____ Section 4.3

TAKING SOCIAL ACTION

One of the purposes of literacy is to make changes and to promote social justice (Vasquez, with Muise, Adamson, Heffernan, Chiola-Nakai, & Shear, 2003). One example of taking social action is when students in Kentucky used reading, writing, speaking, and listening skills to influence those in power to responsibly mine the highest peak in the state (Powell, Cantrell, & Adams, 2001). Taking social action can be one of the most powerful uses of writing that students will experience.

Directions

1. Encourage students to become aware of local social issues in your area, such as the need to clean up vacant yards, the under funding of schools, and so on. Tell students that changes can occur when people are informed and take social action.

2. Read a book to students that illustrates the impact of taking social action. For example, the book *Ida B. Wells: Mother of the Civil Rights Movement* (Fradin & Fradin, 2001) discusses how Ida B. Wells helped to establish the National Association for the Advancement of Colored People (NAACP). Tell students that their own action can also make a difference in their world.

3. Divide the class into groups of two or three students. Tell students to identify an issue that they would like to change or influence.

4. Duplicate and distribute the Taking Social Action sheet that follows. Model how the sheet could be used as follows.

    One of the issues that concerns me is burning leaves in our neighborhood. During the fall and spring, so many people burn leaves and brush that the air is hard to breathe. We have to close the windows in our house because the smoke comes right in. My issue, therefore, is burning leaves.

    I would like to see this changed. The town near us has leaf pick-up, and I think we should have that too. I will target our neighborhood council with a flyer discussing the problems with leaf burning, and I'll develop a leaflet to distribute to my neighbors to educate them on the health risks of breathing too much smoke.

5. Have students write the issue they identified in the blank. Then have students list the change they would like to see. Finally, have students list possible audiences and formats for their writing.

6. Guide students to take social action in a positive and respectful manner. Encourage students to distribute their writings to their audiences.

Name _____ Date _____

Taking Social Action

Issue to be addressed _____

Changes to be made _____

_____

_____

_____

_____

Audiences	Formats
_____	_____
_____	_____
_____	_____
_____	_____
_____	_____
_____	_____
_____	_____
_____	_____

Writing can be either public or private. Journals are examples of private writing: their audience is the writer. Writing can also be public. Writing is public if the teacher reads the work, if other students are the intended audience, or if the writing is published in hard copy or on the Internet. Students rarely get the opportunity to see their work actually published, but in her book *Go public! Encouraging student writers to publish*, Susanne Rubenstein (1998) encourages teachers to help their students take their writing "beyond the grade book." Students can be published in their classroom or to a wider audience. In any case, however, publishing can be very rewarding.

📑 Directions

1. Tell students that even though they have shared their writing in many venues, you would like them to take their writing to a more public audience. Explain to students that one of the purposes for writing is to write for publication.

2. Help students understand what it means to write for publication by saying something like the following.

    How many of you would like to have your writing published? If your writing is published, people you don't know will read your work. It can be rather scary, but it's also lots of fun to think about someone in a different state or province reading something you have written. If you want to write for publication, you will add another step to the writing process.

3. Inform students that when they write for publication they will be using the same writing process that they have been using all year with one exception. Instead of having one purpose for writing, they will really have two purposes. In addition to their primary purpose, one of the purposes will be to write something that could be published

4. Talk with students about the process of publishing. To assist your discussion, duplicate and distribute the Writing for Publication sheet that follows. Discuss each step with students.

5. Tell students that writing for publication takes time and that they might have to submit more than one piece before one is published. Encourage students throughout the year to continue trying to be published.

Writing for publication can take many forms.

Writing for Publication

1. Identify several topics and formats for your writing. Determine whether any of these topics is "cutting edge" or interesting to a wider audience.

2. Look through journals, periodicals, and Internet sites for a venue that publishes the type of writing that you do. Identify the outlet that matches your writing topic most closely.

3. Read the information for authors to give you information about the length of the piece, format, and so on. Follow these directions closely.

4. Write your piece. Refer as needed to the information for authors so what you write has a greater chance of being published.

5. Give your piece of writing to several readers for comments.

6. Revise, revise, revise.

7. Edit and proofread your writing carefully. Have at least one other reader proofread your writing.

8. Read the directions for submitting the manuscript. You might need to send a SASE (self-addressed stamped envelope), a computer disk, or other information.

9. Begin a new piece of writing while waiting for a response.

10. If your writing is not accepted, send it to a different outlet.

Publish Your Story

www.kidpub.org/kidpub/

Students can publish their writing on the web when they log on to this site.

MATCHING PURPOSE TO FORMAT

The purposes for writing will influence the format writers use. The format, in turn, influences the writers' purposes. For example, when a cook writes a recipe, the purpose for the writing is to list the ingredients and directions to make something to eat. Most recipes follow a certain writing format. When a cook writes a recipe, the format will guide the way the cook writes. The recipe will not contain a critique of the cookies. A different writing format would accomplish that purpose. When students learn how to match their writing purposes to the format for writing, they can make their own writing purposes more clear.

Directions

1. Tell students that their writing purposes should match the format they choose for writing.

2. Divide the class into groups of three or four students. Duplicate and distribute the list of 549 Writing Formats that follows. Provide each group with a copy of the list and a dictionary of literary terms. You also may wish to use only a portion of the list.

3. Have students select 10 different writing formats. Tell students that if they aren't familiar with the format to look up its definition in a literary dictionary or an unabridged dictionary.

4. Have students write their lists in alphabetical order on the left-hand side of a piece of paper. Then have students brainstorm writing purposes for each of the writing formats. Have students list the purposes for writing on the right-hand side of the page as in the following example

Formats	Purposes	Formats	Purposes
1. advertisement	to inform	6. guarantee	to promise
2. baby book	to remember	7. junk mail	to persuade
3. caption	to clarify	8. magic spell	to change
4. commentary	to comment	9. plea	to ask
5. euphemism	to improve	10. wager	to predict

5. After the groups have finished listing writing formats and purposes, have members of each group share their lists with the class. Display the lists on a poster. Remind students to match their writing purposes and writing formats.

549 Writing Formats

Margaret E. McIntosh

abbreviation
ABCs of something
abecedarian
abridgment
absolution
abstract
acceptance speech
accolade
account of
acknowledgment
acronym
adaptation
address
address book
advertisement
advice column
agenda
agreement
aha!
allegory
alternative to counting sheep
    (for insomniacs)
amendment
analogy
anecdote
annotation
announcement
anthem
anthology
anything boustrophedonic
anything written in runic
    characters
aphorism
apologue
apology
appeal
application
article
ascription
assembly directions
assertion
assignment

assumption
astrological prediction
autobiography
award
axiom

baby book
baccalaureate address
ballad
ballot
banner
beauty tip
bedtime story
beginning
belief
billboard
bill of lading
bill of sale
biographical sketch
biography
birth announcement
blessing
boast
book
book jacket
book review
bookplate
brochure
bulletin
bumper sticker
business card

calendar
calendar quip
calorie chart
campaign speech
cantata
captain's log
caption
cartoon
case study
catalog description

censure
cereal boxes
ceremony
certificate
certificate of authenticity
chapter
character sketch
charter
checkbook register
cheer
children's book
choral reading
chorus
chronicle
church bulletin
cinquain
cipher
clue
code
collection notice
college application letter
comic strip
commemoration
commendation
comment
commentary
community notice
comparison
complaint
concatenation
confession
confutation
congratulatory note
conjecture
consequence
contest rules
contract
conundrum
conversation
convocation
correspondence (series of)
counterfeit document

couplet
covenant
cover letter
creed
critique
cumulative story
curse
customs

data sheet
date book
declaration
decree
dedication
deed
definition
denunciation
description
dialogue
diary
dictionary
diet
directions
directory
disclosure
ditty
docudrama
document
double-talk
drama
dream script

editorial
elogium
e-mail
emblem
encyclopedia entry
ending
epic
epilogue
episode
epistle
epistrophe
epitaph
epithet
epitome
essay
estimate
euphemism
evaluation
exaggeration
examination

exclamation
excuse
exhortation
expense account
explanation
expose

fable
fabrication
fact
fact sheet
fairy tale
fallacy
falsehood
falsity
family tree
fantasy
farce
farewell
fashion article
fashion show narration
feasibility study/statement
fib
fiction
figure of speech
filibuster
filmstrip
folderol
folktale
folklore
forewarning
formula
fortune
fraud

game rules
generalization
ghost story
gloss
goals
good news/bad news
gossip
grace
graffiti
greeting card
grievance
grocery lists
guarantee
guess
guess what? descriptions
guess who? descriptions
guide to watching TV

habit
hagiography
hagiology
harangue
headline
history
homily
horoscope
how-to-do-it speeches
hyperbole
hypothesis

idea
ideograph
impassioned statement
impromptu speech
impugns (something that . . .)
index
inflammatory statement
inscription
inspirational piece
insult
interview
introductions to books
introductions to people
invective
invitation
invoice
itinerary

jabber (the way it would look
    on paper)
jargon for a particular field or
    profession
job application
joke
journal
jump rope rhyme
junk mail
justification

kudos

l'envoi (or l'envoy)
lab report
label
labeled ichnography
lament
lampoon
lease
lecture
legend

letter
letter gram
letter of acceptance
letter of application
letter of condolence
letter of consent
letter of credit
letter of support
letter of surrender
letters of credence
letters of marque and reprisal
letters of resignation
letters to the editor
lexicon
lexiphanic writing
libel
license
lie
list
list of items for sale at an
   auction
long distance phone bill
love note
luscious words

magazine
magic spell
make a motion
manifest
manifesto
marquee notice
maxim
melodrama
memo
memoir
memory
menu
message
message in semaphore
message to send in a bottle
metaphor
minutes of a meeting
monograph
monologue
monument
motto
movie review
movie script
mystery
myth

news analysis
news release

newscast
newspaper
newspaper "fillers"
nonsense
note
notebook
notes for a debate
notice of employment
notification
nursery rhyme

oath
obituary
observation
ode
one liner
opinion
oration
oxymoron

pact
palindrome
pamphlet
pamphlet to aid sightseeing
parable
paradox
parody
party tips
pedigree
personal reaction
persuasive letter
phone survey
phrase
plaque
play
plea
pledge
poem
political announcement
postcard
poster
prayer
preamble
precis
prediction
preface
prescription
press release exposing
   malfeasance
probability
problem
problem solution
proclamation

product description
profile
proforma
profound saying
prologue
promotional campaign
propaganda sheet
proposal
protest letter
protest sign
proverb
public service announcement
pun
puppet show
purchase order
puzzle

querela
querimony
query
question
questionnaire
quip
quiz
quotation
quote

ransom note
rationale
reaction
real estate description
rebuttal
recapitulation
recipe
record cover
refrain
refutation
remedy
remembrance
renunciation
report
report card
report of an inquisition
request
requiem
resolution
response
resume
retrospective account
review
revision
rhapsody
riddle

rite
road signs
roast
Rolodex™ file
rondeau
rondel
rondelet
RSVP
rule
rules of etiquette
rumor

saga
sale notice
sales pitch
sandwich board
satire
schedule
script
secret
self-description
sentence
sequel
serenade
serialized story
sermon
service agreement
sign
silly saying
skywriting message
slide show
slogan
soap opera
society news
something that needs to be
    shredded
something to be stored on
    microfilm
something with a surprise
    ending
song
speech
speech balloon
spoof
spoonerism
sporting event rules
sports account
sports analysis
stage directions
statement

statute
study guide
style book
style sheet
subjective vs. objective account
    (of the same event)
suggestion
summary
summons
superlatives
superstition
supervisor's report
supply list
supposition
survival guide
suspense
suspicious note
syllabus
syllogism

tall tale
tautologism
tax form
technical report
telegram
telephone directories
test
testimony
textbook
thank you note
theater program
theorem
thumbnail sketches of content
    ideas
thumbnail sketches of famous
    people
thumbnail sketches of historical
    events
thumbnail sketches of places
title
toast
tongue lashing
tongue twister
traffic rules
transcript of a quarrel
transcript of a trial
transcript of an oral recollection
    by someone 10, 20, 30, or
    more years older than you
travel brochure

travel poster
treatise
treaty
tribute
trivia
true-false statements
TV commercial
TV guide
TV program

umpirage
untruth

validation
verse
vignette
vita
voucher
vow

wager
waiver
want ad
wanted poster
warning
warrant
warranty
watchword
weather forecast
weather reports
what you would do with an
    intercalary day each
    week(end)
while you were out
will
wise saying
wish
word
word problem
word search
words/sentences for spelling
    bee
written apology for
    maladroitness
written demonstration of
    know-how

yarn
yearbook inscription
yellow pages

Identifying Audiences

Goal • *To help students identify appropriate audiences for their writing.*

BACKGROUND

If you want to give the best possible gift to a writer, give an audience (Elbow, 1981). An audience is any person who reads a writer's work. Audiences can be small and private, or they can be large and public. Students can write for a pen pal—a known audience of one. They also can write for publication on the Internet—an unknown audience of many. Audiences vary with the purposes that a writer has for a piece of writing. The important thing about audiences, however, is that they exist.

> *An audience is any person who reads a writer's work.*

Writing is primarily a social act. The main purpose of writing is to be read by another person. Students need to have a variety of real audiences for their writing because it is the audience that shapes a piece of writing. As writers visualize their audiences, they decide what to include in a piece of writing, what to omit, and whether their writing needs to be scholarly or conversational. It is the awareness of audiences that drives many writing decisions (Dahl & Farnan, 1998).

Unfortunately, most students in schools write for one audience, the teacher. In a large study, Britton *et al.* (1975) identified four main audiences for students' writings:

- themselves
- the teacher
- a known audience (such as other students)
- an unknown audience (such as for publication).

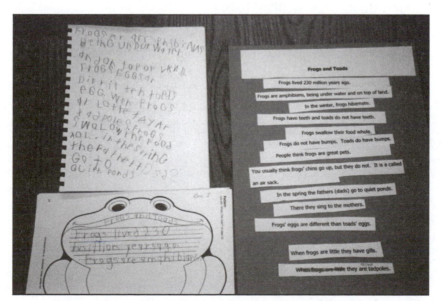

Who could be the audience for these pieces of writing?

Of the 2,000 pieces of writing these scholars read, over 95% of them were written for the teacher as the audience.

Britton and his colleagues also distinguished between the roles a teacher could take as an audience. The teacher could be a real audience, someone interested in reading the piece of writing, or the teacher could be a pseudo-audience, someone who reads the writing as an examiner. Over half of all of the pieces of writing in the study were written for the teacher in the role of teacher-as-examiner rather than for a real audience.

Students understand that when a teacher reads their writings in the role of teacher-as-ex-

aminer, the teacher is not a real audience. When students consistently write for the teacher as their audience, they have difficulty developing a sense of *audience awareness*. Audience awareness is when writers think about their audiences while writing (Rubin, 1998). Writers who think about their audiences care about their writing, because they know that their writing is a vehicle for communicating thoughts and ideas to someone else. It is because of readers that writers write. This section, therefore, contains resources, teaching strategies, ideas, and activities to help students identify appropriate audiences when they write.

*Teaching**1**Strategy* _____

Section 4.4.

TARGETING AN AUDIENCE

When students write for a real audience, they are more deeply motivated to write (Hubbard, 1985). To target an audience is a challenge for students because they frequently write only for their teachers. Therefore, students need to brainstorm a list of audiences for their writing before they can target appropriate audiences for their work. Helping students find audiences for their writing reinforces the real reason for writing—to communicate thoughts and ideas to readers.

Directions

1. Tell students that when they write they should write with the intention that someone else will read their work. Explain that, before students decide exactly what to write, they need to target an audience to read their writing.

2. Duplicate the list of Audiences for Students' Writings that follows and distribute it to students. Tell students that this is a partial list of people for whom they can write.

3. Read the list together in class. Think carefully about the possibilities of the audiences and about whether students could write to a particular audience. List topics for writing after the appropriate audience.

 4. Tell students that this list is not complete, that there are other ideas for audiences for students' writing. Divide the class into groups of three or four students. Have students generate additional audiences to add to the list.

5. Display the amended list in a prominent place in the classroom. Tell students that as they think of additional audiences they should add them to the list.

6. As students begin a piece of writing, have them refer to the list of audiences and choose an audience that fits the topic of their writing.

Audiences for Students' Writings

1. Students in your class
2. Students in other classes in the school
3. Students in other local schools
4. Students in classes in other states
5. Students in other countries
6. Students identified via the Internet
7. Administrators in the school
8. Support staff in the school (cooks, crossing guards, secretaries)
9. School board members
10. Classroom or hall displays
11. Family
12. Relatives or friends
13. Community newspapers
14. Community members
15. City officials
16. State or federal representatives
17. TV stations
18. Governmental officials
19. Local businesses
20. Local organizations
21. Travel bureaus
22. Chambers of commerce
23. Foreign embassies
24. Classroom publications
25. Literary journals
26. Waiting rooms in dentists' or doctors' offices
27. Public libraries
28. Writing contests
29. Authors of books
30. Heroes
31. Pen pals
32. Local radio stations

Section 4.4
WRITING PICTURE BOOKS

Picture books can be created to share with the school library, a class of kindergarten students, or families of young children. Picture books are also a good product of the writing process. Cohle and Towle (2001) state, "If children are truly going to view themselves as writers, it is necessary for them to have authentic purposes for publishing and sharing" (p. 14). Writing picture books is one way for students to have authentic purposes and authentic audiences for their writing.

Directions

1. Tell students that a writing project option is to create a picture book for an audience that you will specify. You might ask a primary grade teacher if the books could be used for a classroom library, or you might have students give the picture books to a relative. Help students determine an appropriate audience.

2. Remind students that a picture book will have some words and colorful pictures. Show students a variety of picture books that they can use as models for their own work. One way to show students picture books is to divide them into three categories as follows.

   One type of picture book is like a list. I'd like to read 31 Uses for a Mom *(Ziefert & Doughty, 2003). In this book you can see that each page is numbered with something that a Mom is. For example, some of the things listed are hair stylist, pet sitter, and banker. If you want to write this type of book, think of a topic, and then start listing words or phrases about that topic. Finally, draw a colorful picture about each word or phrase.*

   A second type of book is an alphabet book. You've read many alphabet books in your life, so you know that they can be about any topic and can contain words, phrases, or paragraphs. You could also write an alphabet book about reading as in the book Read Anything Good Lately? *(Allen & Lindaman, 2003). This book has phrases beginning with each letter of the alphabet that describes a place to read, such as "history in a hammock." Each page also has a picture illustrating the phrase.*

   A final type of picture book is a book with a simple plot. In Hoptoad *(Yolen, 2003), the author uses simple language to describe a toad crossing a road and almost getting hit by a truck. The book has suspense and interest despite its few words. If you write this type of book, think of a plot first, and then try to write the story with very few words. Illustrate the book with colorful pictures.*

3. Have a variety of picture books available for students to browse through. Some examples of appropriate picture books are listed on the Picture Books resource pages that follow. You can use this list to select books for students to see, or you can duplicate and distribute the list and have students find picture books in a library.

4. 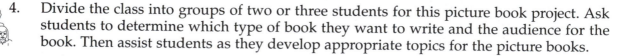 Divide the class into groups of two or three students for this picture book project. Ask students to determine which type of book they want to write and the audience for the book. Then assist students as they develop appropriate topics for the picture books.

5. After the picture books are completed, have a book party where students can share their work with each other and possibly present their books to their audience.

6. Encourage students to continue to create picture books independently. You might decide that students can only write one picture book per semester in writing workshop, but tell students that they can also write these books at home.

Picture Books

Agra Deedy, C. (2000)
The yellow star: The legend of King Christian X of Denmark
Atlanta: Peachtree

Allen, S., & Lindaman, J. (2003)
Read anything good lately?
Brookfield, CT: Millbrook Press

Amis, N. (2003)
The orphans of Normandy
New York: Atheneum

Andersen, H.C. (1990)
The tinderbox
Boston: Little, Brown

Bang, M. (1983)
Dawn
New York: Mulberry Books

Bloom, B. (1999)
Wolf!
New York: Orchard

Bridges, R. (1999)
Through my eyes
New York: Scholastic

Bunting, E. (1997)
I am the mummy Heb-Nefert
San Diego, CA: Harcourt Brace

Cannon, J. (1996)
Verdi
New York: Harcourt

Cech, J. (1991)
My grandmother's journey
New York: Bradbury

Cherry, L. (1993)
The great Kapok tree
San Diego, CA: Harcourt Brace

Cordova, A. (1997)
Abuelita's heart
New York: Simon & Schuster

Cronin, D. (2000)
Click, clack, moo: Cows that type
New York: Simon & Schuster

Feiffer, J. (2001)
I'm not Bobby!
Manhasset, NY: Hyperion

Frost, R. (1978)
Stopping by the woods on a snowy evening
New York: Dutton

Gerstein, M. (1987)
The mountains of Tibet
New York: HarperCollins

Keller, L. (1998)

The scrambled states of America

New York: Scholastic

Keller, L. (2000)

Open wide, tooth school inside

New York: Henry Holt

Lawrence, J. (1968)

Harriet and the promised land

New York: Windmill

Lovell, P. (2001)

Stand tall, Molly Lou Melon

New York: Putnam's Sons

Myers, W.D. (1997)

Harlem

New York: Scholastic

Polacco, P. (1994)

Pink and Say

New York: Putnam

Pulver, R. (2003)

Punctuation takes a vacation

New York: Holiday House

Ryan, P. (1996)

The flag we love

Boston: Charlesbridge Publishing

Scieszka, J. (1995)

Math curse

New York: Viking

Siebert, D. (1991)

Sierra

New York: HarperCollins

Slier, D. (1997)

The enormous turnip

New York: Star Bright Books

St. George, J., & Small, D. (2000)

So you want to be president

New York: Philomel

Tarbescu, E. (1998)

Annushka's voyage

New York: Clarion

Thaler, M. (1989)

The teacher from the Black Lagoon

New York: Scholastic

Williams, S.A. (1992)

Working cotton

San Diego, CA: Harcourt Brace

Wilson. A. (1999)

Magpie magic

New York: Dial

Yolen, J. (2003)

Hoptoad

San Diego, CA: Silver Whistle

Ziefert, H., & Doughty, R. (2003)

31 uses for a mom

New York: Putnam's Sons.

 Picture Book Ideas

http://www.geocities.com/oberry1790/narrativebibliography.htm

This site presents ideas for using picture books to teach narrative and six trait writing.

The optimum type of process writing situation is for students to be paired with more able writers. When students are placed in tutoring situations, they find more support throughout the writing process, and they also are writing for an audience that they know. Topping, Nixon, Sutherland and Yarrow (2000) write that Paired Writing is a system for "peer or parent tutoring (or co-composition) of any sort of writing (creative or technical)—in any language" (p. 81). Topping and his colleagues have developed a structured form of Paired Writing that has been helpful in supporting the writing of students with learning difficulties.

Directions

1. Divide the class into pairs of writers: one struggling and one successful. Tell students that they will be writing for each other.

2. Assign roles for the writers. For the first piece, the successful writer should be the helper and the struggling writer should be the writer. Duplicate and distribute the Paired Writing Outline that follows.

3. Tell students to use the Paired Writing Outline as the basis for the writing process, but encourage students to deviate from the outline as needed.

Writing buddies can be useful.

4. Ask the helper to question the writer about a topic as in the following example. Tell the helper to write the answers that the writer gave.

   - What topic would you like to write about?
   - Do you have any lists or journal entries that could help you decide on a topic?
   - What interests you most?
   - Who would you like to write about?

5. Once the writer has a topic, have the helper ask additional questions to flesh out the piece. Once again the helper should take notes. Some questions could include Who? What? When? Where? How? Why?

6. Tell the two students to read the notes about the topic. Then instruct them to verbalize a story together. As they talk, the writer should begin to draft the piece without concern for the conventions of language.

7. After a draft has been completed, tell both students to read the draft and make suggestions for revisions. Either of the students can make the revisions.

8. Instruct students then to edit the piece to make it conform to Standard English. Encourage both students to use the resources available in the classroom to correct spelling, usage, and punctuation.

9. Finally, have the writer prepare a final copy to present to the helper. The helper is the initial audience for the writing.

10. Have students switch roles and complete a second piece of Paired Writing so that each student has the opportunity to be the helper and each student has the opportunity to be the writer.

Nifty Nibbles: Children's Literacy Magazine

www.angelfire.com/ia/niftynibbles

This site provides a magazine where K–12 authors' materials can be published.

Paired Writing Outline

1. Generate a topic.
   - What topic would you like to write about?
   - Do you have any lists or journal entries that could help you decide on a topic?
   - What interests you most?
   - Who would you like to write about?

2. Write about the topic.
   - Who?
   - What?
   - When?
   - Where?
   - How?
   - Why?

3. Read the notes.

4. Draft the piece.

5. Revise the writing.

6. Edit.

7. Give the piece of writing to the helper.

8. Switch roles and complete a new piece of writing.

Teaching 4 Strategy

PUBLIC AUDIENCES

Some students may deliberately choose to write for publication. At other times, teachers might identify an outstanding piece of writing that is worthy of a wider audience than the student had intended. In any case, writing for publication is a significant and meaningful way for students to understand the concept of audience. Ray with Laminack (2001) state, "For publishing to make any sense at all in our writing workshops, students need to feel the pull of readers waiting for them" (p. 257). Having students write for public audiences helps them feel this pull.

Directions

1. Have students write for publication as described earlier in the chapter (see pages 188–189). Once students have completed their writing, they should try to have their writing read by a wider audience.

2. Obtain an appropriate magazine to share, such as *National Geographic World*. Describe to students the excitement of publishing their writing in a journal, periodical, or a website.

   When you write, you always have an audience in mind. Many times you know your audience; it may be a family member or a friend. You can also write for a wider audience—people you don't know. It's exciting to imagine someone else reading your writing.

   Let's think about the audience for National Geographic World. *What kinds of students read this magazine? How old are they? What are their interests? How are they like you?*

   As you answer these questions, you can visualize your audience. It's exciting to think about someone in your imagination reading your writing.

Writing for a public audience is motivating.

3. Duplicate several copies of the Outlets for Student Writing that follows. Divide students into working groups and give each group a copy of the handout. Have students mark the magazines with which they are familiar.

4. Ask students to find sample copies of the magazines that are appropriate for their age level and that interest them. Your library media center may have some copies; your public libraries may have some; and families may have some. Publishers might also send sample copies. Gather as many different magazines as possible.

5. Tell students that they need to match their writing with the needs of the magazines. If students are able to find a magazine that could be an outlet for their writing, encourage students to read several issues of the magazine.

6. Instruct students to read the submission guidelines. Tell students that they may need to revise their writing so that it fits the submission guidelines of the magazine.

7. If you have Internet access, look for a website of the magazine for further information.

8. Have students submit their writing to the targeted magazine. Remember that it is not ethical to send the same piece of writing to more than one magazine at the same time.

9. Applaud students for taking the risk of submitting a piece of writing to a public audience. Explain that their writing might be rejected for that outlet but that they can resubmit their work to another magazine.

10. Tell students that there are many Internet sites that publish students' work. Encourage students to submit their writing to these sites as well as print copies. You can find some websites throughout this book that publish students' work; however, website addresses change, so it's better to conduct your own search of Internet audiences for your students.

Outlets for Student Writing
Compiled by M. Kristiina Montero

The Acorn (ages 5–18)
Editorial & Ordering Address:
1530 Seventh Street
Rock Island, IL 61201
309-788-3980
(fiction, nonfiction, articles, poetry)

American Girl (ages 8 and up)
Editorial Address:
Pleasant Company Publications, Inc.
8400 Fairway Place
Middleton, WI 53562-0986
608-836-4848
Fax: 608-831-7089
E-mail: ageditor@ag.pleasantco.com

Ordering Address:
Pleasant Company Publications, Inc.
8400 Fairway Place
P.O. Box 62986
Middleton, WI 53562-0986
800-234-1278
(letters, comments, jokes, anecdotes, poems)

Barbie, The Magazine for Girls (ages 5–12)
Editorial Address:
Marvel Entertainment Group, Inc.
387 Park Avenue
New York, NY 10106
212-576-4042
Fax: 212-576-9286

Ordering Address:
Marvel Entertainment Group, Inc.
P.O. Box 10798
Des Moines, IA 50340
515-243-4543
(letters, art)

Black Belt for Kids (ages 5–16)
Editorial & Ordering Address:
Rainbow Publications
P.O. Box 918
Santa Clarita, CA 91380
805-257-4066
(letters, first person accounts, art)

Boodle (ages 6–13)
Editorial & Ordering Address:
Graphic Printing Co.
P.O. Box 1049
Portland, IN 47371
219-726-8141
Fax: 219-726-8143
(stories, poems, puzzles, artwork)

Boomerang! The Children's Audio Magazine about Big Ideas (ages 6–12)
Editorial & Ordering Address:
P.O. Box 261
La Honda, CA 94020
800-333-7858
415-747-0978
Fax: 800-333-7858
(letters, interviews, audio clips)

California Weekly Explorer (ages 9–11)
Editorial & Ordering Address:
285 E. Main Street, Suite 3
Tustin, CA 92780
714-730-5991
Fax: 714-730-3548
E-mail: cwex@aol.com
(area reports, geography, history)

Calliope (ages 8–15)
Editorial & Ordering Address:
Cobblestone Publishing, Inc.
7 School Street
Peterborough, NH 03458
603-924-7209
Fax: 603-924-7380
(letters)

Casper the Friendly Ghost (ages 5–9)
Editorial & Ordering Address:
Harvey Entertainment Company
100 Wilshire Boulevard, Suite 1400
Santa Monica, CA 90401-1110
310-451-3377
Fax: 310-458-6995
(letters, artwork)

Chickadee Magazine (ages 8 and under)
Editorial Address:
Owl Communications, Inc.
179 John Street, Suite 500
Toronto, ON
Canada M5T 3G5
416-971-5275
Fax: 416-971-5294
E-mail: owlcom@owl.on.ca

Ordering Address:
In the U.S.
Chickadee Magazine
25 Boxwood Lane
Buffalo, NY 14227-2780
(stories, poems)

Child Life (ages 9–11)
Editorial Address:
Children's Better Health Institute
1100 Waterway Boulevard
P.O. Box 567
Indianapolis, IN 46206
317-636-8881
Fax: 317-684-8094

Ordering Address:
Children's Better Health Institute
P.O. Box 7133
Red Oak, IA 51591-0133
317-636-8881, ext. 233
(stories, poems, jokes, photos, drawings)

Children's Digest (ages 10–12)
Editorial & Ordering Address:
Children's Better Health Institute
1100 Waterway Boulevard
P.O. Box 567
Indianapolis, IN 46206
317-636-8881
(original stories under 200 words, jokes, poems)

Children's Playmate (ages 6–8)
Editorial & Ordering Address:
Children's Better Health Institute
1100 Waterway Boulevard
P.O. Box 567
Indianapolis, IN 46206
317-636-8881
Fax: 317-684-8094
(drawings, poems, jokes, riddles)

Cobblestone (ages 8–15)
Editorial & Ordering Address:
Cobblestone Publishing, Inc.
7 School Street
Peterborough, NH 03458
603-924-7209
Fax: 603-924-7380
E-mail: http://www.cobblestonepub.com
(stories, poems)

Crayola Kids Magazine (ages 4–8)
Editorial Address:
Meredith Custom Publishing Services
1912 Grand Avenue
Des Moines, IA 50309-3379
515-284-2007

Ordering Address:
Crayola Kids Customer Service
P.O. Box 37198
Boone, IA 50037-0198
800-846-7968
(letters, artwork related to upcoming themes)

Creative Kids (ages 8–14)
Editorial & Ordering Address:
Prufrock Press
P.O. Box 8813
Waco, TX 76714-8813
800-998-2208
Fax: 800-240-0333
E-mail: Creative_kid@prufrock.com
(poems, stories, games, artwork, photography)

Daybreak Star Indian Reader (ages 9–12)
Editorial & Ordering Address:
United Indians of All Tribes Foundation
1945 Yale Place E.
Seattle, WA 98102
206-325-0070
Fax: 206-328-1608
(Native children's artwork, letters, stories,
    puzzles, legends)

Disney Adventures (ages 7–14)
Editorial Address:
Disney Adventures Magazine
114 Fifth Avenue
New York, NY 10011-5690
212-807-5821
Fax: 212-807-5499
E-mail: dazpc@aol.com

Ordering Address:
Disney Adventures Magazine
114 Fifth Avenue, Suite 101
New York, NY 10011-5690
212-973-4173
800-829-5146
Fax: 818-559-7353
(occasional contests for stories)

EarthSavers (ages 6–13)
Editorial & Ordering Address:
National Wildlife Federation
8925 Leesburg Pike
Vienna, VA 22184
703-790-4535
(letters)

Faces (ages 8–14)
Editorial & Ordering Address:
Cobblestone Publishing, Inc.
7 School Street
Peterborough, NH 03458
603-924-7209
Fax: 603-924-7380
E-mail: http://www.cobblestonepub.com
(stories)

Falcon Magazine (ages 8–12)
Editorial & Ordering Address:
Two Worlds Publishing
3060 Peachtree Road, NW, Suite 500
Atlanta, GA 30305
404-262-8921
(book reviews, columns)

Fantastic Flyer Magazine (ages 2–12)
Editorial & Ordering Address:
Delta Airlines, Inc.
Department 790, Admin. Bldg.
1030 Delta Boulevard
Atlanta, GA 30320
404-715-4813
(letters, art, jokes, stories)

Girls' Life (ages 7–14)
Editorial & Ordering Address:
Monarch Publishing
4517 Harford Rd.
Baltimore, MD 21214
410-254-9200
Fax: 410-254-0991
(some stories, poems, artwork)

The Goldfinch (ages 8–13)
Editorial & Ordering Address:
State Historical Society of Iowa
402 Iowa Avenue
Iowa City, IA 52240
319-335-3930
(letters, stories, artwork, poems)

Guide Magazine (ages 10–14)
Editorial & Ordering Address:
Review & Herald Publishing Association
55 W. Oak Ridge Drive
Hagerstown, MD 21740
301-791-7000, ext. 2433
Fax: 301-790-9734
E-mail: 74617.3100@compuserve.com
(stories)

Harambee (ages 7–14)
Editorial & Ordering Address:
Just Us Books, Inc.
356 Glenwood Avenue
East Orange, NJ 07017
201-676-4345
Fax: 201-677-7570
(stories)

Highlights for Children (ages 2–12)
Editorial Address:
803 Church Street
Honesdale, PA 18431
717-253-1080
Fax: 717-253-0179

Ordering Address:
P.O. Box 269
Columbus, OH 43272-0002
800-848-8922
(poems, drawings, stories, letters to the editor)

HiP Magazine (ages 8–14)
Editorial Address:
HiP Magazine
127 Seabridge Court
Alameda, CA 94502
510-523-4221
Fax: 510-523-4081

Ordering Address:
HiP Magazine
1563 Solano Avenue, #137
Berkeley, CA 94707
510-527-8993
(letters, stories, artwork, responses to magazine
   questions, personal profiles)

Hopscotch: The Magazine for Young Girls
   (ages 6–12)
Editorial & Ordering Address:
P.O. Box 164
Bluffton, OH 45817-0164
419-358-4610
Fax: 419-358-5027
(letters to the editor, contests)

Humpty Dumpty (ages 4–6)
Editorial & Ordering Address:
Children's Better Health Institute
1100 Waterway Boulevard
P.O. Box 567
Indianapolis, IN 46206
317-636-8881
Fax: 317-684-8094
(readers' drawings)

Jack and Jill (ages 7–10)
Editorial Address:
Children's Better Health Institute
1100 Waterway Boulevard
P.O. Box 567
Indianapolis, IN 46206
317-636-8881

Ordering Address:
P.O. Box 10003
Des Moines, IA 50340
(jokes, poetry, stories, drawings, special contests)

Junior Scholastic (ages 6–8)
Editorial Address:
Scholastic, Inc.
555 Broadway
New York, NY 10012
212-505-3071

Ordering Address:
Scholastic, Inc.
2931 E. McCarty Street
P.O. Box 3710
Jefferson City, MO 65102-9957
314-636-8890
(letters to the editor, junior reporter news stories)

KSE News (Kids for Saving Earth News)
   (ages 7–13)
Editorial & Ordering Address:
Kids for Saving Earth
P.O. Box 47247
Plymouth, MN 55447
612-525-0002
Fax: 612-525-0243
(artwork, letters, poetry)

Kids Today (ages 8–14)
Editorial & Ordering Address:
1000 Wilson Boulevard
Arlington, VA 22229-0002
703-276-3780
(letters, poems, jokes, recipes)

KIND News (Kids in Nature's Defense News)
   (ages 5–11)
Editorial & Ordering Address:
P.O. Box 362
East Haddam, CT 06423-0362
860-434-8666
Fax: 860-434-9579
Fax Orders: 860-434-6282
(letters, accounts of animals, environmental
   activities)

Merlyn's Pen (ages 10–15)
4 King Street
P.O. Box 910
East Greenwich, RI 02818
(stories, poems, plays, essays)

MetroKids Magazine (13 and under)
Editorial & Ordering Address:
KidStuff Publications, Inc.
1080 N. Delaware Avenue, Suite 702
Philadelphia, PA 19112
215-291-5560
Fax: 215-291-5563
E-mail: metrokids@family.com
(a kids' column each month)

National Geographic World (ages 8–14)
Editorial Address:
National Geographic
1145 17th Street N.W.
Washington, DC 20036
202-857-7000
Fax: 202-429-5712

Ordering Address:
National Geographic
P.O. Box 2330
Washington, DC 20013-2330
800-638-4077
800-548-9797
(artwork, letters)

New Moon (girls 8–14)
Editorial Address:
New Moon
P.O. Box 620
Duluth, MN 55806
(stories, poems, drawings)

Nickelodeon Magazine (ages 6–14)
Editorial Address:
Nickelodeon Magazine
1515 Broadway, 41st Floor
New York, NY 10036
212-258-7388
Fax: 212-846-1766
E-mail: nickeditor@aol.com

Ordering Address:
P.O. Box 0945
Des Moines, IA 50340-0945
515-280-8750
(letters, contests)

Nineteenth Avenue (ages 6–10)
Editorial & Ordering Address:
The Humphrey Forum
301 19th Avenue, S.
Minneapolis, MN 55455
612-624-5799
Fax: 612-624-6351
(essays, letters, fiction)

Odyssey (ages 8–14)
Editorial & Ordering Address:
Cobblestone Publishing, Inc.
7 School Street
Peterborough, NH 03458
603-924-7209
Fax: 603-924-7380
(letters, art, poems, contest entries)

Otterwise: For Kids Who Are into Saving Animals and the Environment (ages 8–13)
Editorial & Ordering Address:
P.O. Box 1374
Portland, ME 04104
207-283-2964
(stories, art, poems, letters)

Owl: The Discovery Magazine for Kids (ages 8 and up)
Editorial Address:
Young Naturalist Foundation
179 John Street, Suite 500
Toronto, ON
Canada M5T 3G5
416-971-5275
Fax: 416-971-5294
E-mail: owlcom@owl.on.ca

Ordering Address:
In the U.S.
25 Boxwood Lane
Buffalo, NY 14227-2780
(drawings, letters, stories, poetry)

Pockets (ages 6–12)
Editorial Address:
The Upper Room
1908 Grand Avenue
Box 189
Nashville, TN 37202-0189
615-340-7333
Fax: 615-340-7006
E-mail: 102615.3127@compuserve.com

Ordering Address:
Pockets
P.O. Box 37146
Boone, IA 50037-0146
800-925-6847
(letters, poems, stories, art)

Racing for Kids (ages 4–16)
Editorial & Ordering Address:
Racing for Kids, LLC
P.O. Box 192
Concord, NC 28026-0192
704-786-7132
Fax: 704-795-4460
Orders: 800-443-3020
(artwork, short stories, poetry)

R-A-D-A-R (ages 8–12)
Editorial & Ordering Address:
Standard Publishing
8121 Hamilton Avenue
Cincinnati, OH 45230
513-931-4050
Fax: 513-931-0904
(letters, stories)

Ranger Rick (ages 6–12)
Editorial & Ordering Address:
National Wildlife Federation
8925 Leesburg Pike
Vienna, VA 22184-0001
703-790-4000
Fax: 703-442-7332
(letters, questions)

Scholastic Math (ages 12–14)
Editorial Address:
Scholastic, Inc.
555 Broadway
New York, NY 10012
212-343-6435
Fax: 212-343-6333
E-mail: mathmag@scholastic.com

Ordering Address:
Scholastic, Inc.
2931 E. McCarty Street
P.O. Box 3710
Jefferson City, MO 65102-3710
800-631-1586
(puzzles, brain teasers, published math mistakes)

School Magazine (ages 8–12)
Editorial & Ordering Address:
Private Bag 3
Ryde, NSW
Australia 2112
02-9808-9598
Fax: 02-9808-9588
(letters)

School Mates (ages 5 and up)
Editorial & Ordering Address:
U.S. Chess Federation
186 Route 9W
New Windsor, NY 12553
914-562-8350
Fax: 914-562-2437
800-388-KING
E-mail: USCF@delphi.com
(letters, art, photos, puzzles, stories, poems, chess
    games students have won)

Signatures from Big Sky (ages 5–17)
Editorial & Ordering Address:
928 Fourth Avenue
Laurel, MT 59044
406-628-7063
(stories, poems, essays, black and white drawings)

Soccer Jr. Magazine (ages 8–16)
Editorial Address:
Triplepoint, Inc.
27 Unquowa Road
Fairfield, CT 06430
203-259-5766
Fax: 203-254-2966

Ordering Address:
Soccer Jr. Magazine
P.O. Box 420442
Palm Coast, FL 32142
(stories, artwork)

Sports Illustrated for Kids (ages 8 and up)
Editorial Address:
Time, Inc. Magazine Co.
1271 Sixth Avenue
New York, NY 10020
212-522-KIDS
Fax: 212-522-0120

Ordering Address:
Time, Inc. Magazine Co.
P.O. Box 830609
Birmingham, AL 35283-0609
800-334-2229 U.S. and Canada
(letters, artwork)

Stone Soup: The Magazine for Children (ages 6–13)
Editorial Address:
P.O. Box 83
Santa Cruz, CA 95063
(stories, poems, book reviews, artwork)

Storyworks Magazine (ages 8–10)
Editorial Address:
Scholastic, Inc.
555 Broadway
New York, NY 10012
212-343-6298
Fax: 212-343-6333

Ordering Address:
Scholastic, Inc.
2931 E. McCarty Street
P.O. Box 3710
Jefferson City, MO 65101-3710
800-631-1586
(children's book reviews, letters)

**Surprises: Activities for Today's Kids and
    Parents** (ages 5–12)
Editorial Address:
Children's Surprises, Inc.
275 Market Street, Suite 521
Minneapolis, MN 55405
612-937-8345

Ordering Address:
Children's Surprises, Inc.
P.O. Box 20471
Bloomington, MN 55405
(letters, artwork, activities)

Tapori (ages 6–13)
Editorial & Ordering Address:
Tapori/Fourth World Movement
7600 Willow Hill Drive
Landover, MD 20785-4658
301-336-9489
(stories about experiences and ideas on how to
    fight extreme poverty)

Troll Magazine (ages 6–12)
Editorial Address:
Marvel Entertainment Group, Inc.
87 Park Avenue
New York, NY 10016
212-687-0680
Fax: 212-986-1849

Ordering Address:
Marvel Entertainment Group, Inc.
P.O. Box 7346
Red Oak, IA 51591
515-243-4543
(letters, photographs)

U*S* Kids (ages 5–10)
Editorial Address:
Children's Better Health Institute
1100 Waterway Boulevard
P.O. Box 567
Indianapolis, IN 46206
317-636-8881
Fax: 317-684-8094

Ordering Address:
Children's Better Health Institute
P.O. Box 7133
Red Oak, IA 51591-0133
(art, poetry)

Winner (ages 9–11)
Editorial Address:
The Health Connection
55 West Oak Ridge Drive
Hagerstown, MD 21740
301-790-9734

Ordering Address:
The Health Connection
P.O. Box 859
Hagerstown, MD 21741
800-548-8700
(artwork, poems, posters on drug education
    themes)

Word Dance Magazine (ages 5–13)
Editorial & Ordering Address:
Word Dance Magazine
P.O. Box 10804
Wilmington, DE 19850
302-328-6834
(letters, poetry, short stories; special consideration
    given to unique group projects and work from
    mentally and physically challenged youths)

ZiNj Magazine (ages 7–14)
Editorial & Ordering Address:
The ZiNj Education Project
300 Rio Grande
Salt Lake City, UT 84101
801-533-3565
Fax: 801-533-3503
(articles, book reviews, questions for Dr. What,
    artwork, activities, photos)

MATCHING TOPICS, PURPOSES, AND AUDIENCES

During process writing, students will decide on their purposes for writing and will self-select writing topics. These papers will then need to go to the appropriate audiences. Audiences can be determined at any time before or during the writing process. Students may, however, need some guidance in considering which audience is best for a particular piece of writing.

Directions

1. Tell students that they need to consider audiences for their writing. Remind students that the audiences they choose should be matched to their topics and purposes.

2. Provide students with examples of writings that match audiences and writings that do not. Some examples follow. Encourage students to think of additional mismatches between pieces of writing and audiences.

   - A poem about sports to the city mayor
   - A request for longer recesses to your grandmother
   - An essay about spring to your baby brother
   - A picture book to your dog

3. Duplicate and distribute the sheet that follows titled Matching Topics, Purposes, and Audiences. Tell students that they can use this sheet to record their thinking about how appropriate a specific piece of writing is for an audience. Explain to students that finding the right audiences for their writing will take time and practice.

4. Have students select a piece of writing. Ask them to record the topics of the paper and the purposes of the paper. Then have students write who some appropriate audiences would be for the piece.

5. Divide the class into groups of two or three students. Have students discuss their topics, purposes, and audiences. Have students give reasons why their audiences would be appropriate.

6. Instruct students to write the reasons why the topic was appropriate for the particular audience. Then have students reflect on the effectiveness of the piece and write that down as well.

Name _____ Date _____

Matching Topics, Purposes, and Audiences

Title _____

1. The topics of this paper were _____
   _____ .

2. My purposes for writing this paper were _____
   _____
   _____ .

3. The audiences for this paper were _____
   _____
   _____ .

4. The reasons why this was a good topic for my audiences were _____
   _____
   _____ .

5. I think this paper was effective because _____
   _____
   _____ .

Assessing Motivation and Content

Goal ● *To assess students' motivation and the content of students' writing.*

BACKGROUND

If writers aren't careful, they can fall into a rut. Teachers see this happen a lot. A student writer begins the year writing adventure stories starring a popular super hero as the main character. By spring, students are writing stories with the same characters and the same plot. Some students tend to write the same thing over and over unless they are urged to vary their writing topics, purposes, and audiences. Because students need a variety of writing experiences to grow as writers, teachers should assess the content of students' writings.

Teachers can assess students' writing content in three different ways:

1. Teachers can compare their students' writings with writings of previous students.
2. Teachers can evaluate how effective students have been in matching topics with authors' purposes and audiences.
3. Teachers can evaluate ways in which students have written a variety of topics for a variety of purposes and audiences.

> *Good assessment should influence instruction.*

Teachers can also assess students' motivation to write. Motivation plays a key role in writing achievement. If students want to write, they will work harder to learn the skills and strategies of writers. Many teachers think that they know how motivated students are without an assessment device. However, when students are asked about their motivation, teachers are sometimes surprised. The students they thought were not motivated were actually having difficulty writing, or the students they thought were motivated actually did not like to write. Knowing this information can assist teachers as they prepare instructional lessons.

Good assessment should influence instruction. Therefore, students should be part of the assessment picture by monitoring their own writing content. Teachers also should have regular input into students' writings by making positive comments on students' papers (Straub, 1997). Additional types of assessment strategies that teachers can use to evaluate students' writing content are presented in this section.

WRITING ATTITUDE SURVEY •————————

The Writing Attitude Survey (Kear, Coffman, McKenna, & Ambrosio, 2000) measures how students feel about writing using the popular Garfield characters. Students circle the different Garfield characters to reflect how they feel about a statement related to writing. This information can be used by teachers to determine how students feel about writing.

📠 Directions

1. Tell students that you want to know more about their feelings about writing. Explain to students that there are no right or wrong answers on this survey but that you want students to answer honestly.

2. Duplicate and distribute the Writing Attitude survey that follows. Point out the four Garfield characters. Show students the Garfield on the left. Ask students how they think Garfield feels. If students do not say something like very happy or enthusiastic, point out Garfield's smile and thumbs-up. If students are unfamiliar with the thumbs-up sign, tell them that it means "yes" or something very positive. Then point out the next Garfield, the one standing with the thumbs-up sign. Suggest to students that this Garfield is happy but not as happy as the Garfield on the left. Point out the two Garfields on the right. Explain to students that the far right Garfield is very unhappy, and the Garfield in the center right position is unhappy.

3. Ask students if they understand how the different Garfields feel. Then have students begin reading the survey questions or read them to students. Instruct students to circle the Garfield that represents how they feel about that statement.

4. Remind students to work independently and repeat that there are no correct answers. Tell students you really want to know how they feel.

5. After students are finished, score the surveys by awarding four points for every very happy Garfield, three points for the happy Garfield, two points for the unhappy Garfield, and one point for the very unhappy Garfield. Add up the points, using the Writing Attitude Survey Scoring Sheet on page 223.

6. The survey contains a total of 28 questions, so students scoring approximately 70 would fall midway between the somewhat happy and somewhat upset Garfield, indicating an indifferent attitude toward writing. Rank the scores of your students to determine which students' scores are above 70 and which are below.

7. Adjust your instruction according to the results of the survey.

Writing Attitude Survey

1. How would you feel writing a letter to the author of a book you read?

2. How would you feel if you wrote about something you have heard or seen?

3. How would you feel writing a letter to a store asking about something you might buy there?

4. How would you feel telling in writing why something happened?

5. How would you feel writing to someone to change their opinion?

6. How would you feel keeping a diary?

7. How would you feel writing poetry for fun?

8. How would you feel writing a letter stating your opinion about a topic?

9. How would you feel if you were an author who writes books?

10. How would you feel if you had a job as a writer for a newspaper or magazine?

11. How would you feel about becoming an even better writer than you already are?

12. How would you feel about writing a story instead of doing homework?

13. How would you feel about writing a story instead of watching TV?

14. How would you feel writing about something you did in science?

15. How would you feel writing about something you did in social studies?

16. How would you feel if you could write more in school?

17. How would you feel about writing down the important things your teacher says about a new topic?

18. How would you feel about writing a long story or report at school?

19. How would you feel writing answers to questions in science or social studies?

20. How would you feel if your teacher asked you to go back and change some of your writing?

21. How would you feel if your classmates talked to you about making your writing better?

22. How would you feel writing an advertisement for something people can buy?

23. How would you feel keeping a journal for class?

24. How would you feel writing about things that have happened in your life?

25. How would you feel writing about something from another person's point of view?

26. How would you feel about checking your writing to make sure the words you have written are spelled correctly?

27. How would you feel if your classmates read something you wrote?

28. How would you feel if you didn't write as much in school?

Writing Attitude Survey Scoring Sheet

Student's name _____

Teacher _____

Grade _____

Administration date _____

Item Scores

1. _____	15. _____
2. _____	16. _____
3. _____	17. _____
4. _____	18. _____
5. _____	19. _____
6. _____	20. _____
7. _____	21. _____
8. _____	22. _____
9. _____	23. _____
10. _____	24. _____
11. _____	25. _____
12. _____	26. _____
13. _____	27. _____
14. _____	28. _____

Full scale raw score _____

From Kear, D.J., Coffman, G.A., McKenna, M.C., & Ambrosio, A.L. (2000). Measuring attitude toward writing: A new tool for teachers. *The Reading Teacher, 54*, 10–23. Reprinted with permission.

WRITER SELF-PERCEPTION SCALE

Teachers can learn about students' writing motivation by having them fill out a self-report survey that measures their perception of themselves as writers. The Writer Self-Perception Scale (Bottomly, Henk, & Melnick, 1997/1998) measures four factors that affect how students perceive themselves as writers: performance (including past experiences), comparison with peers, social feedback, and feelings during writing. When students think about these issues, they become more aware of their writing identities, and teachers are able to glean information about students that they typically wouldn't know.

Directions

1. Tell students that they will be taking a survey that measures how they think about themselves as writers. Inform students that there are no right or wrong answers but that they should answer as honestly as possible.

2. Explain the scoring measure: strongly agree, agree, undecided, disagree, and strongly disagree. Tell students that they should read the survey item and decide how they feel about the item. For example, you could make the statements that follow.

   A sample statement can be found at the top of the survey. It says, "I think Batman is the greatest super hero." Think about whether you agree with this statement. Are you really positive that this is true? If so, you strongly agree. Do you think this is true, but you're not sure? Then you agree. If you can't make up your mind, you are undecided. If you think Batman is not the greatest super hero, you disagree; and if you really are positive that Batman is not the greatest super hero, you strongly disagree.

3. Ask students whether they have questions about the scoring. Some students will find the five-point scale confusing, so answer as many questions as you can before students begin taking the survey. If necessary, use a second example.

4. Duplicate and distribute the Writer Self-Perception Scale that follows to each student.

5. Point out that strongly agree is represented by SA on the survey, and so on.

6. Remind students that there are no correct answers, but that whatever they think, they should mark.

7. Give students time to fill out the surveys. You may need to read the survey to some students.

8. After students are finished, score each survey using the scoring sheet with the scoring key on page 227. Mark a 5 for strongly agree, a 4 for agree, and so on. Add up the scores on the subsections. Look at the scoring interpretation to determine how students think of themselves as writers.

The Writer Self-Perception Scale

Listed below are statements about writing. Please read each statement carefully. Then circle the letters that show how much you agree or disagree with the statement. Use the following scale.

SA = Strongly Agree
 A = Agree
 U = Undecided
 D = Disagree
SD = Strongly Disagree

Example: **I think Batman is the greatest super hero.**　　　SA　A　U　D　SD

If you are *really positive* that Batman is the greatest, circle SA (Strongly Agree).
If you *think* that Batman is good but maybe not great, circle A (Agree).
If you *can't decide* whether or not Batman is the greatest, circle U (Undecided).
If you *think* that Batman is not all that great, circle D (Disagree).
If you are *really positive* that Batman is not the greatest, circle SD (Strongly Disagree).

1.	I write better than other kids in my class.	SA	A	U	D	SD
2.	I like how writing makes me feel inside.	SA	A	U	D	SD
3.	Writing is easier for me than it used to be.	SA	A	U	D	SD
4.	When I write, my organization is better than the other kids in my class.	SA	A	U	D	SD
5.	People in my family think I am a good writer.	SA	A	U	D	SD
6.	I am getting better at writing.	SA	A	U	D	SD
7.	When I write, I feel calm.	SA	A	U	D	SD
8.	My writing is more interesting than my classmates' writing.	SA	A	U	D	SD
9.	My teacher thinks my writing is fine.	SA	A	U	D	SD
10.	Other kids think I am a good writer.	SA	A	U	D	SD
11.	My sentences and paragraphs fit together as well as my classmates' sentences and paragraphs.	SA	A	U	D	SD
12.	I need less help to write well than I used to.	SA	A	U	D	SD
13.	People in my family think I write pretty well.	SA	A	U	D	SD
14.	I write better now than I could before.	SA	A	U	D	SD

From D.M. Bottomly, W.A. Henk, & S. Melnick. (1997/1998). Assessing children's views about themselves as writers using the Writer Self-Perception Scale. *The Reading Teacher*, 51, 286–296. Reprinted with permission.

15.	I think I am a good writer.	SA	A	U	D	SD
16.	I put my sentences in a better order than the other kids.	SA	A	U	D	SD
17.	My writing has improved.	SA	A	U	D	SD
18.	My writing is better than before.	SA	A	U	D	SD
19.	It's easier to write well now than it used to be.	SA	A	U	D	SD
20.	The organization of my writing has really improved.	SA	A	U	D	SD
21.	The sentences I use in my writing stick to the topic more than the ones the other kids use.	SA	A	U	D	SD
22.	The words I use in my writing are better than the ones I used before.	SA	A	U	D	SD
23.	I write more often than other kids.	SA	A	U	D	SD
24.	I am relaxed when I write.	SA	A	U	D	SD
25.	My descriptions are more interesting than before.	SA	A	U	D	SD
26.	The words I use in my writing are better than the ones other kids use.	SA	A	U	D	SD
27.	I feel comfortable when I write.	SA	A	U	D	SD
28.	My teacher thinks I am a good writer.	SA	A	U	D	SD
29.	My sentences stick to the topic better now.	SA	A	U	D	SD
30.	My writing seems to be more clear than my classmates' writing.	SA	A	U	D	SD
31.	When I write, the sentences and paragraphs fit together better than they used to.	SA	A	U	D	SD
32.	Writing makes me feel good.	SA	A	U	D	SD
33.	I can tell that my teacher thinks my writing is fine.	SA	A	U	D	SD
34.	The order of my sentences makes better sense now.	SA	A	U	D	SD
35.	I enjoy writing.	SA	A	U	D	SD
36.	My writing is more clear than it used to be.	SA	A	U	D	SD
37.	My classmates would say I write well.	SA	A	U	D	SD
38.	I choose the words I use in my writing more carefully now.	SA	A	U	D	SD

From D.M. Bottomly, W.A. Henk, & S. Melnick. (1997/1998). Assessing children's views about themselves as writers using the Writer Self-Perception Scale. *The Reading Teacher*, 51, 286–296. Reprinted with permission.

The Writer Self-Perception Scale Scoring Sheet

Student's name _____

Teacher _____

Grade _____ Date _____

Scoring key   5 = Strongle Agree (SA)
4 = Agree (A)
3 = Undecided (U)
2 = Disagree (D)
1 = Strongly Disagree (SD)

Scales

General Progress (GPR)	Specific Progress (SPR)	Observational Comparison (OC)	Social Feedback (SF)	Physiological States (PS)
3. _____	22. _____	1. _____	5. _____	2. _____
6. _____	25. _____	4. _____	9. _____	7. _____
12. _____	29. _____	8. _____	10. _____	24. _____
14. _____	31. _____	11. _____	13. _____	27. _____
17. _____	34. _____	16. _____	28. _____	32. _____
18. _____	36. _____	21. _____	33. _____	35. _____
19. _____	38. _____	23. _____	37. _____	
20. _____		26. _____		
		30. _____		

Raw Scores

Raw score
_____ of 40   _____ of 35   _____ of 45   _____ of 35   _____ of 30

Score Interpretation	GPR	SPR	PC	SF	PS
High	39+	34+	37+	32+	28+
Average	35	29	30	27	22
Low	30	24	23	22	16

From D.M. Bottomly, W.A. Henk, & S. Melnick. (1997/1998). Assessing children's views about themselves as writers using the Writer Self-Perception Scale. *The Reading Teacher, 51*, 286–296. Reprinted with permission.

Writers need to evaluate their writing as they go, but they also should reread their pieces at a later date in order to make decisions about their writing progress (Graves, 2002). To look at writing objectively, writers should step away from their pieces and gain distance, so they can evaluate the good and poor parts of their writing without feeling defensive. Students can self-evaluate their writings in school, too, as long as they keep their pieces over time.

 *Directions*

1. Instruct students to select four pieces of writing from their portfolios and place the papers in order from best to worst. If students have difficulty rating their papers, say something like the following remarks.

   Each piece of writing that you do is different, so it can be difficult to say you like one paper better than another. You might have a folktale, an essay, a letter, and a poem in your selection. To place these pieces in order, read them over carefully and decide which ones have the most impact. As you think about how powerful each piece of writing is, you can order your papers. Don't worry if you aren't certain. You can reorder your papers another time.

2. Tell students that they will be evaluating their own writing at this time. Explain to students that writers need to read their works after they are finished to make decisions about what progress they've made and what skills need additional work. Tell students that they will be evaluating the four pieces of writing that they have chosen.

3. Duplicate and distribute the Student Self-Evaluation sheet that follows. Have students put their names and the date on the top of the sheet.

4. Ask students to write the titles of the four pieces they have selected in order from best to least.

5. Have students write the reasons why they ordered the papers as they did.

6. Ask students to list the topic that they liked best.

7. Have students underline an interesting sentence on each paper and write why the sentences stood out.

8. Have students write what they wish they had done to make the papers more interesting.

9. Ask students to list their strengths as a writer and their writing goals.

10. Repeat the Student Self-Evaluation every two months throughout the school year.

Name _____ Date _____

Student Self-Evaluation

Titles of selected papers in order (1 is your best paper) _____

    1. _____

    2. _____

    3. _____

    4. _____

Reasons why I ordered the papers as I did _____

_____

_____

_____

_____

Topics I liked best _____

_____

Good sentences _____

_____

_____

What would make these papers more interesting? _____

_____

_____

_____

Strengths as a writer _____

_____

_____

_____

Writing goals _____

_____

_____

_____

Many teachers ask students to write to a prompt to assess their writing. Some states even have uniform writing prompts that all students use for a writing test. These tests tend to influence instruction in ways that may not be helpful to writers (Hillocks, 2002). Graves states that "the main reason for having a single stimulus like this is that it makes scoring easier: reviewers can decide rather quickly where the student falls within the rubrics of fluency, use of detail, coherence, use of conventions, and so on" (2002, p. 46). Graves goes on to state what many teachers already have learned: the use of a writing prompt can be unfair for students who have little knowledge about or interest in the topic of the prompt. Therefore, Graves (2002) recommends having students write to their own prompts for classroom assessment.

Directions

1. Tell students that you will be evaluating their writing at the end of the year by asking them to write to a prompt. Explain to students that this evaluation is different from any other local, state, or national writing assessment the students experience. Tell students that you will be tailoring the writing prompts directly to each individual student.

2. Duplicate and distribute the Writing to a Prompt sheet that follows to each student and have students generate a list of potential topics.

3. From time to time before the evaluation period, ask students to write a topic of interest on their Writing to a Prompt sheet. Describe a topic entry as follows.

    When you list your topic entries, please provide a sentence or two that describes your interest. For example, one of the topics that interest me is dogs. As I think about all of the possible areas of interest pertaining to dogs, I can come up with many ideas such as dog health, dog training, dog grooming, types of dogs, and dog shows. As I think about what interests me most, I would choose dog shows, so I'd put dog shows on my list of topics. Dog shows, of course, is also a broad topic, so I'd write a sentence or two that describes my interest in more detail such as: It takes months of work to prepare a dog for a show. You need to train the dog and work with it so that it knows how to act during the show.

4. Explain to students that you will be selecting one of their topics for them to use for their writing evaluation. Tell students that you will choose the topic that you believe will give them the most chance to show off their writing ability.

5. Choose a topic from each student's list for an evaluation. Assess the students' writing on a rubric that fits the assignment.

Name _____ Date _____

Writing to a Prompt

Topic _____

Description _____

_____

_____

Topic _____

Description _____

_____

_____

Topic _____

Description _____

_____

_____

Topic _____

Description _____

_____

_____

Topic _____

Description _____

_____

_____

Writing Genres: Understanding Organizational Patterns

"The art of writing cannot be learned all at once."

—Jean Jacques Rousseau

OVERVIEW

When we read, we often have seemingly intuitive knowledge about what will happen next in a story. For example, when reading a murder mystery, such as Agatha Christie's *Murder on the Orient Express*, we know that some type of crisis will occur that sets the stage for a murder, that a murder will take place, that characters will be developed who could turn into suspects, that red herrings will be introduced, and that the murderer will be found by a clever private eye. When we read, the content of the text may hold surprises, but the text's organization will be fairly predictable.

The reason why we have this knowledge about the text's organization is through many, many experiences with texts. Texts are written

> Students need to become aware of the patterns of texts.

in organizational patterns, called genres, that have been developed in our society over several centuries (Donovan, 2001). Writers have refined different genres over time so that when we read we are aware of the directions in which the text will guide our thinking. Some of the genres that have been fairly stable over time are personal experience stories, works of fiction, exposition, and persuasion.

We become aware of the patterns of texts primarily through reading and writing. As we read, we subconsciously look for texts to move in predictable directions. Writing, however, is another matter. Writers generally need to be taught the genres of texts. Inexperienced writers sometimes think that writing is simply talk written down (Wray & Lewis, 1997). It's not. Writing follows accepted organizational rules so that readers can comprehend content while following the train of thought presented in the text.

Students need to become aware of the patterns of texts. Students who have had many experiences hearing stories will learn the pattern of fictional works easily and apply those organizational features of fiction to their writings (Lancia, 1997). They will easily understand that the story takes place in a particular setting with main characters who are involved in a plot and that the story may have a theme. Fiction is the easiest type of pattern to teach students because of their many experiences with that type of text. Students are usually less familiar with personal experience stories, exposition, and persuasion. Therefore, students need explicit instruction in the ways texts are organized, and they need practice with these types of writings (Kern, Andre, Schilke, Barton, & McGuire, 2003).

Students will probably discover some aspects of text organization on their own while participating in writing activities. For most students, however, the experience of writing will not help them become effective writers of informational texts (Stotsky, 1995). Students who participate in writing workshops for the bulk of their writing instruction still need teachers to help them co-construct strategies for writing (Collins, 1998). For example, students who

Can this teacher help students by sharing his own writing experiences?

want to persuade their parents to give them a larger allowance may need the teacher to help them organize their thoughts so that their arguments are reasonable, logical, and persuasive. Teachers, then, need to develop lessons to help students learn how texts are organized. This chapter provides resources, teaching strategies, ideas, and activities to help you teach students the specific organizational patterns of writing. Ideas for assessment also are included.

Personal Experience Stories

Goal ● *To help students learn the genre of personal experience stories.*

BACKGROUND

"Guess what happened to me?" Students burst into classrooms on a regular basis brimming with stories about their lives. That's because students' lives are filled with events and experiences that they want to share. Students love to tell stories about their lives. They tell stories about themselves to their teachers, to their friends, and even to strangers. Students' lives are filled with stories that they are more than willing to tell others.

Personal experience stories are a natural extension of storytelling. They are the written form of stories of an author's experiences. When students write personal experience stories in schools, they bring their private lives into the classroom. Students' lives and families converge with the public setting of schools through the sharing of personal experience stories, which leads to a stronger sense of community (Buss & Karnowski, 2000). When students share their lives with their teachers and classmates, they reveal new sides of themselves.

The genre of personal experience stories is known to most students through stories they have heard or read. Personal experience stories can be written about any topic, but the story must be a true event or experience of the author. The topic for all personal experience stories, therefore, is the self. Since authors of personal experience stories write about themselves, the stories are written in the first person using the personal pronoun "I." The purpose of personal experience stories is to share the author's feelings about an event or experience. Personal experience stories are organized by a

beginning-middle-end structure. All stories have a beginning that introduces the experiences and the author's reactions to them, a middle that describes the events in a sequence, and an ending that summarizes the events and the author's feelings.

Students will find that personal experience stories are among the easiest types of stories to write. However, many students need instruction in the organizational pattern of personal experience stories. This section presents resources, teaching strategies, ideas, and activities to help students learn the organizational pattern of personal experience stories.

Might this student have an interesting story to share?

Organizational Pattern

Personal experience stories have a specific organizational pattern: beginning, middle, and end. This pattern can be taught to students who may have a vague notion of the way stories are written or told. There are two basic steps to teach story structure:

1. Tell students explicitly the organizational pattern of personal experience stories.
2. Show them an example of a personal experience story that was written by a student at their grade level.

Students can identify patterns in stories that were written at their own developmental level easier than they can in stories that were written by professional authors. Writings that are too complex can discourage students and keep them from learning how to organize their own stories.

Directions

1. Tell students that the stories they hear from others are often personal experience stories. Explain that personal experience stories are stories about the author's own experiences. Tell students that personal experience stories have a beginning, middle, and end.

2. Duplicate and distribute the Organizational Pattern Outline that follows. Tell students that in most cases personal experience stories follow the outline.

3. Divide the class into groups of three or four students. Have students read the Organizational Pattern Outline or read it with them. Discuss the components of a personal experience story. Explain the outline as needed.

4. Tell students that you will show them an example of a personal experience story. Locate a personal experience story that was written by a student at your grade level or, if appropriate, use the Student Example on page 238.

5. Make a transparency of the Student Example of a personal experience story. Identify the features that make the piece of writing a personal experience story rather than a different organizational pattern.

6. Locate additional pieces of writing that could be classified as personal experience stories. Have small groups of students read the stories and look for organizational features.

7. Later, have students write their own personal experience stories. Provide time for sharing.

Organizational Pattern Outline
Personal Experience Stories

Beginning

✓ Has descriptive title

✓ Introduces the event or experience

✓ States author's feelings, reactions, or learning

Middle

✓ Provides events in sequence

✓ Gives details

✓ Includes author's feelings, reactions, or learning

End

✓ Summarizes event or experience

✓ Restates author's feelings, reactions, or learning

Personal Experience Story: Student Example

The Blizzard of '99

The first week of the new year brought a big winter snowstorm. It

snowed over 18 inches in one night. The snow was really deep and very

cold. We all felt stranded because we couldn't get our car out of the drive.

My sister and I started scooping the snow from our driveway. It was

very hard work, and we felt like we were getting nowhere. Next, our

neighbors saw that we were struggling and they came over to help.

Samantha, Elena, Rachel, and I all took turns using shovels and brooms to

move the snow. It was exhausting work! Finally, with everyone working

together we were able to clear our drive. We were really thankful and

happy to have such good neighbors. We could now get out of our drive.

The big winter snowstorm helped us learn to work together as a

team in order to accomplish a certain goal. In conclusion, it's good to

have friends who are willing to lend a helping hand.

Rebecca Mondron
Third Grade

Personal experience stories have a distinct organizational structure. After students have thought of an idea for a topic, they need to develop the idea in the typical story pattern. Students can organize their ideas in many ways. Young students generally are more successful when they organize their ideas with a Writing Frame. Writing Frames provide students with important background knowledge about ways different pieces of writing can be organized. A Writing Frame gives students experience writing with a specific organizational pattern without having to know how to write the transitions.

Directions

1. Tell students that once they have ideas for stories they need to organize their ideas using the organizational pattern of personal experience stories. Remind students that personal experience stories have a beginning, middle, and end.

2. Young students and students who have little background with personal experience stories should begin organizing their ideas with a Writing Frame. Duplicate and distribute the Writing Frame that follows. Tell students that they will be writing their ideas on the Writing Frame.

3. Provide students with a model of a Writing Frame as in the example that follows. Develop your own story or use the example. Make a transparency of the example, show it to students, and explain how the story was developed from the Writing Frame.

4. Have students write their own stories using a Writing Frame.

Writing Frame
Personal Experience Story Example

One day I went fishing in the lake. **First**, my brother rowed us into a small cove where we threw in our fishing lines complete with wriggling worms on the hooks. **Then**, we waited for a fish to bite. **Finally**, we went home with no fish. **It was** a disappointing day for me. **I felt** frustrated **because** we didn't catch any fish. **I learned that** you won't catch fish every time you go fishing. Bummer!

Writing Frame Personal Experience Stories

One day I _____

_____.

First, _____

_____.

Then, _____

_____.

Finally, _____

_____.

It was _____.

I felt _____ because _____

_____.

I learned that _____.

GRAPHIC ORGANIZER

Graphic Organizers are another way to organize information before writing. Graphic Organizers are similar to outlines, but they form a visual representation of the writing's organization. Graphic Organizers can be used before, during, and after writing. Before writing, students can plot their ideas on Graphic Organizers and refer to them when they write. Students also can use Graphic Organizers during writing. As writers complete sections of writing, they can refer to their Graphic Organizers to remind themselves of the pattern of their writing. After writing, students can map out the ideas from their writing on Graphic Organizers to verify that they have all of the components of the writing pattern. Older students especially will find Graphic Organizers useful for learning the organizational patterns of different writing structures.

Directions

1. Remind students that personal experience stories have a specific organizational pattern. Tell students that a Graphic Organizer is a visual representation of the writing pattern.

2. Students who are independent writers can organize their ideas on Graphic Organizers. Once students have thought of an idea for a personal experience story, duplicate and distribute the Graphic Organizer that follows.

3. Have students map out their ideas for their stories on Graphic Organizers. Provide guidance as necessary. Tell students that organizing their ideas before they write will help them organize their writing.

4. Allow students time to plot their ideas on Graphic Organizers. If students have not generated enough ideas before writing, have them partially complete their Graphic Organizers and begin writing.

Could this student use a Graphic Organizer to assist her in writing about learning to ride a bike?

5. Tell students that they also can assess their writing organization by using Graphic Organizers after writing. Have students place several copies of the Graphic Organizer in their writing folders. After students have written personal experience stories, have them use their Graphic Organizers to determine whether they organized their writing according to the writing pattern.

Graphic Organizer Personal Experience Stories

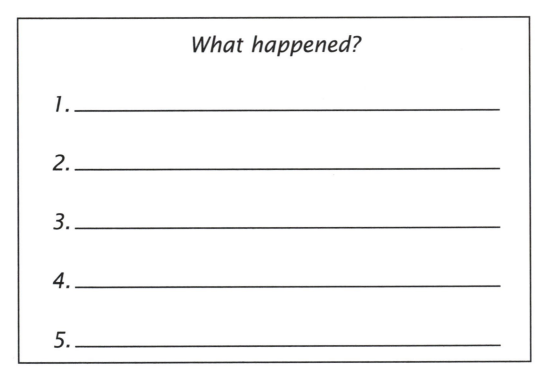

Event or Experience

Feelings, Thoughts, Reactions

What happened?

1. _____

2. _____

3. _____

4. _____

5. _____

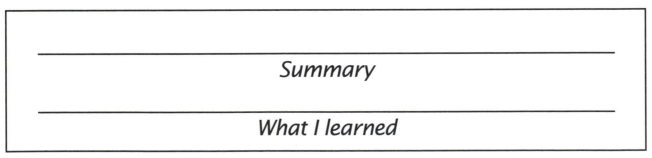

Summary

What I learned

Teaching Strategy 4

REVEALING EMOTIONS

A personal experience story is pretty dull if it doesn't include the author's feelings, reactions, and learning. Often, students have difficulty putting their feelings into words. Many times their vocabularies of feeling words are limited to sad, happy, and mad. To help students add depth to their stories, teach them some of the words that describe the emotional states that everyone experiences. Adding emotions to stories can make the difference between a mediocre story and an interesting one.

Directions

1. Tell students that an element of personal experience stories is the use of the author's feelings, reactions, and learning. Explain that students can improve their stories by adding words that express emotions.

2. Duplicate and distribute the list of Emotions that follows. Have students read the list or read it with them.

3. Have each student select one word from the list of Emotions. Ask students to think of a time when they felt that way. (If students are unsure of the meaning of a word, tell them what the word means.) Have students visualize themselves feeling what the word describes.

4. Select a word yourself, such as downcast. Make your face look downcast. Ask students to guess the word that you are pantomiming. If students have difficulty guessing the word, tell them the letter with which the word begins.

5. Invite students to pantomime the words they chose. Ask other students to guess the words their fellow students are pantomiming.

What words could this girl be using to describe her emotions?

6. Have students look through magazines and newspapers for pictures that have people experiencing the emotions described by the words that they chose. Have students create an Emotions Booklet with pictures next to words describing emotions.

7. When students have a topic for writing a personal experience story, have them use their list of Emotions to find a descriptive word that expresses their feelings, reactions, and learning. Encourage students to use words from the list in their writings.

Emotions

alone	glad	sad
awful	gloomy	scared
	good	sharp
bashful	grand	shy
blue	great	silly
brave		small
bright	happy	starved
	hated	strange
cheerful		stressed
clumsy	important	strong
confident		superb
courageous	joyful	
		terrific
daring	mysterious	thrilled
delighted		timid
depressed	nervous	tough
despised		
downcast	overjoyed	uneasy
downhearted		
dreadful	pleased	warm
	powerful	weak
fantastic	proud	wise
foolish		wonderful
friendly	relaxed	
furious		

Teaching Strategy 5

Section 5.1

ME MUSEUM

Students love to write about their lives, the small events as well as who they are and what they care about. One teaching strategy that students love is called a Me Museum. A Me Museum typically contains a display about the student: photographs, artifacts, timelines, collages, and written descriptions. Students writing about themselves in a Me Museum are motivated to describe the important facts they want their classmates to learn. Me Museums are appropriate for all grade levels and for students who are proficient writers as well as students who are learning English.

Directions

1. Tell students that they will be writing about their lives for their Me Museums. Have students take out other display material that can prompt their memories.

2. Ask students to think about themselves and what is important to their lives. Many students will want to discuss their families and friends as part of this narrative.

3. Read the sample Me Museum pieces on pages 247–248 from two fourth-grade students. Explain that these are examples of what two different students wrote about themselves. Tell students that their writings should be similar to the samples in that students should write about facets of their lives.

4. Discuss the two writings with students. Point out that Tommy's piece has fewer details that does Taylor's story. Explain that some students might just outline areas of interest in their lives, especially if the students are just learning English. Then discuss Taylor's piece, as in the example below.

   Notice the detail Taylor provides the reader in this piece. She tells us about her family, where they live, what she likes to do, her hobbies, and her goals. Taylor's writing lets us understand what kind of person she is.

5. Instruct students to outline their lives. They might use a timeline or another type of graphic organizer. Tell students to provide as many details as they can on their timelines.

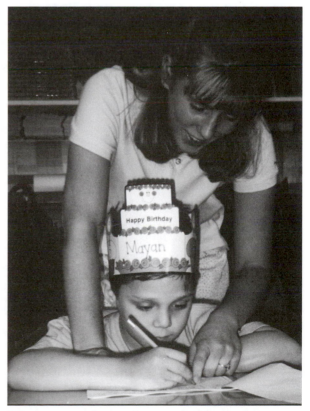

What personal experience can this student share?

245

6. Ask students to share and discuss their timelines with a classmate. Inform students that they should ask each other questions about the timelines. Examples of questions and questioning statements follow.

    - I'd like to know more about your hobbies. What hobbies do you enjoy?
    - Do you like to watch television, play video games, or watch movies? Which ones?
    - What is your favorite subject in school? Why?
    - What do you do on weekends and after school?
    - What is your family like? What do you do as a family?

7. Encourage students to add information based on the questions to their timelines. Then have students write their Me Museum pieces.

8. You might have students share their Me Museum displays on the same day, or you might decide to have students display their Me Museums throughout the school year. Impress upon students that the audience for the Me Museum is their classmates and the display is an example of presenting for an audience.

Writing Instruction Resources

http://7-12educators.about.com/cs/writingresources/

This site contains ideas on grammar, style and mechanics, essays, paragraphs, and papers.

Tommy's ME Museum

HI. MY NAME IS TOMMY THANH NGUYEN, I WAS BORN ON MARCH 25, 1993. I LIVE WITH MY MOM, MY DAD, MY SISTER, AND MY BROTHER. MY BROTHER'S NAME IS TIM NGUYEN. MY SISTERS NAME IS TIFFANY NGUYEN AND MY MOM AND DAD'S NAMES ARE TUN NGUYEN AND THAO TRAN. THEY WERE BOTH BORN IN HO CHI MINH CITY, VIETNAM. I'VE BEEN TO 5 COUNTRIES AND I KNOW 3 LANGUAGES. I'VE ALSO BEEN TO LAS VEGAS, NEVADA, LOS ANGELES, CALIFORNIA, DETROIT, MICHIGAN, AND ST. LOUIS, MISSOURI. THE FIVE COUNTRIES WERE VIETNAM, TOKYO, JAPAN, SEOUL, KOREA, TAIPEI, TAIWAN AND TORONTO, CANADA. I RODE ON (JAL) JAPAN AIRLINES, VIETNAM AIRLINES, KOREAN AIR, AMERICAN AIRLINES, AMERICAN WEST AND EVA AIR. MY HOBBIES ARE COLLECTING STUFF. LIKE MY AIRPLANE COLLECTION, I LIKE TO COLLECT TURTLE STUFF AND I LIKE TO BUILD STUFF. I LIKE TO TRAVEL. I LIKE TO DRAW. I LIKE TO GO TO VIETNAM. MY FAVORITE ANIMAL IS A TURTLE. MY FAVORITE MOVIE IS <u>BEHIND ENEMY LINES</u>.

THAT IS THE END OF MY ME MUSEUM.

ME Museum

My full name is Taylor Marie Smith. My birthday is March 2, 1993. My parents are Tom and Connie Smith. My mom is an RN (Registered nurse) at Methodist Medpointe. My dad is a paramedic at Advanced Medical Transport. So, I guess you could say I'm pretty safe around my mom and dad. I was born at Methodist Hospital about 9:00 PM. I weighed 8 pounts and 13 ounces.

My family and I live in Galena by Mark Twain School. I live in a brick house. I have lived in this house my whole life. I have a big back yard with a Jungle Jim swing set. My neighbors on one side of our house are Pete and what's her name. On the other side of our house is the Jones family. Shelby and I sometimes play together in our back yards. I have lots of fun in the summer riding my bicycle in the neighborhood. Sometimes I'll ride to Alex Robert's house, or sometimes we'll meet by the big oak tree at the end of our street. Sometimes we go hiking in the woods southeast from our house. It is very neat in the woods. I love being in the woods because it is peaceful.

I go to St. Alexa's church and I go to CCD on Sundays. CCD is like Sunday school. I had my First Communion two years ago in May. My mom and dad had a party for me afterwards. My whole family came, plus some of my neighbors.

My family and I like to go on a lot of vacations. My favorite one was to Gulf Shores, Alabama. That was my favorite vacation because I got to see dolphins and see what Alabama culture was like. We went on a dolphin cruise where we got to see live dolphins swimming in the ocean. It was fun seeing them chase the boat. Whenever we take a vacation near a beach, it's a tradition that my dad and I build a turtle or an alligator in the sand. We also went to Disney world and I got lots of autographs from Disney characters.

Usually we will go boating in the summer. I have been on our boat every summer since I was a baby. In 2002, I learned to water ski. I also like to go "tubing" behind our boat. It's a lot of fun! My cousins Kylee and Trevor came for a visit last summer. We spent the whole afternoon on our boat water skiing and tubing. I like to sit in the front of the boat with the wind in my hair. I like to sit up front because the front of the boat bounces up and down.

Other things I like to do in the summer are play softball. My favorite position is short stop. My least favorite position is center field. I don't like center field because there is not much action there. On the last game of our tournament, I got a triple and two doubles.

My favorite things to play with are my dolls. Molly and Lindsey. Molly and Lindsey are American Girl dolls. Each one of the dolls is sort of a theme doll. Molly is a character from around World War II, and Lindsey is from more modern times. I have a nurse doll that goes with my doll Molly. Sometimes, my mom and dad take me to the American Girl Doll store when we're in Chicago. It is a really neat store and they have a café there. My dad calls Molly "Molly the dolly."

I take dance at Debbie's School of Dance. I have taken lessons there since I was 4 years old. I have so much fun! I like learning new moves and performing them on stage in front of people. I take tap, jazz and tumbling. Every year in June, I perform in a dance recital at the Civic Center.

I want to be a veterinarian because I really like animals. I have loved animals my whole life. I like learning about animals in their natural habitat. I had a lot of goldfish. When I was little, their names were Rainbow, Simba, Nala, Goldie and Gus. Those are only a few. I also had a dog named Oreo and a hamster named Snickers. Now I have a dog named Bailey. She is a Golden Retriever and she is about 2 years old. She is a very good dog, but she like to chew on things like our remote for the TV. She is very hyper and likes to play fetch. She takes me on walks, instead of me taking her on walks. My dad is the only one that my dog minds.

My Mom and Dad are very cool. We have so much fun together. I like to go to my dad's work because we can play basketball. I like playing board games with him when I'm sick. My mom and I go shopping a lot. We also read together. I like scrap booking because we give each other ideas.

I just told you about 10 years of my life in about 10 minutes. I have a great family and lots of great friends. I just told you about me and my family and some of my friends. I have had a great life so far. I hope it only gets better.

Fictional Stories

Goal ● To help students learn the genre of fictional stories.

BACKGROUND

Fictional stories have a unique structure that is similar to personal experience stories but different from expository and persuasive writing. Unlike other types of writing, fictional stories are not true. They are figments of writers' imaginations. Writers can shape and develop their stories in any way they want, letting their imaginations take them to distant places. Fictional stories, therefore, will vary widely. However, all fictional stories have roughly the same type of organizational pattern.

The structure of fictional stories is well-known to most children and adults in our society. Not only do students read and hear fictional stories, but they also view them on television and at movies. Television stories and movies have the same elements as do print materials. Both books and movies have characters, a plot, a setting, a theme, and a point of view.

The *characters* of fictional stories are the people or personified animals who are the focus of the story. These characters have qualities which are revealed through their thoughts, actions, appearances, and sayings. Stories can have a single character or many characters. The characters of fictional stories are involved in some sort of plot. The *plot* is the action that takes place in the story, usually in a series of events that begins with a problem to be resolved and that ends with a resolution. The problem may be as simple as deciding where to find a kitten to buy or as complex as surviving an arctic storm. Every fictional story, however, has some sort of problem to be resolved. The characters and the plot take place in a setting. The *setting* of a fictional story is the time and place of the story. Through the character, plot,

and setting, the author of a fictional story frequently introduces a thought or idea. This thought or idea is called the *theme* of the story. Themes also can range from simple to complex. Finally, all stories are written from a *point of view*.

Most fictional stories are written in the third person with the author relating the story using the characters' names and the pronouns "he," "she," "they," etc. Some fictional stories are written in the first person. These stories are written as if the author is telling the story as in *Sarah, Plain and Tall* (MacLachlan, 1985). First-person fictional stories seem to be true, but they're not.

Writing fictional stories takes a lot of thought.

Fictional stories have a distinct organizational structure. By teaching students how to write stories with characters, plots, settings, themes, and from a point of view, students can write more vivid sto-

Fictional stories have a distinct organizational structure.

ries. This section includes resources, teaching strategies, ideas, and activities to help teach students to learn the organizational structure of fictional stories.

Teaching 1 Strategy

ORGANIZATIONAL PATTERN

Even though students are familiar with the organizational pattern of fictional stories from reading and hearing books, they should be taught the organizational pattern of fictional writing. Many students know some of the aspects of fictional stories from their background knowledge. However, learning the basics of writing fiction can help students develop plots more completely so that they can write interesting stories.

Directions

1. Tell students that fiction is the type of writing they most frequently have read in books. Explain that fictional stories are not true, that they have characters in them, and that they have a plot. Remind students that fictional writing can take the form of stories other people tell, television plots, or movies.

2. Duplicate and distribute the Organizational Pattern Outline for fictional stories that follows. Tell students that fictional stories follow the outline in most cases.

 3. Divide the class into groups of three or four students. Have students read the Organizational Pattern Outline or read it with them. Discuss the components of fictional writing with students.

4. Tell students that you will show them an example of fictional writing. Locate an example of fictional writing written by a student at your grade level or, if appropriate, use the Student Example on page 252.

5. Make a transparency of the Student Example. Identify the features that make the piece of writing fictional rather than a different organizational pattern.

6. Locate additional pieces of writing that could be classified as fictional. Have small groups of students read the stories and look for their organizational features.

Organizational Pattern Outline
Fictional Stories

Introduction

- ☐ Introduces the main character and the setting
- ☐ Introduces the main problem that will be resolved
- ☐ Introduces the theme

Interior Paragraph (may be more than 1)

- ☐ Develops the plot by giving events in sequence
- ☐ Uses the setting to provide details
- ☐ Develops the problem through events
- ☐ Develops characters through events
- ☐ Develops the theme through characters' actions

Conclusion

- ☐ Resolves the characters' problem
- ☐ Restates the theme in a subtle or explicit way

Fictional Story: Student Example

The Picnic

Yesterday Tanya got to play with Alissa. How did Tanya

get to play with her? Tanya spotted a familiar bike. It was

Alissa's! Tanya was on her bike. She was fast. She knew where

Alissa's house was. But Alissa was in the house. She came back

out and Tanya and Alissa had a little picnic. They got the food

and put the food in a wagon. Then they went to a shady place

to eat. They saw a butterfly and squirted their drink in the air.

They had a fun picnic.

Erin Bohlin
First Grade

Introduces main characters

Introduces problem

Resolves problem

Conclusion

Fictional stories have a distinct organizational structure. One of the challenges of writing fictional stories is to organize ideas so that the story is told clearly. After students have thought of the key elements of a plot, they need to develop the idea in the typical fictional organizational pattern. Students can organize their ideas in many ways. Young students generally are more successful when they organize their ideas with a Writing Frame. Writing Frames provide students with important background knowledge about ways different pieces of writing can be organized. A Writing Frame gives students experience writing with a specific organizational pattern without having to know how to write the transitions.

Directions

1.   Tell students that once they have ideas for their stories they need to organize their ideas using the organizational pattern of fictional stories. Remind students that fictional stories have a plot that is developed through the use of characters and a setting.

2.   Young students and students who have little background with fictional stories should begin organizing their ideas with a Writing Frame. Duplicate and distribute the Writing Frame that follows. Tell students that they will be writing their ideas on the Writing Frame.

3.   Provide students with a model of a Writing Frame as in the example that follows. Develop your own story or use the example. Make a transparency of the example, show it to students, and explain how the story was developed from the Writing Frame.

4.   Have students write their own fictional stories using a Writing Frame.

Writing Frame **Fictional Story Example**
Jeremy **lived in** a crowded neighborhood in a large city. Jeremy **wanted to** learn how to play soccer. **That was a problem because** there was very little room to run and play in his neighborhood. Jeremy **solved the problem by** asking his neighbors to help him clear the trash from a vacant lot. Jeremy and his neighbors cleared enough space to construct a half-sized soccer field.

Writing Frame Fictional Stories

_____ **lived in** _____
Character

_____ .
Setting

_____ **wanted to** _____
Character

_____ .

That was a problem because _____

_____ .

_____ **solved the problem by**
Character

_____ .

_____ .
Ending Sentence

Graphic Organizers are another way to organize information before writing. Graphic Organizers are similar to outlines, but they form a visual representation of the writing's organization. Graphic Organizers can be used before, during, and after writing. Before writing, students can plot their ideas on Graphic Organizers and refer to them when they write. Students also can use Graphic Organizers during writing. As writers complete sections of writing, they can refer to their Graphic Organizers to remind themselves of the pattern of their writing. After writing, students can map out the ideas from their writing on Graphic Organizers to verify that they have all of the components of the writing pattern. Older students especially will find Graphic Organizers useful for learning the organizational patterns of different writing structures.

Directions

1. Remind students that fictional stories have a specific organizational pattern. Tell students that a Graphic Organizer is a visual representation of the writing pattern.

2. Students who are independent writers can organize their ideas on Graphic Organizers. Once students have thought of an idea for a fictional story, duplicate and distribute the Graphic Organizer that follows.

3. Have students map out their ideas for their stories on Graphic Organizers. Provide guidance as necessary. Tell students that organizing their ideas before they write will help them organize their writing.

4. Allow students time to plot their ideas on Graphic Organizers. If students have not generated enough ideas before writing, have them partially complete their Graphic Organizers and begin writing.

5. Tell students that they also can assess their writing organization by using Graphic Organizers after writing. Have students place several copies of the Graphic Organizer in their writing folders. After students have written their stories, have them use their Graphic Organizers to determine whether they organized their writing according to the writing pattern.

Name _____ Date _____

Graphic Organizer Fictional Stories

_____
Title

Setting
_____
Time   Place

Characters

Major   Minor

_____ _____

_____ _____

_____ _____

Problem
_____

Events

1. _____
2. _____
3. _____
4. _____

_____
Resolution

Tell students that fictional stories employ characters who have the same qualities as real people. Characters in stories should be described by their actions, their feelings, their appearances, and the things that they say. Help students develop characters in fictional stories by using Character Webs.

Directions

1. Explain to students that characters in fictional stories should be described by their actions, their feelings, their appearances, and the things that they say. Tell students that using Character Webs can help them develop their characters.

2. Duplicate and distribute the Character Web that follows. Point out the sections for characters' acts, feelings, appearances, and sayings.

3. Have students refer to stories they are writing. Ask students to highlight on their drafts the actions of their characters. Then have them list the actions on the Character Webs. Repeat the process for the characters' feelings, appearances, and sayings.

4. After the Character Webs are completed, have students analyze the balance of information they have given about their characters. If students have not described how their characters look, have them write ideas on their Character Webs. Give students 5 to 10 minutes to complete their Character Webs.

5. Tell students that Character Webs can help them as they revise their stories. Remind students to supply enough information about their characters so that the characters live in the minds of readers.

6. Provide extra copies of Character Webs to students as they develop additional stories. Tell students that they can use the Character Webs before writing or after they have finished a draft of a story.

Character Web
Fictional Stories

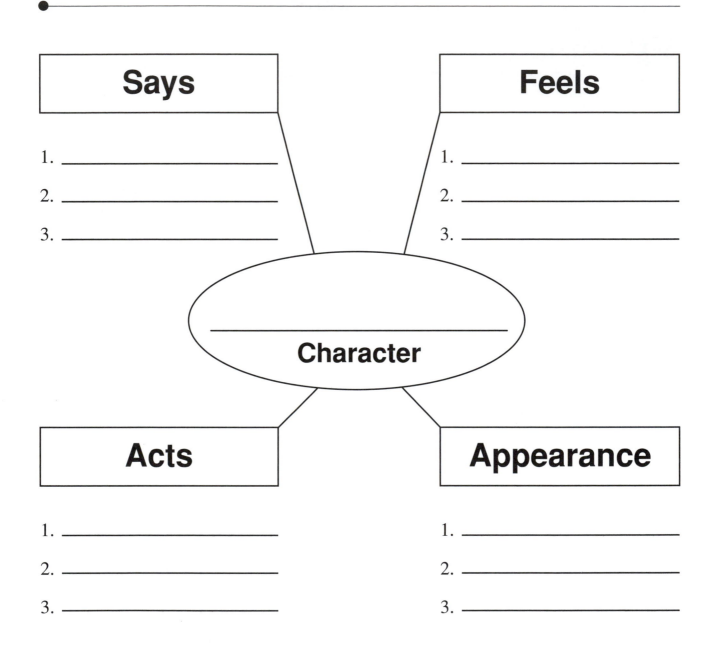

Says

1. _____
2. _____
3. _____

Feels

1. _____
2. _____
3. _____

Character

Acts

1. _____
2. _____
3. _____

Appearance

1. _____
2. _____
3. _____

Teaching Strategy 5

PLOT CUBE

One of the most difficult aspects of writing fictional stories is organizing the elements of the genre: characters, setting, problem, actions, solution, and ending. Many students begin writing but get bogged down in the details of the characters and never move on with the plot. Plot Cubes, however, can help students think about the story as a whole before beginning to write.

Directions

1. Tell students that they will be developing the elements of a fictional story. Many students will have ideas already generated for previous lessons or from their journals. For students who do not have an idea, show them the pictures of Chris Van Allsburg's (1984) book, *The Mysteries of Harris Burdick*. Explain to students that they can develop a story using the pictures as a guide.

2. Duplicate and distribute copies of the Plot Cube that follows. Explain to students that they will be outlining their stories on this Plot Cube. Point out the areas of the Plot Cube: characters, setting, problem, actions, solution, and ending. Tell students that they will be using the Plot Cube to plan their stories.

3. Tell students that the first thing they need to consider is the setting and the characters for their story. Remind students that a setting is the time and place of the story. Have students write one or more key words for the setting on that section of the cube. Then have students write key words for the main character.

Plot cubes make excellent displays.

4. Explain to students that the plot is an important aspect of fictional stories. Read the student sample, "The Ship," on pages 262–264. Discuss with students the elements of the plot as in the following conversation.

> *Teacher: What is the problem of this story?*
>
> *Student: The ship was bombed.*
>
> *Teacher: Yes, the ship was bombed. Why was John concerned about that?*
>
> *Student: The police thought his father was involved.*
>
> *Teacher: Yes, that's the kernel of the plot: John was worried that his father was implicated in bombing the ship. What actions occurred in the story?*
>
> [Students supply list of actions.]
>
> *Teacher: The most important part of a fictional story is the sequence of actions. As you plan your story, remember to list actions that solve the problem. Stories will also have a solution to the problem. You need to know how the problem will be solved before you write. Stories also have an ending. Think of your ending during your planning session.*

5. Encourage students to ask any questions about the elements of fictional stories. Take sufficient time to answer their questions.

6. Have students complete the remaining sections of the Plot Cube. Some students may want to illustrate the sections. Then have students cut the Plot Cube, fold the edges, and make a cube.

7. Inform students that they should use their Plot Cubes as they develop their fictional stories.

Lesson Plans

http://www.proteacher.com/070037.shtml

Writing lesson plans for elementary level teachers are provided on this site.

Plot Cube

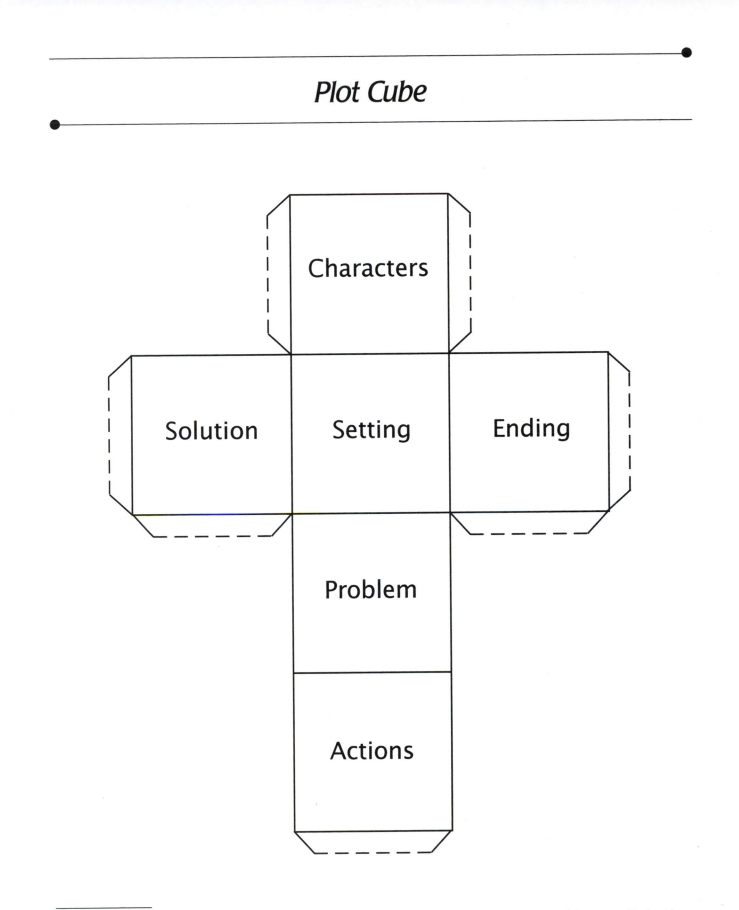

The Ship

Chapter 1

Even with her mighty engines in reverse, the ocean liner was pulled further and further into the canal. The ocean liner was headed strait for the city. Smash! The first tower of a building came crashing down. The ocean liner kept being pulled father into the canal, destroying everything in its path. The captain could not figure out why and how they were being pulled into the canal, even with the engines in reverse. Everyone on the ship was in a state of panic. By now they were almost halfway down the canal. The captain had noticed that the entire time they had been gaining speed. The captain could see people in the buildings along the canal running for their lives. Other small boats along the canal were crushed by the ocean liner's massive hull and intense weight. The captain was going crazy! All those years it took to build all those grand buildings were being wasted away. Suddenly the captain saw a figure standing on the shore. He was not running. Strange. He appeared to be holding some sort of device. Suddenly there was a scraping sound. The captain continued to look at the man on the shore. He was smiling. The captain yelled out, Boom!

Chapter 2

"Hi Mom, I'm home," yelled John.

"Hi sweetie." My mom is very busy. She works for one of those major companies that is located across the world.

"How was school?"

"All right I guess."

My mom came down the stairs.

"Have you listened to the news?"

"What news?"

"The news about the ocean liner that drove into the canal and exploded," said my mom.

"It what!" exclaimed John.

"Come here and look at the television." John watched the television and couldn't believe it. "This morning an ocean liner drove into the canal at the north end of town. It was here that the ocean liner exploded, wiping out everything around it. It is said that the port was expecting an ocean liner to be delivering food today. We will keep you updated with any news as soon as it is in. Wait! This just in! We have a detailed description of a strange man who apparently wasn't running when the ocean liner was driving through the canal. We have gotten this information from a man who was running, but turned to look back at the ship and saw the man standing there holding some sort of device. The man was a dark skinned man with a beard and long hair. He was wearing a very ripped and beat up jacket and very trashed out pants. We will keep you updated with any further news as soon as it is in. This is Peter Jennings with CBS 31 World News Tonight. Good night.

"Hey," yelled John, "that's Dad's description!"

Chapter 3

"I don't believe it! Dad wouldn't do anything like that! He wouldn't! And besides, why would he even do anything like that?" screamed John. His mother stood there, perplexed, amazed, not believing that her husband would do such a thing. They changed the channel and continued to watch the news.

"More news has just come in. Someone has seen a strange man doing something to the ship's hull while it was still in the port. The person, we aren't giving out any names, thought that it was just a repairman fixing the ship. The person who did this had to have known the exact time and place the ship was going. If you see anyone who matches this description, please contact us immediately."

Knock-knock.

"I'll get it," said John. He opened the door.

"Hello. Is this the Robinson family?"

"Ah year." It was the cops.

"We've gotten reports that a man who matches the description of the man who blew up the ocean liner lives here," said the officer.

"Listen," said John, "My father did not blow that ocean liner up!"

John was furious.

"John, what are you doing?" cried his mother, "Invite them in."

They all went in and sat down on the couch. They started discussing why they had come and what they were going to have my dad do. Then we heard the door open.

"Hello?" It was my dad.

Chapter 4

Dad walked into the living room.

"Oh, what's going on here?" He was very puzzled.

"I'm sorry sir, but we're going to have to take you under arrest," said the officer.

"What! For what!" said my dad.

"For blowing up that ocean liner. You match the description perfectly," the officer told him. So the officers took my dad down to the police station and questioned him. That night we turned on the news again to see the weather so that I could figure out what to wear tomorrow.

"Our main story tonight is the police seemed to have captured the person responsible for the explosion of the ocean liner. Another story we have is a sailor seems to have survived the explosion and told us that the ocean liner was approaching the dock faster than it should have been and that when it was driving through the canal that it's engines were trying to go backwards. We will keep you updated on anything that we get. Good night."
"What do you think could have happened?" I asked my mom.
" I don't know" she said, "but whatever it was, it wasn't good."

Chapter 5

Down at the police station, they knew dad wasn't telling the truth. They were threatening to lock him up in jail if he didn't tell the truth. Finally, he gave in.
"I didn't do it. It was my twin brother. He found out that another man was calling his wife, and he got mad. He strapped giant magnets to the front of the ship and on a building in the canal. Then he put a bomb in the water and when the ship drove over it he blew it up. It turned out the person who was calling his wife was the captain."
"Thank you," said the officer, " you can go home now."
My dad came home and the police went and arrested my dad's twin brother. He was sentenced to life in prison and we all lived happily ever after.

Daniel

This story and title are taken from a writing prompt about the book, *The Mysteries of Harris Burdick*, by Chris Van Allsburg.

Expository Writing

Goal ━━● *To help students learn the genre of expository writing.*

BACKGROUND

Expository writing is the kind of writing that gives directions, explains a situation or event, or tells how a process happens. Expository writing has a specific organizational structure:

> *Expository writing is a big part of our lives.*

- The main point is usually clearly stated or implied;
- The main point is then developed and supported by facts;
- The facts are presented in an orderly way; and
- The writing is directed toward a specific audience (Buss & Karnowski, 2002).

All types of expository writing have these characteristics, but there are a variety of organizational patterns that are typically considered to be expository writing. Among the most common expository writing patterns are simple explanation, steps-in-a-process, compare and contrast, and cause and effect. Each of these types of expository writing has a slightly different organizational pattern, but all are nonfiction with main ideas and details.

There has been an increasing interest in teaching expository writing in schools because so much of the print we read in life is one kind of expository writing or another. Examples of expository writing with which all of us are familiar

> **Expository Writing Patterns**
> Simple Explanation
> Steps-in-a-Process
> Compare and Contrast
> Cause and Effect

include directions for income taxes, computer manuals, and labels on cans. Letters can also be expository when they describe or explain a situation or event. Expository writing, therefore, is a big part of our lives.

Students in schools should learn the various organizational patterns of expository writing, both to help them construct meaning from text and so that they can become writers of this common type of written communication (Ryder, 1994). Before students can write expository text effectively, however, they need to have knowledge about a specific subject. Expository writing entails knowledge that is organized and shared. For example, if students are writing a paper comparing the African animal population today with the animal population of the early twentieth century, they would have to know some information about that topic. That information may be part of students' background knowledge. If students have to find information from other sources, they engage in research (Harvey, 1998). Then they can organize information in any of the accepted patterns of expository writing. This section provides information to help students learn the organizational patterns of expository writing through various resources, teaching strategies, ideas, and activities.

Teaching **1** *Strategy*

EXPLANATION/DEFINITION WRITING

Explanation/Definition Writing is one of the kinds of expository writing with which students are probably familiar. Many trade books and textbooks have sections that are organized by simple explanation. That means the writing begins with a main idea, details are given to support the main idea, and examples are given to illustrate the details. Although the main idea of any paragraph can be anywhere in the paragraph, or not even directly stated, most explanation writing that students will read or hear has the main idea stated in the first sentence. Explanation/Definition Writing is one of the easiest types of expository writing to teach students.

Directions

1. Tell students that you will be introducing Explanation/Definition Writing. Tell students that writers choose the explanation/definition organizational pattern of writing when they want to explain a point or define a concept. Remind students that writers decide on writing patterns based on their topics, purposes, and audiences.

2. Describe Explanation/Definition Writing by using the Organizational Pattern Outline on page 268. Make an overhead transparency of the outline and point out the various components of the pattern. Remind students that Explanation/Definition Writing will follow the outline in many respects but that writing can deviate from the outline.

3. Tell students that you will show them an example of Explanation/Definition Writing. Locate an example of Explanation/Definition Writing written by a student at your grade level or, if appropriate, use the Student Example on page 269.

4. Make a transparency of the Student Example. Identify the features that make the piece of writing Explanation/Definition rather than a different organizational pattern.

5. Locate additional pieces of writing that could be classified as Explanation/Definition Writing. Have small groups of students read their writings and look for organizational features.

6. After students have seen how Explanation/Definition Writing is organized, help them develop a topic for writing that can be organized in a Writing Frame or on a Graphic Organizer. Young students and students who have little background with expository writing should begin organizing their ideas with a Writing Frame.

7. Provide students with a model of a Writing Frame by developing your own piece of writing or by using the example that follows. Make a transparency of the example, share it with students, and explain how the example was developed from the Writing Frame. Duplicate and distribute the blank Writing Frame on page 270. Tell students that they will be writing their ideas on the Writing Frame.

Good habits are an important part of leading a healthy life. Getting regular exercise, eating nutritious foods, and getting plenty of sleep all are important components of a healthy life. **First**, most people need to have regular exercise to feel good and to stay healthy. **Another** part of staying healthy is eating nutritious foods. Eating plenty of fruits and vegetables is an essential part of good nutrition. **Finally**, sleeping is important. Getting seven or eight hours of sleep every night is part of healthy habits. **Habits such as regular exercise, eating nutritious foods, and getting plenty of sleep make up a healthy lifestyle.**

8. Students who are more independent writers can organize their ideas on Graphic Organizers. Once students have thought of ideas for writing, duplicate and distribute the Graphic Organizer on page 271.

9. Have students map their ideas for their stories on their Graphic Organizers. Tell students that organizing their ideas before they write will improve their writing.

10. Before students write their Explanation/Definition papers, tell them that certain transition words help connect their sentences. Write the list of Explanation/Definition Writing Transition Words on the chalkboard or on an overhead transparency. Introduce one transition word at a time by writing it in a sentence. Encourage students to try to use transition words in their writing. Remember, though, that students will misuse words frequently. Encourage many attempts and help students learn from their mistakes.

Explanation/Definition Writing Transition Words	
also	first, next, then, finally
and	for example
another kind	for instance
another way	here's how
are made up of	in addition
as an example	is
consists of	it means
described as	like

Organizational Pattern Outline
Explanation/Definition Writing

Introduction

► States the main idea and purposes for writing

► Gives three details that support the main idea

Interior Paragraph #1

► Restates the *first* detail

► Gives examples that illustrate this detail

Interior Paragraph #2

► Restates the *second* detail

► Gives examples that illustrate this detail

Interior Paragraph #3

► Restates the *third* detail

► Gives examples that illustrate this detail

Conclusion

► Restates the main idea

► Restates how the details support the main point

Explanation/Definition Writing: Student Example

Living in a city would be fun. There would be more

places to ride my bike, more places to go, I would have more

friends, and there would be more shopping. One of the reasons

I would like living in a city is that I could ride bikes around

the city. The city has sidewalks and bike paths to ride on.

Main idea and preview of details

Another reason I would like the city is that my family could go

to more places in a city. Big cities have museums, parks, and

baseball games. I would also have more friends to play with

because there are so many more people living in a city. Finally,

there would be more stores to buy things in. Cities have shop-

ping malls and really big stores. I would find living in a city

fun because all of these things are relaxing for me.

Details with examples

Conclusion

Josh Liming
Third Grade

Writing Frame
Explanation/Definition Writing

_____

_____
Main idea sentence

_____ .

_____
Sentence giving three details

_____ .

First, _____

_____ .

Another, _____

_____ .

Finally, _____

_____ .

_____
Concluding sentence repeating three details

_____ .

Name _____ Date _____

Graphic Organizer
Explanation/Definition Writing

_____
Topic

Detail #1	_____
Examples	_____
	_____
	_____

Detail #2	_____
Examples	_____
	_____
	_____

Detail #3	_____
Examples	_____
	_____
	_____

_____
Conclusion

 *Teaching Strategy*

STEPS-IN-A-PROCESS WRITING

The type of expository writing that is organized as Steps-in-a-Process Writing is familiar to many teachers. Teachers frequently have students give step-by-step directions, such as directions to make a sandwich or directions to make a paper airplane. All of these writings are Steps-in-a-Process Writing. The important part of Steps-in-a-Process Writing is to give clear, concise directions that are sequential. It's fun to watch students follow each other's directions for making cookies when the directions start with placing the pan in the oven, but when you are writing directions for real, being accurate is important. Students can easily learn how to write accurate directions using Steps-in-a-Process Writing.

Could a student this young complete a "Steps-in-a-Process" writing assignment?

Directions

1. Tell students that you will be introducing Steps-in-a-Process Writing. Tell students that writers can choose this type of organizational pattern when they want to state clear directions. Remind students that writers decide on writing patterns depending on their topics, purposes, and audiences.

2. Describe the Steps-in-a-Process Writing by using the Organizational Pattern Outline on page 274. Make an overhead transparency of the outline and point out the various components of the pattern. Remind students that Steps-in-a-Process Writing will follow the outline in many respects but that writing can deviate from the outline.

3. Tell students that you will show them an example of Steps-in-a-Process Writing. Locate an example written by a student at your grade level or, if appropriate, use the Student Example on page 275.

4. Make a transparency of the Student Example. Identify the features that make the writing a Steps-in-a-Process piece of writing rather than a different organizational pattern.

 5. Locate additional pieces of writing that could be classified as Steps-in-a-Process Writing. Have small groups of students read their writings and look for organizational features.

6. After students have seen how Steps-in-a-Process Writing is organized, help them develop topics for writing that can be organized in a Writing Frame or on a Graphic Organizer. Young students and students who have little background with expository writing should begin organizing their ideas with a Writing Frame.

7. Provide students with a model of a Writing Frame by developing your own piece of writing or by using the example that follows. Make a transparency of the example, share it with students, and explain how the example was developed from the Writing Frame. Duplicate and distribute the blank Writing Frame on page 276. Tell students that they will be writing their ideas on the Writing Frame.

Writing Frame Steps-in-a-Process Example
Here is how a chocolate cake **is made**. **First**, you gather all of the ingredients exactly, such as flour, sugar, chocolate, and shortening. **Next**, you mix them up until they form a smooth batter. **Then**, you pour the batter into cake pans and bake it in the oven for 35 minutes. **Finally**, you eat your chocolate cake with lots of ice cream.

8. Students who are more independent writers can organize their ideas on Graphic Organizers. Once students have thought of ideas for writing, duplicate and distribute the Graphic Organizer on page 277.

9. Have students map their ideas for their stories on their Graphic Organizers. Tell students that organizing their ideas before they write will improve their writing.

10. Before students write their Steps-in-a-Process papers, tell them that certain transition words help connect their sentences. Write the list of Steps-in-a-Process Writing Transition Words on the chalkboard or on an overhead transparency. Introduce one transition word at a time by writing it in a sentence. Encourage students to try to use transition words in their writing. Remember, though, that students will misuse words frequently. Encourage many attempts and help students learn from their mistakes.

Steps-in-a-Process Writing Transition Words
after as before finally first, second, next, then, last not long after now when

Organizational Pattern Outline
Steps-in-a-Process Writing

Introduction

- States the topic and purposes for writing

Interior Paragraph #1

- Describes the *first* part of the process
- Gives examples that illustrate this part

Interior Paragraph #2

- Describes the *second* part of the process
- Gives examples that illustrate this part

Interior Paragraph #3

- Describes the *third* part of the process
- Gives examples that illustrate this part

Conclusion

- Restates the topic

Steps-in-a-Process Writing:
Student Example

How to Make a Cookie Burger

States topic

If you want to make a cookie burger, you need to follow these steps. The first step is to get some chocolate frosting. You can make your own or buy the kind in a can. Next you need to get some vanilla wafers. You'll need lots of

Steps with examples

them because you might want to eat some as you work. After that you need to make sure you have an even number of wafers for the cookie burgers. You can eat any leftovers. Next you need a knife to put on the frosting. Then you place the cookies flat side up.

Before you begin frosting the cookies, make sure you have placed them in groups of two. Then you put the frosting on each and every cookie, flat side up. The very last thing you do is put each pair of cookies together to

Conclusion

make the frosting sides touch. Then you have cookie burgers to enjoy!

Justin Stickney
Sixth Grade

Writing Frame
Steps-in-a-Process Writing

Here is how a _____

is made. First, _____

_____

_____.

Next, _____

_____

_____.

Then, _____

_____

_____.

Finally, _____

_____.

Name _____ Date _____●

Graphic Organizer
Steps-in-a-Process Writing

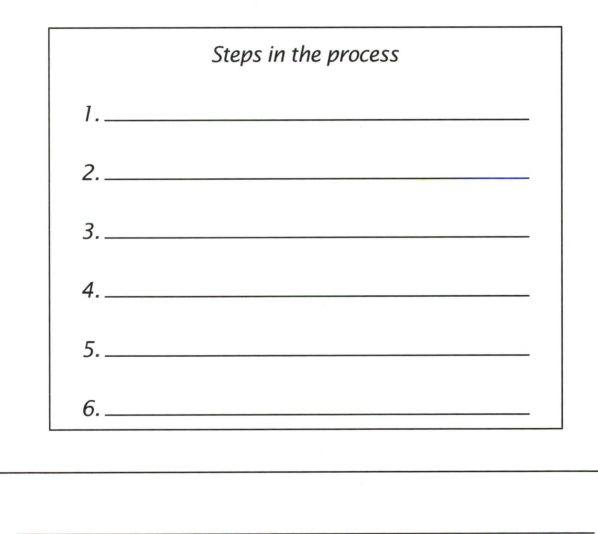

_____
Name of process

Steps in the process

1. _____

2. _____

3. _____

4. _____

5. _____

6. _____

_____
Conclusion

COMPARE AND CONTRAST WRITING

The Compare and Contrast Writing pattern is another type of expository writing that students frequently see. We compare and contrast things all of the time. We may compare and contrast prices in stores, models of cars, or even breeds of dogs. Because our society compares and contrasts things often, students may be familiar with the thinking process that is needed for Compare and Contrast Writing. They will, however, need instruction in this type of writing so that they can express their thoughts more clearly.

Directions

1. Tell students that you will be introducing a type of writing called Compare and Contrast Writing. Tell students that writers choose this type of organizational pattern when they want to compare and contrast two or more things. Remind students that writers decide on writing patterns depending on their topics, purposes, and audiences.

2. Describe Compare and Contrast Writing by using the Organizational Pattern Outline on page 280. Make an overhead transparency of the outline and point out the various components of the pattern. Remind students that Compare and Contrast Writing will follow the outline in many respects but that writing can deviate from the outline.

3. Tell students that you will show them an example of Compare and Contrast Writing. Locate an example written by a student at your grade level or, if appropriate, use the Student Example on page 281.

4. Make a transparency of the Student Example. Identify the features that make the piece of writing a compare and contrast pattern rather than a different organizational pattern.

5. Locate additional pieces of writing that could be classified as Compare and Contrast Writing. Have small groups of students read their writings and look for organizational features.

6. After students have seen how Compare and Contrast Writing is organized, help them develop topics for writing that can be organized in a Writing Frame or on a Graphic Organizer. Young students and students who have little background with expository writing should begin organizing their ideas with a Writing Frame.

7. Provide students with a model of a Writing Frame by developing your own piece of writing or by using the example. Make a transparency of the example, show it to students, and explain how the example was developed from the Writing Frame. Duplicate and distribute the blank Writing Frame on page 282. Tell students that they will be writing their ideas on the Writing Frame.

Writing Frame
Compare and Contrast Example

Fairy tales **and** tall tales **are alike in several ways**. **Both** fairy tales **and** tall tales **are alike because** they aren't true. **They are also alike because** they have talking animals. Fairy tales **and** tall tales **are also different**. **They are different because they** have different settings. **They are also different because** they make different uses of exaggeration. Fairy tales **and** tall tales **are similar and different**.

8. Students who are more independent writers can organize their ideas on Graphic Organizers. Once students have thought of ideas for writing, duplicate and distribute the Graphic Organizer on page 283.

9. Have students map their ideas for their stories on their Graphic Organizers. Tell students that organizing their ideas before they write will improve their writing.

10. Before students write Compare and Contrast papers, tell them that certain transition words help connect their sentences. Write the list of Compare and Contrast Writing Transition Words on the chalkboard or on an overhead transparency. Introduce one transition word at a time by writing it in a sentence. Encourage students to try to use transition words in their writing. Remember, though, that students will misuse words frequently. Encourage many attempts and help students learn from their mistakes.

Compare and Contrast Writing Transition Words

alike	however
also	in comparison
as well as	in the same way
both	instead
but	on the other hand
different	same
either . . . or	similar
have in common	unlike

Organizational Pattern Outline
Compare and Contrast Writing

Introduction
- States the things being compared
- States how they are alike and how they are different

Interior Paragraph #1
- States one or more of the similarities
- Provides examples that illustrate the similarities

Interior Paragraph #2
- States one or more of the differences
- Provides examples that illustrate the differences

Conclusion
- Restates the things being compared
- States whether they are mainly alike or mainly different

Compare and Contrast Writing:
Student Example

Two Tribes

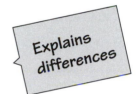

States things being compared

The Plains Indians and the Anasazi Indians were alike in some

ways and different in other ways. I learned that both of the tribes made

their own clothes. They also were careful about using the environment.

Explains similarities

For example, the Plains Indians didn't just kill buffalo when they didn't

need them, and the Anasazi used water carefully. The tribes were also

Explains differences

different. The Plains Indians lived on flat grassy land. The Anasazi lived

in the southwest in the desert. The Plains Indians lived in teepees, and

the Anasazi Indians lived in the cliffs of Mesa Verde. The Plains Indians

Conclusion

killed their food like buffalo, and the Anasazi had to grow their food like

corn, beans, and squash. The two tribes, the Plains Indians and the

Anasazi Indians, were alike in some ways but different.

Lauren Board
Third Grade

Writing Frame
Compare and Contrast Writing

•_____

_____ and _____

are alike in several ways. Both_____

and _____ are alike because _____

_____.

They are also alike because _____

_____.

_____ and _____

are also different. They are different because they_____

_____.

They are also different because_____

_____.

_____ and _____

are similar and different.

_____

Graphic Organizer
Compare and Contrast Writing

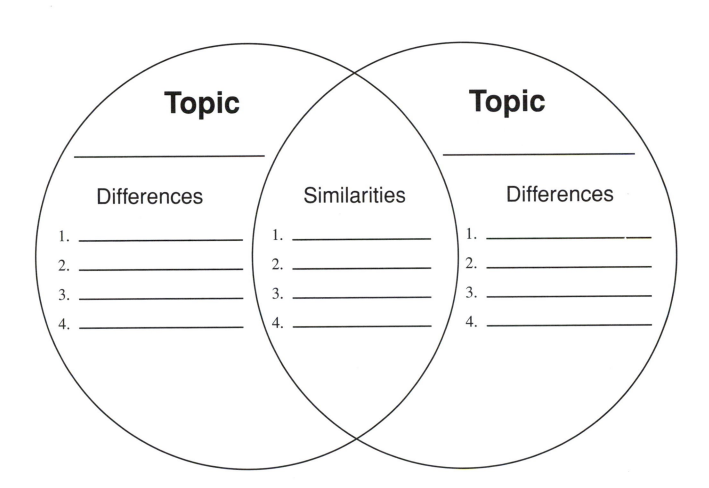

Topic
_____

Differences

1. _____
2. _____
3. _____
4. _____

Similarities

1. _____
2. _____
3. _____
4. _____

Topic
_____

Differences

1. _____
2. _____
3. _____
4. _____

Cause and Effect Writing is a bit more subtle than the other types of expository writing. In this type of writing, a cause is stated with its effect. Students typically have more difficulty with this type of writing. Cause and Effect Writing, however, is an important organizational tool for students to learn. Throughout their lives, students have learned that there are consequences for actions. In Cause and Effect Writing, students can learn the thinking and writing processes behind actions and consequences. With instruction, even young students can learn how to compose Cause and Effect Writing.

Directions

1. Tell students that you will be introducing Cause and Effect Writing. Help students understand cause and effect by using a concrete example, such as when they go out in the rain, they will get wet. Tell students that writers can choose this type of organizational pattern when they want to show the causes and effects of something. Remind students that writers decide on writing patterns depending on their topics, purposes, and audiences.

2. Describe Cause and Effect Writing by using the Organizational Pattern Outline on page 286. Make an overhead transparency of the outline and point out the various components of the pattern. Remind students that Cause and Effect Writing will follow the outline in many respects but that writing can deviate from the outline.

3. Tell students that you will show them an example of Cause and Effect Writing. Locate an example written by a student at your grade level or, if appropriate, use the Student Example on page 287.

4. Make a transparency of the Student Example. Identify the features that make the piece of writing a cause and effect pattern rather than a different organizational pattern.

5. Locate additional pieces of writing that could be classified as Cause and Effect Writing. Have small groups of students read their writings and look for organizational features.

6. After students have seen how Cause and Effect Writing is organized, help them develop topics for writing that can be organized in a Writing Frame or on a Graphic Organizer. Young students and students who have little background with expository writing should begin organizing their ideas with a Writing Frame.

7. Provide students with a model of a Writing Frame as in the example that follows or develop your own piece of writing. Make a transparency of the example, share it with students, and explain how the example was developed from the Writing Frame. Duplicate and distribute the blank Writing Frame on page 288. Tell students that they will be writing their ideas on the Writing Frame.

Writing Frame
Cause and Effect Example

Because of pollution it is no longer safe to swim in many lakes and rivers. The dumping of wastes from factories **has caused** lakes and rivers to become polluted. **Therefore,** swimmers can contract a variety of diseases if they swim in these waters. Motor oil **has also caused** pollution in lakes and rivers. The gasoline from motor boats spills into the lakes and rivers. **This explains why** the lakes and rivers are so polluted.

8. Students who are more independent writers can organize their ideas on Graphic Organizers. Once students have thought of ideas for writing, duplicate and distribute the Graphic Organizer on page 289.

9. Have students map their ideas for their stories on their Graphic Organizers. Tell students that organizing their ideas before they write will improve their writing.

10. When students write their Cause and Effect papers, tell them that certain transition words help connect their sentences. Write the list of Cause and Effect Writing Transition Words on the chalkboard or on an overhead transparency. Introduce one transition word at a time by writing it in a sentence. Encourage students to try to use transition words in their writing. Remember, though, that students will misuse words frequently. Encourage many attempts and help students learn from their mistakes.

Cause and Effect Writing
Transition Words

as a result
because
consequently
due to
for that reason
if
leads to
so
then
when

Organizational Pattern Outline
Cause and Effect Writing

Introduction

◆ States the cause and its effects

Interior Paragraph #1

◆ Restates the *first* effect

◆ Gives examples that illustrate this effect

Interior Paragraph #2

◆ Restates the *second* effect

◆ Gives examples that illustrate this effect

Interior Paragraph #3

◆ Restates the *third* effect

◆ Gives examples that illustrate this effect

Conclusion

◆ Restates the cause and its effects

Cause and Effect:
Student Example

The Effects of Pollution

Cause and effect introduced

Pollution and abusing the natural environment are ruining the earth. Too many people drive by themselves and don't carpool or take public transportation. Because of the exhaust from these extra cars, there is more car exhaust in the air than there should be. Car exhaust, in turn, has caused acid rain which pollutes water, and has caused damage to buildings like the Statue of Liberty. The amount of exhaust in the air may also be responsible for the hole in the ozone layer. Burning trash has also caused pollution by contaminating the air we breathe.

Cause and effect described

There are many ways to change the increasing amounts of pollution in the earth. If each town collected everything that needed to be burned once a month and took the trash to a place where no one lived and burned it there, we wouldn't be hurt as much by contaminated air.

If people would carpool, take buses, planes, and taxis, we wouldn't have near as much car exhaust which in turn would mean less acid rain.

Conclusion

Changing the way we look at our environment can make important changes in our earth's environment.

Josh Wurmnest
Seventh Grade

Name _____ Date _____●

Writing Frame
Cause and Effect Writing

●_____

Because of _____

_____ .

_____ **has caused** _____

_____ .

Therefore, _____

_____ .

_____ **has also caused** _____

_____ .

_____ .

This explains why _____

_____ .

Graphic Organizer
Cause and Effect Writing

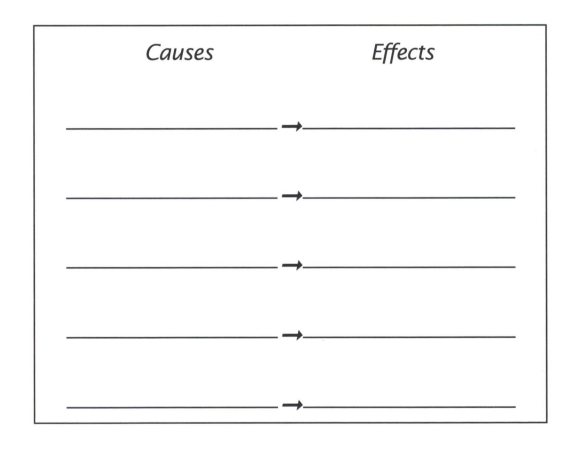

_____	
Topic	

Causes	Effects
_____ → _____	
_____ → _____	
_____ → _____	
_____ → _____	
_____ → _____	

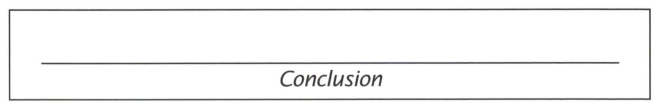

_____

Conclusion

Expository writing is not merely a way to organize impersonal thoughts. Writers can present facts using the expository writing genres and still incorporate their own opinions. In the past, writers were discouraged from using the first person in expository essays. Now, however, there are times when using the first person is acceptable, especially in Personal Essays.

 Directions

1. Remind students of the expository writing genres you have introduced. Explain to students that those genres are ways to organize facts and ideas, but they can also include personal thoughts at times.

2. Discuss with students the ways that personal thoughts are written. Guide students into talking about personal pronouns, especially the first person pronouns *I, me, we, us, they,* and *them.* Have students volunteer a sample sentence for each pronoun.

Personal Essays are an easy type of writing for most students.

Activities in English

www.syvum.com/english/

This site provides activities and games for children of all ages related to grammar, reading, spelling, and vocabulary.

3. Explain to students that some writers incorporate personal thoughts within expository structures. Tell students that at times this strategy is acceptable and at times it is discouraged. For example, you could explain as follows.

    There are different types of writing. Some writing is very formal, such as encyclopedia entries and some reports. In these pieces of writing, the authors do not use personal pronouns. They never state their opinions. Another example is our state test. Some teachers have suggested that you refrain from using personal pronouns when you write using the expository genre on the state test.

    There are other situations in which you can use personal pronouns when writing within the expository genre. We call these Personal Essays. In this type of writing, you are writing facts and also including some opinion statements.

4. Duplicate and distribute one of the writing samples that follow. The three writing samples reflect different ages and abilities of writing. Show your students the sample that best reflects the type of writing you expect of your students.

5. Discuss the piece of writing. Explain that the writer is using the expository genre but has also written at least one opinion statement. Draw students' attention to the sentences that use the first person.

6. Tell students that you want them to write an essay about a topic of their choice. Have students gather facts and then write using the genre that fits the topic. Encourage students to add one or more sentences stating their opinions in this piece.

Spring Break

Books! No school! Sleep late! Candy! Candy! And more candy! All of these activities happened over my Spring Break. These activities were the three best activities that happened to me. During my Spring Break I got to read a book, there was no school so I got to sleep late, and I also got tons of Easter presents. You may think that all of these activities were boring but it was nice just to sit back and relax for a while.

Do you like reading books? Well I really don't like to but I was bored and I needed some accelerated reader points. So I read a book called *Sang Spell*. It turned out to be a pretty good book. It was a very weird mystery. During the time that I was reading this book I was sitting outside on my deck's lawn chairs. While I was reading it was a very nice day outside but very windy.

Over Spring Break I had ten days with absolutely no school. I got to do whatever I wanted to. The only bad part about all of this was having to watch my little brother and sister. Overall it was fun watching them and getting to play with them. Though there was a lot of stuff over Spring Break the best part was sleeping in late for a change.

Another one of the best things that happened to me over Spring Break was all of the candy that I got. I got tons and tons of candy for Easter. I got so much candy for Easter that I still have over half of it left. For Easter I also got makeup, softball stuff, and clothes. Now all I have to worry about is getting fat.

Throughout my Spring Break there were a lot of good times but yet there were a lot of boring ones too. I spent so much time at home that it was getting really boring. Even though that happened I am still glad that I got to get out of school. So as I was setting my alarm for the next day of school I thought to myself that maybe my Spring Break wasn't so bad after all.

Tasha

Wolves

Pups are wolf babies. They are born in nine weeks in a breed of two to ten pups. In two to three weeks pups can see, hear, walk, eat and drink by themselves. They meet the den when they are one month old. They are watched by the whole pack. The pups are friends with the whole pack even though they are adults. The pack gives the pups the food and other needs. They also watch for enemies like the eagle. Once the pups are nine weeks old the pack moves on. When the female is breeding, the males hunt alone. The pups wrestle and pounce on each other to practice to hunt.

Wolves are close to extinction. Wolves are followed and killed for fun. Many wolves roam North Asia. The snow wolves were almost extinct from being killed for fun. People thought it would be a good idea to bring the snow wolves back to Alaska. The white wolf is almost identical to the snow wolf and close to extinction. When wolves mate they mate for life.

A pack is a group of wolf families. A pack starts with one female and one male. In a pack some wolves are not the same species. The leader of the pack is called the alpha male. The alpha can punish any wolf in the pack, even its mate.

I found wolves interesting and harmless animals. I like wolves.

Sharadyn

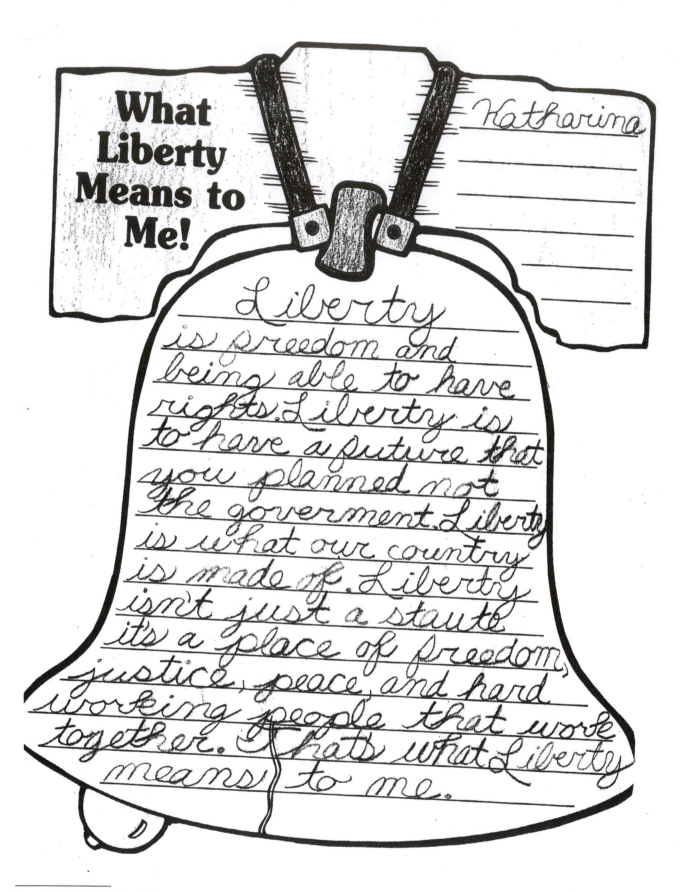

What Liberty Means to Me!

Katharina

Liberty is freedom and being able to have rights. Liberty is to have a future that you planned not the goverment. Liberty is what our country is made of. Liberty isn't just a staute it's a place of freedom, justice, peace, and hard working people that work together. Thats what Liberty means to me.

From Susan Davis Lenski and Jerry L. Johns, *Improving Writing K–8: Strategies, Assessments, and Resources* (2nd ed.). Copyright © 2004 by Kendall/Hunt Publishing Company (1-800-247-3458, ext. 4 or 5). May be reproduced for noncommercial educational purposes within the guidelines noted on the copyright page.

Persuasive Writing

Goal ● *To help students learn the genre of persuasive writing.*

BACKGROUND

The art of persuasion and creating effective arguments is not a natural human ability but must be learned (Fulkerson, 1996). Frequently, students come to teachers with requests or opinions with little substantiating rationale. For example, a student may say to a teacher, "We need a hamster in our class." When queried about the reasons for this opinion, a student may respond, "Because." In general, students haven't had experience forming opinions that are based on sound reasoning.

Some types of persuasion, such as the kinds of advertising campaigns we see on television and the Internet, use visual cues to transform viewers' opinions. Often the picture "sells" more than the text does. Creating an effective argument in writing, however, is much more difficult. Writing persuasive essays requires instruction and practice.

Persuasive writing is written in a genre that is similar to expository writing (Jago, 2002). To persuade, writers must

- make a claim,
- offer reasons for that claim, and
- provide examples or details that illustrate the reasoning.

Students rarely have had these types of experiences in their lives. In addition, they rarely have read the type of persuasive essays they are expected to write in schools. For these reasons, students need extra time to learn the organizational pattern of persuasive writing so they can learn to think and write using logic and reasoning. Once students have become comfortable with persuasion, watch out! They will have persuasive reasons for getting that class pet. This section provides resources, teaching strategies, ideas, and activities to help students learn how to organize and write persuasive essays.

> *The art of persuasion and creating effective arguments is not a natural human ability but must be learned.*

Teaching **Strategy**

ORGANIZATIONAL PATTERN

Persuasive writing has a specific organizational pattern: subject, reasons, and examples. Students often are unfamiliar with the organizational pattern of persuasive writing because it is a form that is used only in a certain type of writing. There are two basic steps to teach the structure of persuasive writing.

1. Tell students explicitly the organizational pattern of persuasive essays.
2. Show them an example of a persuasive essay that was written by a student at their grade level.

Students can identify patterns in essays that were written at their own developmental level easier than they can in essays that were written by professional authors. Writings that are too complex can discourage students and keep them from learning how to organize their own pieces of persuasive writing.

Directions

1. Tell students that they hear persuasive arguments frequently but that they may not have read persuasive essays. Explain to students that when they hear commercials on television, read them on the Internet, or see advertisements, they are experiencing an author trying to persuade a listener or a reader. Tell students that these modes of persuasion can use pictures, sounds, and words. Explain that when writing persuasive essays students will be using words only.

2. Duplicate and distribute the Organizational Pattern Outline that follows. Tell students that persuasive writing usually follows the outline.

3. Divide the class into groups of three or four students. Have students read the Organizational Pattern Outline or read it with them. Discuss the components of persuasive writing with students.

4. Tell students that you will show them an example of persuasive writing. Locate an example of persuasive writing written by a student at your grade level or, if appropriate, use the Student Example on page 298.

5. Make a transparency of an example of student writing. Identify the features that make the piece persuasive writing.

6. Locate additional pieces of writing that could be classified as persuasive writing. Have small groups of students read the stories and look for the organizational features of persuasive writing.

Organizational Pattern Outline
Persuasive Writing

Introduction
- States the subject and the purposes for writing
- Gives three reasons that support the view
- States the opinion in one sentence

Interior Paragraph #1
- Restates the *first* reason that supports the point of view
- Gives examples and details that support this reason

Interior Paragraph #2
- Restates the *second* reason that supports the point of view
- Gives examples and details that support this reason

Interior Paragraph #3
- Restates the *third* reason that supports the point of view
- Gives examples and details that support this reason

Conclusion
- Restates the subject of the paper
- Summarizes how the reasons support the point of view
- Concludes with a summary of the opinion

The Best Grandpa in the World

I have the best Grandpa in the world because he loves me. He makes a lot of things for me, he lets me do things that I can't do at home, and we have a lot of fun together.

First, Grandpa makes a lot of things for me. For example, he made my brothers and me a tire swing and an inner tube for the creek. I can climb to the top of the swing. Another example is that when there's something wrong with our go-cart, he fixes it.

Next, Grandpa lets me do things I can't do at home. Once I got to drive his truck around their drive. I wrote my name on the floor of his shed when the concrete was still wet. After he's done using his skid steer, I get to drive it around.

Last, we have a lot of fun together. He always makes me laugh. Sometimes he pretends he's going to run me over. One year after my birthday he told me he had next year's present already. I had to wait a whole year for it.

My Grandpa is the best Grandpa ever. He makes a lot of stuff for me, he lets me do things I can't do at home, and we have a lot of fun together. What a wonderful man!

Koree Larimer
Sixth Grade

Persuasive writing has an organizational structure that is similar to expository writing. The key difference between persuasive writing and expository writing is that persuasive writing expresses an opinion rather than stating facts or explanations. Writing Frames help students understand how persuasive writing is organized. After students have generated opinions and reasons for those opinions, they should organize their ideas into the organizational pattern of persuasive writing. Students can organize their ideas in many ways. Young students generally are more successful when they organize their ideas with Writing Frames. Writing Frames give students experience writing with a specific organizational pattern without having to know how to write the transitions. They also give students important background knowledge about ways different pieces of writing can be structured.

Directions

1. Tell students that once they have an opinion they need to organize their ideas using the organizational pattern of persuasive writing. Remind students that persuasive writing should have a subject or opinion, reasons for that opinion, and examples to support the reasons.

2. Young students and students who have little background with persuasive writing should begin organizing their ideas with a Writing Frame. Duplicate and distribute the Writing Frame that follows. Tell students that they will be writing their ideas on the Writing Frame.

3. Develop a Writing Frame example or make a transparency of the example that follows. Share the Writing Frame example with students and explain how the essay was developed from the Writing Frame.

4. Have students write their own pieces of persuasive writing using a Writing Frame.

Writing Frame
Persuasive Writing Example

I think that we should have a class pet **because** a class pet would be a great learning experience. **I think this because** pets need care, they are good topics for observational logs, and pets are lovable. **First**, to care for a pet would be good for us. We would learn responsibility because we would need to feed it and give it water. **Second**, a pet would be interesting to watch and write about. We could record how much it eats, when it sleeps, and how it plays. **Third**, it would be good for us to have something else in the class to love. Some students are shy and they could love and talk to the pet. **I believe that** a class pet would be a good decision **and** I hope you do too.

Writing Frame
Persuasive Writing

●_____

I think that _____

because _____ .

I think this because _____

_____ .

First, _____

_____ .

Second, _____

_____ .

Third, _____

_____ .

I believe that _____

and _____ .

Teaching Strategy 3

GRAPHIC ORGANIZER

Graphic Organizers are another way to organize information before writing. Graphic Organizers are similar to outlines, but they form a visual representation of the writing's organization. Graphic Organizers can be used before, during, and after writing. Before writing, students can plot their ideas on Graphic Organizers and refer to them when they write. Students also can use Graphic Organizers during writing. As writers complete sections of writing, they can refer to their Graphic Organizers to remind themselves of the pattern of their writing. After writing, students can map out the ideas from their writing on Graphic Organizers to verify that they have all of the components of the writing pattern. Older students especially will find Graphic Organizers useful for learning the organizational patterns of different writing structures.

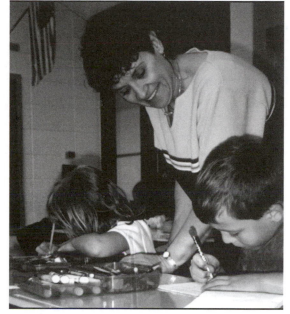

Do you have copies of the Graphic Organizer ready to help students organize their writing?

Directions

1. Remind students that persuasive writing has a specific organizational pattern. Tell students that a Graphic Organizer is a visual representation of the writing pattern.

2. Students who are independent writers can organize their ideas on Graphic Organizers. Once students have thought of an idea for a persuasive essay, duplicate and distribute the Graphic Organizer that follows.

3. Have students map out their ideas for their essays on Graphic Organizers. Provide guidance as necessary. Tell students that organizing their ideas before they write will help them organize their writing.

4. Allow students time to plot their ideas on Graphic Organizers. If students have not generated enough ideas before writing, have them partially complete their Graphic Organizers and begin writing.

5. Tell students that they also can assess their writing organization by using Graphic Organizers after writing. Have students place several copies of the Graphic Organizer in their writing folders. After students have written persuasive essays, have them use their Graphic Organizers to determine whether they organized their writing according to the writing pattern.

Name _____ Date _____

Graphic Organizer
Persuasive Writing

_____

_____

Opinion

Reason #1 _____

Examples _____

_____

_____

Reason #2 _____

Examples _____

_____

_____

Reason #3 _____

Examples _____

_____

_____

_____

Conclusion

I HAVE MY REASONS

Students are more likely to understand how to write using the persuasive writing genre if they have the opportunity to use persuasive writing to make an actual difference. Many students do not understand that different viewpoints can have valid reasons and that explaining these reasons is the basis for persuasion. When students use the strategy I Have My Reasons, they formulate their own reasoning to use in writing a persuasive essay.

Directions

1. Tell students that each person has his or her own opinions and that these opinions may vary within a class. Explain to students that what one person believes may be different from what other people believe. Tell students that in order to persuade others they need to understand that other people will have different opinions.

Students can be very persuasive.

2. Choose a topic that is of interest to your students. For example, you might consider the following topics.

    School parties

    Field trips

    School uniforms

    Music videos

    Sports equipment

    Plays and concerts

    Pets

3. Write the name of the topic on the chalkboard or on an overhead transparency. Ask students individually to develop a series of statements about the topic. For example, if your topic was school uniforms, some of the statements could be as follows.

    School uniforms would restrict our sense of fashion.

    School uniforms are boring.

    School uniforms equalize students' appearance.

    School uniforms save money.

4. Give students several minutes to write at least five statements about the topic. After students have finished their lists, divide the class into groups of two or three students and have students read each other their lists. Have students point out the similarities and differences between the lists.

5. Tell students to choose which side they want to take about the issue and to revise their lists to include only those statements.

6. Reproduce one of the persuasive papers that follow. Choose the piece that is closest to the ability level of your students. Read the piece as an example of a persuasive piece of writing.

7. Give students adequate time to write their persuasive pieces. Have students who have taken the same side of the issue compare their pieces of writing. Encourage students to notice that different points can be made about the same topic and still be persuasive.

Homophone Zone

www.cooper.com/homophonezone/

This site provides an alphabetical list of many homophones. It includes quizzes to test knowledge of definitions of homophones.

The Halloween Party

I think we should not ban Halloween parties because all of the children like them and it's a good opportunity for the kids that cannot go out on Halloween to have fun on the holiday. It will also give us a chance to see the other kids' costumes.

For example, we have fun doing the parade and the parents have fun watching. We like getting the candy and exchanging. Making crafts are always fun and it gives me new ideas.

Halloween parties are a great opportunity for the kids that cannot go out on Halloween to have fun and get candy. They also get to see the other kids' costumes.

Halloween parties also give us a chance to be something we're not and to see what it would be like. It helps the kids to figure out what they want to be when they grow up. It also gives us a chance to use our imagination.

We need Halloween because it is a chance for us to have fun and it brings us joy. It also gives us a chance to use our imaginations.

Emily

The Halloween Party

I agree with taking away the Halloween party. I agree because it's a lot of money to buy costumes every year. I hate dressing up, and I don't like eating a whole lot of candy. Now I'm telling some reasons why.

My parents and I don't like spending money every year buying costumes because it's too much money. Also, I do not think you should spend money every year on costumes because the costumes are only for one day, so why buy? So you shouldn't spend too much money.

I hate dressing up because some people might make fun of what you dress up in. Also, I hate dressing up because I outgrew dressing up. You can only dress certain things so many times before it gets boring.

I don't like eating too much candy because it can rot my teeth. It also can give me a stomachache. Candy is also bad for you because it's junk food.

Now, that's why I agree to take away the Halloween Party. I don't like spending any money buying costumes every year, I hate dressing up, and I don't like eating too much candy.

Rebecca

Baseball Equipment

We need cheaper baseball equipment! Baseball is very fun and expensive. Some reasons we need it cheaper is because we can't afford some of the stuff, we need new equipment, and for the love the game.

First of all, we can't afford a lot of equipment. It we want to be the best of our ability, then the equipment should be more affordable. A lot of people love baseball and are good at it, but could be better with more things. If anyone didn't have money and liked baseball, the only way they would play is by a donation from someone.

Second of all, we need more baseball equipment. Most schools have baseball teams and are very good. They could be better if they could afford more things that help them field and hit better. For catchers, some don't have knee savers, and would really help their legs if they had them.

Last, but not least is for the love of the game. Many people's favorite sport is baseball and they love the game. It could become their worst sport if they don't have the right equipment they needed to play. If you love the game, then you should play it.

In conclusion, we need cheaper baseball equipment. We need it because more people can't afford it. We need more and new equipment, and for the love of the game. Baseball is awesome!

Jeremy

Assessing Genre Writing

Goal • *To assess students' genre writing.*

BACKGROUND

Students' writing can be assessed in a number of ways. The purpose of assessment should dictate which type of assessment strategy is used. "While every piece of writing is *evaluated* by someone, even if that someone is the writer, only selected pieces of writing need to be *graded*, and then with specific criteria known to the writers from the beginning of the assignment" (Hughey & Slack, 2001, p. 79).

PRIMARY TRAIT ASSESSMENT. To assess students' genre writing, you need to remember that you are looking only for the organization of the papers. To assess organizational patterns, you can use a primary trait assessment such as the game What's the Structure? When using a primary trait assessment strategy, assess only the organizational patterns of the writing.

HOLISTIC SCORING. Teachers frequently like to assess more than one trait of a piece of writing. Because teachers' time is limited, they frequently assess many aspects of a piece of writing at the same time. One way to look at the entire piece of writing, the organization as well as the content and mechanics, is through holistic scoring. When you assess a piece of writing in its entirety to get a general sense of the quality of the writing, you are engaging in holistic assessment. Anchor papers can provide a helpful basis for assessment when you use holistic assessment (Wolcott & Legg, 1998). An anchor

paper gives you an example of the quality of writing that you expect from students.

ASSESSING WITH RUBRICS. A final way to assess students' ability to organize writing as well as other writing skills is through a rubric. A rubric details the criteria you will use in assessment. You can use a rubric to assess one aspect of students' writing, or you can use a rubric to assess several aspects of their writing. A rubric can be tailored to your assessment expectations.

Finally, you need to teach students how to write for writing assessments. When students are familiar with writing assessments, their writing scores are more valid. This section provides four assessment strategies to help you assess students' genre writing.

> *Organization Assessment*
>
> Primary Trait Assessment (What's the Structure?)
>
> Holistic Scoring (Anchor Papers)
>
> Assessing with Rubrics

Assessment can help students identify strengths in their writing.

WHAT'S THE STRUCTURE? •————————

What's the Structure? is a game to introduce and assess students' ability to identify and write different organizational patterns (Richards & Gipe, 1995). You can use this game with students' writings, textbook passages, or teacher-written passages. Students can use What's the Structure? to review writing genres before they are assessed by the teacher.

Directions

1. Collect examples of the different kinds of writing: personal experience stories, fictional writing, expository writing, and persuasive writing. You can use examples from students' writings, textbooks, passages from literature books, and other sources.

2. Number the passages and place them on a large table. Place 12 passages on the table.

3. Give students a sheet of paper numbered from 1 through 12. List the names of the writing organizational patterns you used for the game. For example, if the passages are personal experience stories, persuasive writing, steps-in-a-process, and explanation, write these names on the paper.

4. Tell students that you will be giving them time during the day to go to the table, read the passages, and write on their papers the various types of writing organizational patterns used in the passages.

5. After students have finished writing the names of the organizational patterns, collect and assess their papers. Notice the types of writing that students were able to identify and unable to identify. Review the types of writing with which students had difficulty.

ANCHOR PAPERS

Anchor Papers are examples of writing that can be scored using holistic scoring methods (Wolcott & Legg, 1998). An Anchor Paper can be an exemplary paper, or it can be a typical paper done by students at your grade level. Anchor Papers help you determine the quality of your students' writings compared with writings done by other students.

Directions

1. Determine whether you want to assess students' personal experience stories, expository writing, or persuasive pieces. Tell students that you will be assessing a particular type of writing.

2. Give students a writing prompt from the lists that follow. Choose a writing prompt about which you believe students will have some background knowledge.

   If you are developing your own prompt, use the recommendations developed by Hughey and Slack (2001) to create writing prompts that are appropriate for your students. The characteristics of these prompts are noted below.

   - Realistic—the prompt reflects the type of writing that students will encounter in other texts.

   - Appropriate—the prompt is appropriate for the students' age and can be completed in the time allocated.

   - Understandable—the wording of the prompt can be understood by the students.

   - Personal—the assignment appeals to students' personal lives.

   - Reliable—the prompt will be interpreted the same way on different occasions.

   - Feasible—it is possible for students to be successful.

   - Fair—the topic is fair for all students and does not privilege any particular group.

3. Tell students to write one draft responding to the prompt. Give students from 30 to 45 minutes to write.

4. Collect students' writings. Read the papers and divide them into three stacks: excellent writing, typical writing, and poor writing. From each of the three stacks choose four papers that seem typical for your class. Take the 12 pieces of writing and arrange them from excellent to poor. From the 12 papers, delete five papers that seem to overlap in quality with the other papers. You should now have seven papers to arrange in order of quality. Number the papers from seven for the best paper to one for the poorest paper. These are your Anchor Papers.

5. As students write new pieces, occasionally score them using the Anchor Papers as benchmarks. Read students' writings and decide the quality of the paper by assigning it a number from one through seven depending on which Anchor Paper is the most similar to students' writings.

Personal Experience Writing Prompts

1. Your class has just read a selection from the book *Rufus M.* by Eleanor Estes. As you read about Rufus's childhood, you learned that he was persistent in getting what he wanted. The editor of your local newspaper has been advertising for citizens to submit personal life stories that show determination. The top three winning stories will be published in the paper. Write a narrative paper that describes three instances in your life when you were determined to get or do something. For each of the three instances, include your own definition of determination and be sure to describe where, when, why, and how you were determined.

2. Think about a family trip you took to a special place. It might have been a trip to a forest preserve, a park, a relative, a zoo, or anything you thought was special. Write a story about going on that special trip. Tell how and why you remember the trip. Describe how you felt before, during, and after the trip. We will place all of the stories in a class book.

3. Think about a specific time when you felt awkward or embarrassed. It could have been at school, at home, or with friends. Write about that time. Explain the situation, what happened, and why you felt awkward or embarrassed. Give details surrounding the situation and be sure to explain how you felt during this experience. After you finish writing your stories, we will read them in the class writing groups.

4. Think about a special time when you celebrated a holiday or event. It could have been with your family or your friends. Choose only one event or holiday about which to write. Identify the occasion in the beginning of your paper. Tell when, where, and why the event occurred. Give specific details. Explain the feelings you experienced at that time. Give the reasons why it was special. After completing the stories, you will place them in your portfolios to show your family.

5. Think about a time when you celebrated your birthday in a special way. Identify which birthday you have selected in the beginning of your paper. Explain why it was special. Give specific details or events that led to that special birthday and explain how those events made you feel. Describe the importance or significance of your experiences. You may want to include other people who helped make this birthday special. After you finish the papers, we will include them in a class book.

6. Tell about a time when you and your family, friends, or classmates spent the day together. Perhaps it was on a special holiday or maybe a day when you planned an activity together. Identify one time about which to write. Describe your activities that day. Write who was included in the event and exactly what you did that day. Explain how you felt and why this particular day stands out in your memory. After you finish writing, you will give the stories to family or friends who were involved in the activities.

7. Think about an experience you have had that you will never forget and tell how or why it was memorable. It might have been when you saw a particular person or went to a special event or place. It might be a time when you felt that you were treated unfairly or a time when you were frightened. Choose one experience that you will never forget. Identify that special experience and tell why it was memorable. Tell what happened by giving details about the people, the situation, and how you felt. We will place the completed papers in a class book.

8. Think about a time when you learned a new skill. It may have been learning to ride a bike, learning how to read, or learning how to Rollerblade. Choose a skill that took some practice before you were able to learn it. Think of a specific skill that you learned. Include events that helped you learn the skill. Tell how you felt as you were learning. Include things you learned about yourself as a learner. After you complete the papers, you will read them to younger students.

9. Think about a time when you were a good friend or someone was a good friend to you. It could be a time when you were nice or did a special favor for someone. It could be a time when someone helped you out with a problem. Identify what you did to be a good friend. Explain the situation fully. Tell what happened during the situation and how you felt about what you did. Explain what you learned from the situation. We will put all the papers in a friendship book.

10. Think about things you have done or things that have happened to you that make your life interesting. It could be a place you have lived, an interest you have, or something you have done. Choose one aspect of your life that could be considered interesting. Describe that one situation by writing about how you felt, what you said, and who else was present. Explain why you think this situation is interesting. We will place the papers in our class museum.

11. Think about a time when you were scared. It could be a time when you were afraid as a young child, or it could be a more recent time. Identify the time when you were scared. Be sure to tell what scared you, what happened, and how you felt while and after you were scared. Use images that will help the reader feel what you felt. We will read these papers on Halloween.

12. Think about your favorite or best day at school this year. It could be a day you learned something new, a day you were recognized for an accomplishment, a day someone did something nice for you, or a day something special happened. Write about your special day by identifying the event that made the day your favorite day. Fully explain why this day was your favorite. Include the other people who were involved, your feelings about the event, and the details of the day. After you finish the papers, we will compile a classroom book about the memories of the class.

13. Think about your best Saturday ever. It could be a time when you went someplace special, when you relaxed, or when you were involved in a particular sporting event or activity. Identify the Saturday that was excellent for you. Tell why it was so special. Tell about the activities of the day in the order they occurred. Explain in detail what happened and why it happened. Tell how you felt about all of the things that happened and explain why it was your best Saturday.

14. Think about a time when you watched a terrific television program, played a video game, or found something interesting on the Internet. It could be a time when you were alone, with family members, or with friends. Identify a time when you really enjoyed viewing something. Describe the situation, who was there, and why you found it interesting. Explain how you felt. We will put all of the papers in our class media book.

Expository Writing Prompts

1. In science class, you have just finished learning about the different biomes that are found on Earth. The local newspaper recently has added a new travel section and has asked for your help in writing the first column. That column is titled "Biomes of the World: A Visitor's Paradise." Select a biome that you think would be an interesting place for a visitor to see and write a news article about it.

2. Your community is planning an Earth Day celebration. Your classroom teacher is requesting that all students in the class write a paper explaining how people can help conserve the resources of our Earth. You are asked to include several things that people should or should not do to help conserve our Earth's resources. The community newspaper will print the three best papers.

3. You have been studying about health care for cats and dogs. One of the local veterinarians has expressed a need for an easy-to-read brochure that he can give to new dog and cat owners. Based on the knowledge you have gained from learning about caring for animals, write an essay explaining three important components of a pet care program for either a dog or a cat. Discuss in detail what parts of the program will provide an appropriate environment, good health care, and proper training in order to have a healthy, happy pet. Two veterinarians will pick the essays that they believe will be easy to understand and the most helpful to pet owners.

4. Families who live in the country are used to open spaces, trees and grass, fields of corn and wheat, and many different animals. Families who live in the city have buildings, trucks, buses, playgrounds, and many different kinds of people. Write an essay about the differences between city and country living for a group of city students who are going to spend a week on a farm.

5. You have been learning in school about the structure of the federal government in Washington, D.C. As part of a Global Government Awareness Program, the President requests that students in schools across the country write to their foreign classmates and explain to them as accurately as possible the structure of the United States government. Write a letter explaining what you know about the United States government.

6. The cafeteria recently has hired a new head cook who is looking for students' input on menu planning. Using your knowledge of nutrition, suggest three general nutritional guidelines to follow while planning school lunch menus. Consider, also, foods students enjoy that meet these guidelines. Write a paper explaining the guidelines the new head cook should use to prepare menus.

7. You have been learning in school about dental health. The school nurse is holding an assembly for children who don't know how to care for their teeth. The nurse wants to know how children who are informed about dental health care for their teeth. Write a paper about how people can keep their teeth healthy, including examples of things to do to keep teeth healthy, and explain how each example helps maintain dental health.

8. We have been learning about fire safety. The fire department is having a writing contest for students. Think about what you would do if there were a fire at your house. Tell the firefighters step by step what you would do to safely get out of your burning house. Be sure to include the safety rules we have learned. We will enter our work in the fire department contest.

9. You have just moved to a new town and have returned home from your first day at your new school. Your parents asked you what your new school is like. Write a paper comparing your old school with your new one. In the beginning of your paper, state whether you believe that your old and new schools are very alike or very different. Give three examples to support your belief.

10. Your science unit has been about matter. Your teacher asked you to write a paper that includes everything a classmate who has been on vacation needs to know about matter to pass the science test. Include the definition of matter, describe the three kinds of matter, and give examples of the different kinds of matter.

11. An out-of-town builder has decided to build houses where a local woods is right now. In order to build the houses, the builder must cut down over 200 trees. In class we have learned about the importance of trees in the environment. The city council doesn't seem aware of the importance of the trees; they just want the new homes in the town. Write the members of the city council a letter telling them at least three ways trees help the environment.

12. In science class, you have been learning about relationships in ecosystems. A zoologist is coming to our school to present a program on harmful and helpful relationships in ecosystems. She has requested that you become experts on the topic so that you can help her during her presentation. Write an expository paper that describes three harmful or three helpful relationships within ecosystems. Include the importance of relationships in ecosystems, the animals in each ecosystem relationship, and the names of the relationships you will discuss.

13. A member of your family recently has received some money and wants to spend some of it on a three-week family vacation to one of the 50 states. You were asked to give your opinion about where you should go, because this family member knows you have been studying the United States. Think about which state you would like to visit, why it would be a good choice, and how you could persuade your family to choose that state for your family vacation. Write a paper telling which state you want to visit, why it would be the best state to vacation in, and give examples to support your reasons.

14. Your teacher is new to your school. This teacher would like to know more about the school and would appreciate information about school traditions, school stories, and school rules. Write a paper explaining what you know about your school. State how your school has developed an identity and explain the types of things that your teacher should know. Give specific examples to support your ideas.

Persuasive Writing Prompts

1. The superintendent of our school recently asked the parents of our district whether the children should have an additional 40 minutes of school each day. Now the superintendent wants to know the students' opinions on lengthening the school day. The superintendent will read the students' papers to help her decide whether school will last 40 minutes longer next year. Write an essay for your superintendent in which you try to get the superintendent to agree with you about whether the school day should be longer.

2. Your principal is thinking about eliminating lunch recess because many discipline problems occur at that time. Think about all of the reasons for keeping or eliminating lunch recess and how you could persuade your principal to keep or eliminate it. Write an essay explaining the reasons for your position.

3. Your parents have agreed to talk to you about whether you may have a pet for your birthday. Write an essay to convince them that you will take care of your pet. In the essay, state the kind of pet you want, give reasons why you should have a pet, and explain how you would take care of your pet.

4. Your class has earned an extra field trip. Each student will vote on whether the class goes to the zoo, the park, or the YMCA to do activities. Decide which place you would like to visit and write an argument to persuade your classmates to vote your way.

5. Pretend you are living in the 1860s. You and your family spent your entire fortune starting a new homestead. A plague of locusts destroyed the crop that your family planted and planned to live on for the next year. Write a letter to a distant family member to plead for help and money to get your family back on its feet again. Decide to whom you want to write, describe the details of the event, make reasonable requests, and provide details about repayment.

6. Our classroom pet, a Russian dwarf hamster, unexpectedly gave birth to six babies. Your teacher has offered a baby hamster to those children who can convince their parents to let them have one as a pet. Write a letter to your parents to convince them that you can take care of this new pet. In your letter, give at least three reasons for your parents to let you have a hamster, give examples of how the pet would be good for you and your family, explain how you would take care of it, and conclude by summarizing the reasons you have given.

7. Your reading class has just finished reading the book *Tuck Everlasting*. The book discussed the topic of living forever. Some of the characters in the book believed they would live forever if they drank the spring water. Others believed that people were not destined to live forever and shouldn't drink the water. Write a paper for your reading teacher that tells your view. Explain why you would or would not drink the water. Support your belief by giving three reasons for it and support each reason with three details.

8. The mayor has decided to cancel the annual Halloween parade. The mayor believes the parade takes time away from school children to learn in class. We need to write the mayor a letter to explain why we should have the Halloween parade. We need to include three reasons why we should have the parade, and we need to give examples to support our reasons. Write that letter.

9. NASA has decided it will let one student ride to the moon on the next space shuttle mission. The panel in charge of the expedition has recommended asking you to be that person. Write an essay convincing NASA to let you ride the space shuttle.

10. Your city leaders have banned in-line skating from downtown sidewalks and from shopping centers. The city leaders feel that sidewalks should be solely for people who want to walk and that skaters are dangerous to walkers, especially in crowded city areas. Decide whether you agree or disagree with a law about banning skates from sidewalks. In the beginning of your paper, state your opinion clearly. Give reasons for your opinion and examples for each reason. Be sure to conclude your paper so that the reader clearly understands your opinion. We will give these essays to the city leaders to read.

11. Your parents are having a garage sale and have informed you that they would like to sell your stuffed animal collection. Think about whether you agree with this idea. State your opinion in the beginning of the paper. Then explain your feelings about your stuffed animals and their importance to you. Give specific examples that describe your feelings. Conclude your paper so that your parents understand your opinion.

12. Your school is having a spring concert. The music teacher thinks that everyone should attend the event to support the musicians and to learn more about music. Think about whether you agree with this decision. State your opinion in the beginning of the paper. Then tell why you think as you do. Be sure to give specific examples.

13. The governor of your state has decided that a large bike path will run through your state. Thousands of people will be able to enjoy this path while biking, jogging, or walking. You have just learned that this path is scheduled to run through your backyard and will eliminate your favorite soccer field. Think about whether you agree that a bike path should be developed. State your opinion and give detailed reasons for your opinion.

14. Chocolate was first manufactured in the United States in 1765. Now the people in the United States consume about half of the world's production of chocolate. In recent years, doctors have been concerned that too much fat from chocolate in our diets is harmful and that chocolate should be eliminated from our diets. Decide whether you agree or disagree with the doctors. Think about specific reasons for your opinion and give examples that support your reasons. Conclude your paper by restating your opinion.

Rubrics are becoming the most popular method of assessing students' writings. Rubrics clarify teachers' expectations and guide students' writings by detailing criteria for assessment (Hill, Ruptic, & Norwick, 1998). Rubrics assess specific aspects of students' writings according to a predetermined set of criteria. These criteria can be set by the teacher or in partnership with students. Rubric assessment can inform teachers about the ability of students to write, and they also can help students self-assess their writing.

📑 Directions

1. Determine the areas you want to assess and list the criteria. Arrange the criteria on a four-point table as in the example that follows. Make sure the criteria match your assessment goals and your instruction.

2. Duplicate and distribute copies of the rubric of your choice. Tell students that their writings will be assessed using the criteria on the rubric. Give students time to discuss the rubric with each other.

3. Ask students whether they have questions about the criteria stated on the rubric. If students have questions about the criteria, take time to teach the information that students need.

4. After you are certain that students understand the criteria, tell them that their next piece of writing will be assessed using the rubric. Remind students as they become immersed in writing to remember the criteria on the rubric.

5. After students have finished writing, have them self-assess their own writings using the rubric. Then assess students' writings using the rubric. Use a different color of ink to note your assessments. Then compare similarities and differences between the students' assessments and your assessments.

Name _____ Date _____

Writing Rubric

Title _____

	Ideas & Content	Organization	Mechanics & Style
4	Stays on topic Many examples Interesting	Organized logically Evident sequence Opening and closing	Excellent word choice Fluent Standard English
3	Mainly on topic Some examples Fairly interesting	Organized loosely Some sequence Opening or closing	Good word choice Fairly fluent Mostly Standard English

2	Topic evident
	A few examples
	Attempt at interest
		Some organization
		Sequence attempt
		Attempt at opening
		   or closing
			Fair word choice
			Somewhat fluent
			Some Standard
			   English

1	Topic confusing Few examples Little interest	Organization poor Sequence confusing No opening or closing	Poor word choice Not fluent Many mechanical errors

Writing Assessment Guide

Focus/Ideas	☐ The writing is extremely clear and purposeful. ☐ Main idea is maintained throughout. Topic is narrow and manageable. ☐ Writer's knowledge, experience, insight is convincing.	☐ The writer is making a strong beginning focusing the topic. ☐ General information is provided. ☐ Writer summarizes events with a few word pictures to show what happened. ☐ The writer may need to add more or get rid of unneeded information.	☐ No main idea stands out although possibilities exist. ☐ Subject may be vague or repetitive. ☐ Unrelated ideas prevent clear focus. ☐ Several possible ideas may be present which could become central theme.	☐ Insufficient writing to show that criteria are met.
Support and Elaboration	☐ Descriptive detail and powerful reasons expand the main topic giving the whole piece a strong sense of focus. ☐ Many details and reasons support the main idea. ☐ Appropriate, original choices of words are used. ☐ Text is lively, expressive, and engaging.	☐ Easy to see where the paper is headed, though more expansion is needed. ☐ Some specific details are used but may be general or repetitive. ☐ Most words are correct and adequate, even if not striking. ☐ Reader has some connection to the writer.	☐ Missing, limited, or unrelated details. ☐ Everything is as important as everything else. ☐ Language is vague. ☐ Voice cannot be discerned.	☐ Insufficient writing to show that criteria are met.
Organization	☐ The structure is compelling and guides the reader. ☐ Writer uses an attention-getting introduction. ☐ Ideas flow logically in well-developed paragraphs. ☐ Writer uses an appropriate ending. ☐ Sentences flow and vary in the beginning structure and length. ☐ Transitions are used.	☐ Sequencing seems reasonably appropriate with few gaps. ☐ Transitions are usually present. ☐ Structure may be too dominant or predictable. ☐ Recognizable introduction though it may not create a strong sense of anticipation. ☐ Conclusion may not tie up all loose ends.	☐ The writer has some structure, but the reader must infer it. ☐ Writer uses limited paragraphing and a random sequence of ideas. ☐ Introduction and/or conclusions are missing.	☐ Insufficient writing to show that criteria are met.
Conventions	☐ Writer shows excellent control over standard writing conventions (spelling, punctuation, capitalization, grammar, usage, paragraphing) and uses them with accuracy to enhance meaning. ☐ Text appears clean, edited, and polished. ☐ Writer creates text of sufficient length and complexity to demonstrate control of conventions appropriate for age and experience.	☐ The writer shows reasonable control over the most widely used writing conventions. ☐ Errors may distract but do not impair readability. ☐ Moderate editing is required.	☐ Writer demonstrates limited control even over widely used conventions. ☐ Errors are serious enough to distract. ☐ Paper needs editing.	☐ Insufficient writing to show that criteria are met.

Adapted from District #87, Bloomington, Illinois.

From Susan Davis Lenski and Jerry L. Johns, *Improving Writing K–8: Strategies, Assessments, and Resources* (2nd ed.). Copyright © 2004 by Kendall/Hunt Publishing Company (1-800-247-3458, ext. 4 or 5). May be reproduced for noncommercial educational purposes within the guidelines noted on the copyright page.

PLAN and WRITE •

Students who are familiar with writing tests tend to do better on them (De La Paz, Owen, Harris, & Graham, 2000). When students know what is expected of them, they are usually able to comply. When a test is unfamiliar, however, students spend precious cognitive energy trying to figure out how to take the test. Therefore, it's important to give students practice with the types of tests they will be taking, and De La Paz, Owen, Harris, and Graham (2000) have developed a strategy called PLAN and WRITE.

Directions

1. Tell students that they will be taking a practice writing test. Reinforce the idea that the test will be similar to the type that students will be taking at a later date. Tell students that the reason for the practice test is to teach them how to PLAN and WRITE the test.

2. Duplicate and distribute the PLAN and WRITE bookmark that follows. You might duplicate it on colored paper so that it is visible in students' materials.

3. Discuss each of the elements of PLAN and WRITE by saying something like the following remarks.

   Before you begin writing on a test, you need to plan what you will write. We've done lots of prewriting in this classroom, and you know that you brainstorm ideas before prewriting. For the test, you can think of the acronym PLAN as you plan your answer.

   The first thing you have to do is to pay attention to the prompt. You might want to read the prompt several times making sure that it makes sense to you. Look for key words that describe the main points of the prompt. Underline these words if you can write on the test paper.

   Then list your main ideas. As you think about the prompt, brainstorm at least three main ideas for your writing.

   Add supporting details. Think of at least three details for each main idea. List them next to the main idea.

   Number your ideas. Decide how you will use your main ideas and prioritize them by numbering.

4. Ask students if they have any questions about PLAN. Answer their questions and then give them time to plan their answers. Remind students to use the steps in PLAN.

5. After students have planned their writing, tell them that they can use the steps in WRITE to write their essays. Explain the steps of WRITE as follows.

   After you have planned your essay, you can begin to write. The first thing to remember is to work from your plan. Then remember the goals you have for your piece. Every piece of writing has a main purpose, and you need to remember your goals as you write. As you write, remember to include transition words, try to use different kinds of sentences, and write with exciting, interesting words. These steps can help you as you write your test.

6. Give students time to ask questions about WRITE and then have them write their test answers.

7. Encourage students to use the steps in PLAN and WRITE when they are given writing tests.

PLAN and WRITE

P	Pay attention to the prompt
L	List main ideas
A	Add supporting details
N	Number your main ideas
W	Write from your plan
R	Remember your goals
I	Include transition words
T	Try to use different kinds of sentences
E	Exciting, interesting words

Writing Style and Mechanics: Revising and Editing

"Everyone needs an editor."

—Tim Foote

OVERVIEW

The purpose of writing is to express ideas for an audience. The degree to which readers are able to construct meaning from a piece of writing, however, depends on the way the piece is written. Clear writing written in a lively style that conforms to standard usage is easier to read than writing that is unclear, dull, and full of errors. In order for writers to make their meanings clear, they must pay attention to the details of writing and learn strategies for rewriting, revising, and editing.

Not all papers that students write should be revised and edited (Graves, 1994). Students should write so much in schools that they simply don't have time to take every piece of writing to the sharing stage. If students are writing

> *Rewriting is the tough part of writing.*

every day (sometimes writing for self-discovery, sometimes writing to learn, and sometimes writing to communicate with an audience), most of their writing should not be rewritten. However, when students are writing for an audience or when their writing will be read by someone else, they need to make their writing as clear and readable as possible. That's when they need to rewrite.

Writing for an audience usually needs to be completed over a period of days. Rewriting doesn't mean that students merely recopy their papers; it means that they use their initial drafts as a lens to make clear what they really want to say (Heard, 2002). Rewriting is the tough part of writing; it takes time, attention, and instruction.

Finding the right words to express thoughts is not always easy for writers. Even though there are times when writing flows, there are other times when writers need to rely on the craft of writing. Writing is a craft as well as an art. When words don't come easily, writers can rely on strategies such as rethinking, varying sentences, creating images, and using writers' tools. These strategies help writers shape ideas so that their meanings are clear.

In the past, writing instruction has emphasized editing rather than the craft of rewriting. Editing is only a small part of the rewriting process.

Teaching strategies can help students learn how to rewrite.

Writing Strategies
Rethinking
Varying Sentences
Creating Images
Using Writers Tools

- Teachers can help students learn the craft of writing beyond getting words correct.
- Teachers can help students imagine their audiences so they write with the appropriate style.
- Teachers can help students learn how to write engaging first sentences and powerful conclusions.
- Teachers also can help students learn how to use writers' tools so that the writing conforms to Standard English usage.

"Good writing is largely a matter of rewriting."

Rewriting doesn't take place at a certain time during the writing process. Even though the bulk of rewriting generally takes place after drafting, the writing process is recursive (Lenski & Johns, 1997). Rewriting takes place all of the time. When students begin pieces of writing that will be read by audiences, they need to be conscious of crafting sentences that fit their writings. As students draft ideas, for example, they might stop and rewrite a phrase, sharpen an image, or check the spelling of a word. Students can learn how to stop and think while writing to find a concise noun or a strong verb. Rewriting can take place throughout the writing process.

Before students' writings are given to their audiences, they need to be edited with a careful eye. Students are novice writers who do not know all of the rules that govern the English language. Therefore, students need to spend time polishing their writing by making sure all of the conventions of language are correct. To produce writings that are correct, students will need their teachers' assistance. Teachers can be copy editors and proofreaders for students who have not yet learned all of the conventions of language.

"Good writing is largely a matter of rewriting" (Britton, 1996, p. 323). Rewriting turns a string of sentences into a stirring piece of prose or an engaging story. This chapter contains resources, teaching strategies, ideas, and activities to teach students how to rewrite papers so that their writing expresses their ideas in ways that are readable for audiences. Ideas for assessment also are included.

Are your students writing every day?

Revising Thoughts and Ideas

Goal ● *To help students revise thoughts and ideas during and after writing.*

BACKGROUND

Revision is revisioning or rethinking a piece of writing. During writing, writers often put down words that do not completely capture their thoughts and ideas. Instead, these initial drafts reflect the surface thoughts of the writer. After writing an initial draft, writers often re-read their original sentences and change them to make the words express their intentions more clearly.

Revision is labor intensive. That means revision takes a lot of time, thought, and work. Since revision is so time-consuming, not every piece of writing that students do in school should be revised (Graves, 1994). Students in school should be writing so much that only a portion of their work, not every piece of writing, should be placed in the revision cycle.

Revision, however, is an important part of writing. Students need to write often to increase their writing fluency. Students also need to learn about the organizational patterns of writing, but if they are to grow as writers, students need to revise some of their pieces of writing. It is through revision that students learn the craft of writing and the recursive nature of the writing process (Fearn & Farnan, 2001).

In a model of the revision process, Hayes (1996) suggests that rereading during revision is essential. Writers reread their work during drafting to make decisions about words, events, spelling, and ideas. Writers also revise their work after the completion of a first draft. They reread and rethink their pieces on many levels, examining their logic, ideas, sentences, grammar, words, and sequence. Revision is necessary to produce high-quality writing.

Even writers in kindergarten need to learn about revision. Young students should learn that written words can be changed. Students in first grade and beyond can learn how to re-work, or revise, their writings. They should think of revision during drafting and after drafting. Students should revise independently and with writing partners. While they are revising, though, students need to learn to think about their writing and follow where their minds lead.

Donald Murray (1991, p. 85) wrote, "I believe that if I attend to the draft, read it carefully, and listen to what it says, the draft will tell me what a reader needs." His words are good advice. This section contains resources, teaching strategies, ideas, and activities to help students learn how to revise, during and after writing, the thoughts and ideas they have.

Revision is labor intensive.

Grammar Lady

www.grammarlady.com

This site offers many tips about correct language usage for students of all ages.

GROW A SENTENCE

Young students can learn to revise sentences by participating in the strategy Grow a Sentence. When you Grow a Sentence, you show students that writing can be changed even after you have finished writing a sentence. Young students often think that once they have written something it should not change. Your instructional purpose in using the strategy Grow a Sentence, therefore, is to show young students that writing can be changed. When students learn that writing can be changed, they are more likely to understand the principles behind revision.

Directions

1. Write a simple sentence on the chalkboard or on an overhead transparency. Use only a simple subject and a simple predicate, such as the example "Dogs run."

2. Tell students that you will Grow a Sentence by adding one word or phrase at a time. Stress the idea that after writers finish parts of writing they read over what they have written and decide whether or not they want to make any changes.

3. Tell students that you will add one word to the sentence, such as "Big dogs run." Explain that when you were thinking about the sentence you were not thinking about all dogs, only *big* dogs. Write the new word in a different color or underline the word so that it stands out.

4. Read the new sentence aloud to the class. Tell the class that you want to change the sentence some more. Have students volunteer words and phrases that would change the sentence. Write the new sentence under the second sentence as in the example that follows.

5. After revising the sentence three or four times, draw a triangle around the sentences. Point out to students how the first sentence was changed to become the final sentence. Remind students that when writers write they can make changes to their writing.

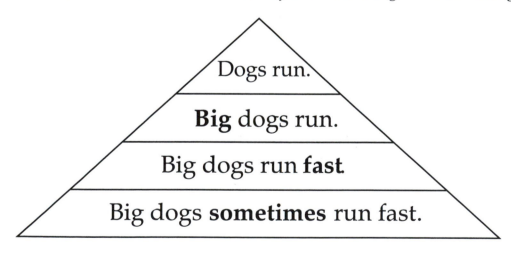

Assessment

Identify students who are able to write long, descriptive sentences. Use these sentences as models for the class.

Teaching Strategy 2

Writers do not revise their writing only after a piece is complete; they revise as they go. Stop and Think is a strategy to remind students to revise during writing and to monitor their revisions. Teachers can model the Stop and Think strategy for young students. Older students should revise their work independently.

 ## Directions

1. Introduce the revision strategy Stop and Think by explaining to students that when they write they need to frequently stop what they are doing and make writing decisions. Tell students that the brief pauses they make while writing in order to choose just the right word or to reread a sentence to see if it makes sense are part of writing and revision. Remind students that *writers revise as they write*—not only after a draft is complete. Tell students that the Stop and Think strategy makes explicit some of the writing decisions they are making during writing.

2. To use the Stop and Think strategy, have students make a tally mark each time they stop and think during the drafting process. Ask them to jot down a word or phrase that will help them remember what made them stop and what they were thinking. Discuss these stopping points and develop a classification scheme using ideas such as the ones that follow.

Are you encouraging your students to "Stop and Think" while writing?

   - stopped to figure out the spelling of a word
   - stopped to think what happens next
   - stopped to think of a million dollar word
   - stopped to decide if what I wrote made sense

3. Create a grid or a table for students to use the Stop and Think strategy on their own. See the example that follows. Duplicate the grid on page 329 and distribute it to students. Have students use the Stop and Think grid while they are writing their next pieces.

4. Every few weeks, revisit the Stop and Think grid. Ask students whether the categories on the grid should remain the same or change. Make changes suggested by students and create a new Stop and Think grid.

Assessment

Work individually with students to assess their ability to revise while writing. Students will need many experiences with this strategy before they will use it independently.

Stop and Think		
Stopped to figure out the spelling of a word	Stopped to think about what happens next	Stopped to think of a million dollar word
Stopped to see if the words made sense	Stopped to admire a sentence	Stopped to think about a conclusion

Teaching Strategy 3

Section 6.1

SELF-REVISION

One of the crucial parts of revision is Self-Revision. Writers need to read their own writing to decide whether their purposes are achieved. As writers revise, they need to find value in their writing, thinking about what they did well (Hansen, 2001). As writers reflect on their writing, they also can set new writing goals by determining in what ways this particular piece of writing exemplified "good writing" and in what ways they want to improve their next piece of writing.

📖 Directions

1. Tell students that writers revise their writing during writing, as in the previous Stop and Think strategy, but that writers also revise their writing after they have completed a draft. Tell students that after drafting a piece of writing they should reread their writing, looking for substantive ways to make the writing clear and compelling.

2. After students have finished drafting a piece of writing, tell them that you will give them the opportunity to revise this writing by using the Revision Suggestions on page 330. Duplicate and distribute the Revision Suggestions so that all students have a copy.

3. Model the revision process using your own piece of writing. Make a transparency of a piece of writing you have drafted, place it on the overhead projector, and read the piece for students.

4. Read each of the suggestions for revision. Apply the suggestions as appropriate to your own writing. Tell students that only some of the Revision Suggestions should be used for each piece of writing, not all of them. Model changes to your writing.

5. Have students use the Revision Suggestions to make changes to their own writing. Provide ample time for students to reread their pieces, to read the Revision Suggestions, and to make appropriate changes. Tell students that you expect them to apply at least one or two of the Revision Suggestions.

Stop and Think

●_____

Revision Suggestions

☐ Read your paper aloud. Listen for places that are awkward. Rewrite sections that caused you to stumble while reading.

☐ Picture your audience. Think about whether your reader could understand your message or story.

☐ Think about your purpose for writing. If your purpose is not clear, revise sections so that a reader will understand your purpose for writing.

☐ Reread your paper, looking for passages that are confusing because you need more information. Add more explanation or details if needed.

☐ Look for places in your writing that don't fit the topic. Delete sections that wander from your main point.

☐ Make sure your paragraphs are in logical order. If the events in the paper do not make sense in the order in which you wrote them, change the order.

☐ If necessary, revise your first sentence to grab the reader's attention.

☐ Underline words that have punch. Replace overused words with Million Dollar Words.

☐ Add figurative language where you can. Think of comparisons, similes, metaphors, and examples that help your reader understand your message.

☐ Read each sentence individually, looking for errors in grammar and usage. Use your writing tools to find out how to write words and sentences in Standard English.

From Susan Davis Lenski and Jerry L. Johns, *Improving Writing K–8: Strategies, Assessments, and Resources* (2nd ed.). Copyright © 2004 by Kendall/Hunt Publishing Company (1-800-247-3458, ext. 4 or 5). May be reproduced for noncommercial educational purposes within the guidelines noted on the copyright page.

Teaching Strategy 4

WRITING PARTNERS

Writing is a social activity. Writers need readers, and readers need writers. Both reading and writing are dependent on others. Since writing will be read by an audience of one or more readers, it helps writers to have a writing partner to give advice on the piece during the revision process. There are generally four functions of writing partners (Mohr, 1984). Writing Partners can offer writers choices. They also can give writers responses, show writers different possibilities, and speed up revision by their suggestions. Writing Partners are very useful for improving students' writing.

Directions

1. Tell students that a valuable resource for revision is a Writing Partner. Explain that Writing Partners can offer useful suggestions during a writer's revision process. You may want to model the process for students.

2. Have students choose a Writing Partner or divide the class into groups of two students. Tell students that the Writing Partners will change in three or four weeks.

3. Duplicate and distribute the Questions to Ask Writing Partners that follow. Tell students that the questions are designed to help the writer discuss a piece of writing and make decisions about ways to revise the piece.

4. Tell students that Writing Partners sometimes are at a loss for things to say about a piece of writing. Duplicate and distribute the list of Comment Ideas for Writing Partners on page 333. Tell students that they can use an appropriate comment from the list if they don't know what to say.

5. Have students move to various parts of the room with their Writing Partners, their pieces of writing, and their handouts. Tell Writing Partners that one of them will begin reading his or her piece of writing. Explain that the other partner should listen carefully during the reading. After the reader is finished, the second student should ask at least three questions, make at least three positive comments, and offer one suggestion. The Writing Partners then should trade roles.

Do these students know the "Questions to Ask Writing Partners"?

Questions to Ask Writing Partners

▲ How do you feel about your writing so far?

▲ Are you finished? If you want to write more, what do you plan to write?

▲ Which part is your favorite? Why?

▲ Could you tell me more about . . .?

▲ What do you mean by . . .?

▲ Why did you choose this topic?

▲ Does your first sentence grab the reader's attention?

▲ Did you say what you wanted to say in this piece?

▲ Who is your audience?

▲ What is your purpose for writing this piece? Did you accomplish your purpose?

▲ Does the piece end the way you want it to end?

I Don't Know What to Say!
Comment Ideas for Writing Partners

Positive Comments	Suggestions
Style	
Excellent first sentence.	You might try a different first sentence.
Many interesting sentences.	Vary sentence length.
Many interesting words.	Use Million Dollar Words.
Transitions apparent.	Add transitions.
Imagery used.	Add similes or metaphors.
Conversation natural.	Omit or revise some conversation.
Content	
Logical order of events.	Change the order of events.
Interesting situation or problem.	Strengthen the main situation or problem.
Clear plan.	Make the story plan more clear.
Interesting events.	Add details to events.
Ending solves the problem.	Change the story's ending.
Characters seem real.	Add details to the characters.
Setting is vivid.	Add details to the setting.
Mechanics	
Capitalization mostly correct.	Revise capitalization.
Punctuation mostly correct.	Revise punctuation.
Spelling mostly correct.	Revise spelling.
Grammar mostly correct.	Revise grammar.
Handwriting easy to read.	Write more neatly.

Teaching Strategy 5

PICK A CARD

Many students have difficulty with revision; they don't know what to do to make deep changes in their writing. Often students rely on their knowledge of spelling and punctuation as they revise. Hughey and Slack (2001) suggest that teachers help their students fine-tune their writing with the strategy Pick a Card. In this strategy, the teacher develops cards with writing terms listed on them, such as "sentence variety." Students use these cards to prompt their thinking during writing conferences.

Directions

1. Tell students that you want them to make suggestions about certain writing strategies that you have taught in the past. Explain to students that when they revise their writing, they need to take into account all of these strategies, not just spelling and punctuation.

2. Duplicate the Pick a Card sheet on page 336 and cut the paper into sections or make your own sheet containing strategies you have taught.

3. Divide the class into groups of four or five students. Ask one of the students to volunteer to read his or her piece of writing. Then give the other students directions as follows.

   I'm going to set these cards on the table. You get to choose one of the cards to use as a revision prompt. The cards listed are all writing strategies that we have studied: sentence variety, beginning sentence, conclusion, vivid details, strong verbs, and organization. One of you will read your piece of writing. As that person reads, the rest of you should think of advice that you can give the writer about the topic that is listed on your card.

4. Model how to give advice about writing. Tell students that they should give the writers a compliment and then proceed to giving advice. The following demonstration exchange uses the piece of writing "Holiday Celebrations" written by Ranah found on page 337.

   Ranah: (Reads Holiday Celebrations.)

   Kim: [vivid details] I was really interested in the way you celebrate Ideai. I've never heard of it. I wonder if you could add some more vivid details to this part of your writing. I'd like to know more about the reasons for this holiday.

   Jose: [beginning sentence] I really liked the beginning of your paper. You started with a question and that made me want to read your story. I don't have any advice about the card I chose "beginning sentence," because you wrote a really good one.

   Scott: [conclusion] Yes, I liked your beginning sentence too, and I also liked the way you ended your story. You said you'd write more about your religion, and I'd like to hear that. But maybe you could change your ending a bit. Instead of ending with "Hope you like it," I think it would be better to end with something that wraps up the story better. The sentence you wrote before that would be a good one to end the entire story.

5. After students have given advice to one of the writers, have students exchange cards before a second writer reads his or her piece.

6. Reassure students that it can be difficult to give advice to another student about writing, but if they continue to practice, they'll become better during the year. Stress that the goal of advice is to help strengthen the piece of writing.

Will this student be happy to share his writing with the group?

Words at Funbrain

www.funbrain.com/words.htm

This site offers many different online language games that help students master everything from spelling to grammar.

Beginning Sentence	Vivid Details
Sentence Variety	Conclusion
Strong Verbs	Organization

How do you celebrate holidays? Here is how my family celebrates birthdays, fasting, and Ideai.

This is how my family celebrates my birthday. We first bring a cake and after we are done eating, we have a party. The next day we go out some place to eat. Last year we went to the Par-a-Dice Buffet.

We celebrate fasting by not eating in the morning, only at 6:30 and at night. My mom wakes me up in the middle of the night and we eat food, and when it is close to morning I eat fast. It starts at 3:00 in the morning.

One of my favorites holidays would be what's called Ideai. What that is would be people that come over to your house and give you money and you do too. Last year my cousin gave me a $50 check and I still have it.

So, if you enjoyed my story I'll write some more to you about my religion. That's the end about how my family celebrates holidays. Hope you like it.

Ranah
Fourth Grade

Teaching Strategy

HANG TEN

Students often have difficulty thinking of just the right word when they write. Writers often use whatever word pops into their head as a placeholder for a more descriptive word realizing that they can spend time during revision to come up with the word they want. Students, however, also have difficulty thinking of replacement words during revision. Hughey and Slack (2001) recommend using the Hang Ten strategy to help students think of rich vocabulary words during revision. Hang Ten is a way for students to get assistance from their classmates for word changes.

Directions

1. Tell students that they need to replace overused words with more descriptive words during the revision cycle of their writing. Explain that writers often use resources to help them think of words as they revise.

2. Remind students that they can be resources for each other's writing because each student has knowledge of different words. Tell students that as a community of writers they should be willing to help each other think of exciting words to use.

3. Ask students for an example of an overused word that is common in their writing. Write the words that the students volunteer on the chalkboard. Some examples might be the following words.

    Nice
    Went
    Play
    Friend
    Go
    Said

4. Have students choose one of these words to use as a demonstration. Say something like the following comments.

    We've chosen the word "nice" as an example of an overused word in our writing. What are some words we could use in place of "nice?" What do you really mean by that word?

5. Students should think of a variety of words such as agreeable, pleasant, enjoyable, amusing, attractive, and so on. Remind students that each of these synonyms means something slightly different and that they need to consider which one really fits their intended meaning.

Internet Park: Online Interactive Word Games

www.internet-park.com/

This site allows students to play various word games live on the Internet.

6. Duplicate and distribute the Hang Ten sheet that follows. Tell students that if they want assistance when they revise a piece of writing they should write the overused word in the middle square and place the Hang Ten sheet on the table in the room.

7. Tell students that when they see a Hang Ten sheet on the table, they should try to think of alternate words for the word in the center square. Encourage students to write at least one word on each Hang Ten sheet that they see.

Hang Ten

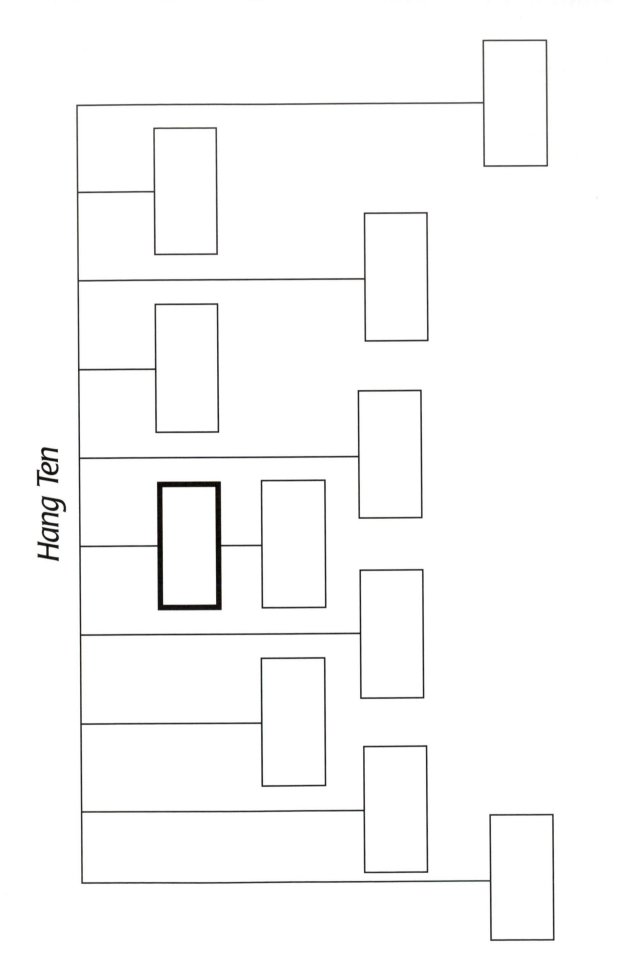

Developing Style and Voice

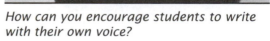

Goal ● To help students develop an engaging writing style.

BACKGROUND

"I love Avi's writing style." This comment refers not to the content of Avi's books but to the way he uses language. Style is the way writers craft sentences and paragraphs in fresh, unique ways. Writing style, however, is elusive and subtle (Harris & Hodges, 1995). It's hard to pinpoint what style actually is.

Style is individual and unique.

Because writing style is hard to define, we tend to ignore the teaching of style. Some teachers believe that each writer's writing style is inherent, fixed, and unchangeable. Teachers who believe writing style is a part of writing talent tend to give their students opportunities to write and let style take care of itself. It's very likely that some of our writing style is part of our personality, part of our verbal talent. But there are other aspects of writing style that are amenable to instruction. The part of writing style that consists of word choice and sentence arrangement can be taught to students throughout the grades.

Good style is subjective. Writing style that appeals to some readers is abhorred by others. For example, some readers love Charles Dickens's writing: the long flowing sentences, the use of semicolons. Other readers prefer Hemingway's short, abrupt sentences. We can't legislate style. But we can help students select appropriate language for the purpose of a piece of writing.

Style is individual and unique. It is like voice, the imprint of ourselves on our writing (Graves, 2003). Teachers can motivate students

to use words in new ways; they can help students write with crisp, clear prose; and they can teach students how to vary words and sentences so that their writing expresses their personality. This section provides resources, teaching strategies, ideas, and activities for you to use as you help your students develop an engaging writing style.

How can you encourage students to write with their own voice?

As students explore their own personal writing style, they can expand their writing choices by becoming a Language Detective. A Language Detective observes "how and why we use language in certain situations and with particular people, investigating how language is used to confer or deny power, and considering the many voices that we adopt as speakers and writers" (Monahan, 2003). As students learn about different ways various groups use language, they can incorporate these codes into their own writing as necessary.

Directions

1. Help students become aware of different ways language is used by having them participate in role playing. Begin the role playing activity as follows.

   You can tell what roles people are filling by their language. For example, your parents use different ways of expressing themselves than do your friends. Your teachers express themselves in certain ways when they are speaking to you, to other teachers, and to the principal. We use language differently depending on our social group. This is called code-switching. *Most people can code switch fairly easily.*

2. Write the term *code-switching* on the chalkboard or on an overhead transparency. Ask students to think of social groups that require them to switch codes from the ways they talk with their peers. Some examples of possible responses follow.

Parents	Babies
Church or synagogue leaders	Grandparents
Teachers	Animals
Police	Principal
Bus driver	Unknown adult
Girlfriend or boyfriend	New peer
Younger children	

3. Have students brainstorm different scenarios in which they would interact with members of the different social groups they have listed. Some examples might be inviting a friend to a party, asking the teacher for directions on homework, meeting a friend of your parents, and teaching a dog to sit. Have students role-play some of these scenarios.

4. After each scene, discuss with students how their voices and vocabularies changed depending on their interactions with the different social groups. Tell students that these are examples of *code-switching*.

5. Explain to students that their writing will be more realistic if they write with the language common to the group. Tell students that *code-switching* is especially important when they write stories with characters of different social groups and that it is also useful when writing expository text. Remind students that when they write expository text they can incorporate quotations and short conversations in them and that these conversations should be as similar to real life as possible.

6. Tell students that writers need to become aware of their writing style and that becoming a Language Detective can help them improve their style.

7. Duplicate and distribute the Language Detective sheet that follows. Model how the sheet could be used as follows.

    Your assignment is to become observant about the types of language that different people use in their speech that could be incorporated into your writing. Listen to those around you tonight and record the people and an example of their words. For example, your grandmother might say, "Wash your hands before dinner." In that case, write "grandmother" in the column labeled "people" and "Wash your hands before dinner" under the column labeled "quotation." Try to find quotations that are typical of that social group.

8. Have students find quotations and fill out the Language Detective sheet. After students have found several quotations, make a list on a bulletin board of the different quotations they've found. Encourage students to use these different codes as they write.

Name _____ Date _____

Language Detective

Person	Quotation

WORD CHOICE: MILLION DOLLAR WORDS

The words writers choose to use as they write are a large part of their writing style. Million Dollar Words can make the difference between ho-hum writing and writing with verve. Some writers seem to have a talent for using colorful words. Other writers need to use writing tools such as a thesaurus as they search for strong verbs and precise nouns. When students are aware that they need to try to write with Million Dollar Words, their writing can become much more exciting.

Directions

1. Tell students that when they write they should try to use words that capture the images they have in their minds. Explain that sometimes writers need to search for the right word, because not just any word will do in a given situation. Tell students that they need to try to use Million Dollar Words when they write.

2. Write the following groups of sentences on the chalkboard or on an overhead transparency. Have students read the sentences independently.

   1. He **held** the bat tightly.
   2. He **gripped** the bat tightly.

   1. She stared in **surprise** at the Grand Canyon.
   2. She stared in **awe** at the Grand Canyon.

3. Ask students to identify the differences between the two sentences in each pair. Encourage students to discuss the more vivid words in the second sentences.

4. Create several Million Dollar Word Posters to display in the room so students have Million Dollar Words easily accessible. To create Million Dollar Word Posters, duplicate and distribute the list of words on the following page. Tell students that all of these words could be used in lieu of the word "said." Explain to students that each word has a slightly different connotation and that the words cannot necessarily be used interchangeably. Instead, the Million Dollar Word Posters list words that have different shades of meaning for the targeted word.

5. Divide the class into groups of three or four students. Have each group develop a Million Dollar Word Poster. You can use the following list of ideas for posters or have students think of the topics for their posters. Tell students that Million Dollar Words can be found in thesauruses and, if possible, secure several for your classroom library.

   Million Dollar Words for "nice."
   Million Dollar Words for "good."
   Million Dollar Words for "went."
   Million Dollar Words for "fun."

6. Encourage students to use Million Dollar Words as they write and share examples of students' use of Million Dollar Words in their writing.

Assessment

Occasionally evaluate students' writing solely on their choice of words. Look for interesting and appropriate words that fit the paper's content.

Million Dollar Words for "Said"

added
admitted
agreed
announced
answered
asked

badgered
barked
begged
bellowed
blabbered
broadcasted

cackled
chattered
chuckled
coaxed
commented
complained
confessed
congratulated
cried

declared
decreed
demanded

echoed
exclaimed

gasped
giggled
grinned
groaned
grumbled

hectored
hinted
hollered
howled

informed
inquired
intimated

jabbered

laughed

mentioned
moaned
mumbled
murmured
muttered

nagged

ordered

persuaded
pleaded
proclaimed
prompted
proposed
protested

questioned

recited
remarked
reminded
repeated
replied
responded

screamed
shouted
shrieked
sighed
snarled
sniveled
stated
stormed
stuttered
suggested

taunted
teased
told

urged
uttered

wheedled
whined
whispered

yelled
yelped

Teaching Strategy 3

OPENING SENTENCES

Opening sentences can be a killer. They can make or break a piece of writing. The first sentence of a story can invite a reader to continue, or it can throw up a roadblock that hinders the reader. Many writers prefer short openers; others use a variety of different first sentences to grab the reader's interest. Most writers, however, don't automatically know how to write a first sentence. Many young writers begin their writing with sentences that tell the entire story in one fell swoop. All writers, however, can learn how to write catchy first sentences. Learning how to write good opening sentences is a part of style that can be learned.

Directions

1. Tell students that the first sentence in a piece of writing can either invite readers to continue reading or keep them from reading more of the piece.

2. Write the following sentence on a chalkboard or on an overhead transparency.

   It was a dark and stormy night.

3. Many students have heard this famous opening sentence. Ask students to discuss what makes this sentence interesting or boring.

4. Read to students several opening sentences from familiar books or write the first sentence of *Drummond* (Odgers, 1990) on the chalkboard or on an overhead transparency. Read the sentence with students. Discuss why this sentence is a good opening. Explain that writers consciously determine how to begin a piece of writing.

   Sarah Jordan and her brother Nicholas were perfectly ordinary people until the day they met Drummond.

5. Ask students to find other opening sentences that they like, either from published books or from their own writing. Have students share these sentences with the class.

6. Tell students that writers can choose to use a variety of opening sentences. Explain that there are 10 types of opening sentences that writers most frequently use. Duplicate the list of Opening Sentences on the following page and distribute it to students.

 7. Read and discuss the 10 opening sentences with the class. Then divide the class into groups of three or four students. Have each group choose two types of opening sentences. Ask each group to write a sample sentence for the two types of opening sentences they chose.

8. Invite students to share their sample opening sentences. Post the sentences along with the sentence types on a display in the room. Encourage students to use the display as they compose opening sentences for their next piece of writing.

Assessment

Informally note which students are successful writing opening sentences and which are not. Work with students individually or in small groups to help them write interesting opening sentences.

Opening Sentences

1. **Ask a question.**

   Example: Where did all of these ants come from?

2. **Use a lively quotation.**

   Example: "Eating carrots will grow hair on your chest," Grandpa boomed.

3. **Create a sense of drama.**

   Example: The solitary figure limped along the rocky trail.

4. **Mention a strange or interesting detail.**

   Example: The temperature can drop to 50 degrees below zero on the summit of Mount Everest.

5. **Begin with action.**

   Example: The basketball circled the rim and wobbled maddeningly before dropping through the hoop.

6. **Use exclamations.**

   Example: Fifty dollars! You must be kidding!

7. **Use humor.**

   Example: He emptied his pocket: a few loose coins, a house key, a handkerchief, and a dead mouse.

8. **Present a problem.**

   Example: As the warriors crossed the narrow bridge, they spotted their enemies shooting fire arrows.

9. **Present an opinion.**

   Example: All students should do one hour of homework a day.

10. **Start with a single word.**

    Example: Lice. How I hate lice. Six of the students in my class have lice. It was only a matter of time.

IT'S A WRAP: WRITING CONCLUSIONS

Conclusions are one of the most difficult parts of writing. Many students simply write "The End" or "I hope you like my story" even when they know that these endings aren't very effective. There are many ways to write conclusions to stories that teachers can demonstrate for students as is evidenced by the strategy It's a Wrap.

Directions

1. Have students select a piece of writing that they have not yet completed. Tell them that you will be discussing a variety of ways for students to end their stories.

2. Compare the ending of a story to the ending of a film. Students are familiar with television programs and films and can use this knowledge to write conclusions for their stories. Have students share examples of endings of television programs and films.

3. Tell students that at the end of producing a film the director says, "It's a wrap." Say that you will be asking students to use this same thinking as they write conclusions for their own stories.

4. Tell students that a story feels like it ends when the action stops, the readers knows how the character feels, the problem is resolved, or the description is complete.

5. Use the story that follows or a story you have written to demonstrate concluding sentences. Write one sentence at a time on the chalkboard or make a transparency of the story and show one sentence at a time.

6. Have students write and decorate cards that say "It's a Wrap!" Tell students to hold their cards in the air when they believe the story is concluded.

7. Ask students how they knew when the story was complete. Guide students to understand that most stories have circular patterns in which they end with the same type of idea as they began.

8. Have students generate as many different endings for this story as they can. If they are unable to think of many concluding sentences, model several for them.

9. Tell students to write a concluding sentence for their own story. Encourage students to write a sentence that wraps up the action or the ideas in their piece.

The Case of the Missing Dog

By
Mayan Laredo

One day my dad and I were playing golf in the backyard and we forgot to close the gate.

After I came in I let my dog, Max, out.

Max likes to run around the yard when he is outside, and he barks when he wants to come in.

He began to bark to come in but as soon as we were going to let him in, he saw the gate open.

He ran out the gate and he wouldn't come when we called him.

Dad and I looked for Max in the forest behind our house.

We were in the front yard looking for Max when the phone rang.

It was two girls who said that they had found Max in the middle of the hill leading to McDonald's.

They told us to come to the hill and get him.

Max had been in the middle of the road when the two girls came along in their car.

They stopped in front of him and looked on his tag.

They waited for us to come to the hill.

When we got to the hill we thanked them for finding our dog.

Then we brought him home and gave him some ice cream because he was all tired out.

Dad decided to put a lock on the gate so Max couldn't get out again.

SENTENCE VARIETY

Sentences have rhythm just like music does. When writers vary their sentences, the writing takes on a rhythm, a beat. A piece of writing that is full of sentences that begin with a simple subject and end with a simple predicate, such as "The kind woman gave us some candy," can lead to very monotonous reading. Reading is more enjoyable when some sentences are long, some are short, and some are in-between. Varying sentence length is another aspect of writing style. As with other stylistic components, some writers naturally vary sentence length while others need to learn that sentence variety adds spice to writing.

 *Directions*

1. Tell students that the flow of words in a piece of writing is like music; sentences have rhythm. Ask students to discuss their viewpoints about sentence rhythm. Then tell students that the length of sentences and the way sentences are organized can create a rhythmic piece of writing.

2. Duplicate the Student Example on the following page and distribute copies to students in the class. Point out the various types of sentences in the writing.

3. Tell students that they can vary sentences by using different types of sentences and by varying sentence beginnings. To help students vary types of sentences, show students how to combine two short sentences into sentences of different lengths, as in the following example.

   Sentences: The clouds began to move in. The day suddenly turned cold.
   Variation 1: Suddenly, the clouds began to move in, and the day turned cold.
   Variation 2: The clouds began to move in, and the day suddenly turned cold.
   Variation 3: When the clouds began to move in, the day suddenly turned cold.

4. Have students combine the following groups of sentences in different ways. Then discuss their groupings.

   I'll never forget that day. We went to the circus.
   I admire my father. He is a wonderful man.
   We thought we were going to lose. The score was 7 to 3.

5. Tell students that they also can vary sentences by writing sentences with different beginnings and lengths. The Sentence Variety list on page 353 provides examples of a variety of sentences. Duplicate the list and distribute it to students. Remind students to vary sentences as they write.

Sentence Variety: Student Example

The Magic Lizard

Once upon a time a lizard was born. Soon the mother found out

that it was no ordinary lizard. It was a magic lizard that had no name.

So the mother thought it was time to name him. She thought and

thought, and it finally came to her. She named him Gex. Well, when Gex

was six, he had no friends, so he made friends with his magic, imaginary

friends anyway. When Gex was eleven, he had a few real friends. He

learned new magic, such as how to fly, breathe fire, and change colors.

When Gex was twenty, he knew every magic trick.

Gex had a lot of friends now. There were small friends, fast friends, sly

friends, smooth friends, and even slick friends. Gex was the most popu-

lar lizard in school. One day Gex got married. His wife's name was

Gexalena. A few years later they had a baby lizard. They named it Gex

Jr., and, well, you know what happened next.

Mark Watson
Third Grade

> Fairy tale opening

> Compound sentence

> Short sentence

> Complex sentence

Million Dollar Words

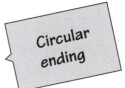

Circular ending

Sentence Variety

1. **Begin with an adverb.**

   Example: Slowly, Bobby backed away from the creaking door.

2. **Use words in a series.**

   Example: Last night Jason got a short, stand-up, wild hair cut.

3. **Add at least one adjective to a noun in your sentences.**

   Example: Amanda hiked up the rugged mountain trail.

4. **Include one simile.**

   Example: Although Wanda was a great grandmother, she felt as young as a spring chicken.

5. **Write a compound sentence.**

   Example: Crissy lost her ring, but she didn't tell her boyfriend about it.

6. **Write a complex sentence.**

   Example: When Jerry retires, he's going to go on four cruises each year.

7. **Write a partial sentence.**

   Example: I love ice cream. Really love it.

8. **End with a dependent clause.**

   Example: Fran traveled to Papua New Guinea because he wanted to see the Birds of Paradise.

Teaching Strategy

Children's literature can be a powerful model of variations of writing styles (McElveen & Dierking, 2000/2001). Some children's books are written with vivid detail, some have strong verbs, and so on. When you teach about the stylistic elements of writing, using models that students can read helps them contextualize the lessons that you teach. In addition, when students become aware of the choices they can make in writing, they begin to think like writers and look for other examples of style independently.

Directions

1. Tell students that you will be using picture books to demonstrate some of the writing strategies students have already learned. For example, you could make the following comments.

    Last week we discussed effective opening sentences, and many of you have experimented with different types of leads. I'd like to read a book for you that has a really interesting beginning sentence.

2. Look at the list of children's books that follows and choose a book that illustrates the skill or strategy that you have taught to your students. In the case of strong leads, you might read *Wilfred Gordon McDonald Partridge* (Fox, 1985) and *What Is the Sun?* (Lindbergh, 1996).

3. Read those two books to students and discuss the opening sentences. Discuss with students the reasons why these leads are considered effective. Guide students to understand that leads that are interesting attract the readers' interest.

4. Have students find examples of the skill or strategy from their own writings. In this example, you'd ask students to find beginning sentences that engage the reader.

5. Tell students that they can find effective beginning sentences in many other books. Encourage students to look for this stylistic element as they read.

6. Create a bulletin board listing the writing skills and strategies that you have taught. Place book jackets of examples of that skill or strategy under the heading. Encourage students to add to this display as they find examples of the stylistic elements that you've taught.

Examples of Children's Literature
for Teaching Writing Style

Baylor, B. (1985)
I'm in charge of celebrations
New York: Scribner's
Using strong verbs for description

Bell, K.M. (1992)
Grandma according to me
New York: Dell
Describing a person

Blume, J. (1974)
The pain and the great one
New York: Dell
Comparing and contrasting two people

Brett, J. (1996)
Comet's nine lives
New York: Putnam
Using cause and effect and strong transitions to sequence a story

Brown, M.W. (1949)
The important book
New York: HarperCollins
Focusing on a topic using specific details

Cooney, B. (1982)
Miss Rumphius
New York: Dial
Developing a strong character

Crews, D. (1991)
Bigmama's
New York: Mulberry
Organizing with an obvious beginning, middle, and end

Curtis, J. L. (1993)
When I was little
New York: HarperCollins
Brainstorming personal topics to write about

Fox, M. (1985)
Wilfred Gordon McDonald Partridge
New York: Dial
Using effective lead sentences

Heller, R. (1989)
Many luscious lollipops
New York: Grosset & Dunlap
Using a variety of verbs

Himmelman, J. (1997)
A slug's life
Danbury, CT: Children's Press
Describing an animal

Johnson, A. (1989)
Tell me a story, mama
New York: Orchard
Brainstorming personal topics

Krauss, R. (1945)
The carrot seed
New York: Harper & Row
Story in the voice of first person

Lindbergh, R. (1996)
What is the sun?
Cambridge, MA: Candlewick Press
Using questions as leads

Numeroff, L. (1994)
If you give a mouse a cookie
New York: Scholastic
Using cause and effect

Numeroff, L. (1996)
If you give a moose a muffin
New York: Scholastic
Focusing on a topic

Numeroff, L. (1998)
If you give a pig a pancake
New York: Scholastic
Using a full circle: the story beginning and ending in the same place

Paulsen, G. (1995)
The tortilla factory
New York: Harcourt Brace
Explaining how to make something

Pratt, K. J. (1992)
A walk in the rainforest
Nevada City, CA: Dawn
Using alliteration in the format of an ABC book

Redhead, J. S. (1985)
The big block of chocolate
New York: Scholastic
Focusing on a topic

Rylant, C. (1982)
When I was young in the mountains
New York: Dial
Brainstorming topics to write about

Showers, P. (1961)
The listening walk
New York: HarperCollins
Integrating onomatopoeia throughout a text

Van Allsburg, C. (1979)
The garden of Abdul Gazasi
New York: Houghton Mifflin
Narrative with open endings

Van Allsburg, C. (1981)
Jumanji
New York: Houghton Mifflin
Narrative with open endings

Van Allsburg, C. (1985)
Polar express
New York: Houghton Mifflin
Narrative with open endings

Viorst, J. (1972)
Alexander and the terrible, horrible, no-good, very bad day
New York: Scholastic
Brainstorming topics to write about

Yolen, J. (1988)
Owl moon
New York: Scholastic
Describing a setting using similes

Yolen, J. (1996)
Welcome to the sea of sand
New York: Scholastic
Elaborating through the use of strong verbs

Teaching Strategy **7**   *Section* 6.2

FINDING MY VOICE

"The human voice underlies the entire writing process" (Graves, 2003, p. 162). All too often, however, students don't realize that their writing should be an example of a more formal version of their own voice. Voice in writing is the subtle message that a piece of writing is the product of one person rather than another. Many of the texts students read, such as textbooks, have a stilted voice, which makes it more difficult for students to understand the use of voice in their own writing. After you teach students about the purpose of voice in writing, however, most students will understand and feel free to write with their own voices.

Directions

1. Explain to students that writing can be formal or informal, and when they write certain types of pieces, students should make sure their voices are "heard" in the writing. You might elaborate on this idea by explaining as follows.

    Writers often have different purposes for writing. Some writers produce textbooks, which are very formal pieces of writing. You can't "hear" the author writing in textbooks. When writers construct stories, however, they put their personalities behind the words they write. When they do this, you can "hear" their voices, even though they're not speaking to you.

2. Duplicate and distribute the list of Voice Descriptors that follows. Tell students that this list contains some of the ways voice is "heard" when reading. Read the list with students and explain any words that are new to them.

3. Select several short pieces of writing from a variety of sources, such as greeting cards, textbooks, letters, stories, e-mails, and newspaper articles. Read the pieces and have students discuss the voices they "hear" in the writing.

4. Have students vote on which voice descriptor matches each writing most closely. If students think of additional voice descriptors, add them to the list.

5. Tell students to think about their own writing and to try to make their own voices heard as they write.

Voice Descriptors

Amusing

Bland

Caring

Clever

Concerned

Critical

Cruel

Curt

Delightful

Detached

Dismal

Earnest

Entertaining

Frightened

Funny

Gracious

Happy

Insightful

Joyful

Kind

Mean

Profound

Rude

Sarcastic

Sensitive

Smart

Sympathetic

Thoughtful

Timid

Witty

Adapted from Culham, R. (2003). *6+1 traits of writing*. New York: Scholastic Professional Books.

Editing to Conform to Standard English

Goal — To help students edit their writing so that it conforms to Standard English.

BACKGROUND

"Poor spelling in the midst of a good piece of writing is like attending a lovely banquet but with the leavings of grime and grease from the previous meal still left on the table" (Graves, 1983, p. 18). Editing is polishing a piece of writing, putting the piece of writing into its final form by correcting its surface features, or mechanics. Correct mechanics, such as spelling, usage, punctuation, capitalization, paragraphing, sentence structure, and handwriting/typing, can make the difference between a banquet and a dirty table.

> Most students tend to be poor editors.

Writers need to attend to the mechanics of writing. Published words require precision because writing doesn't offer the second chance that spoken words do (Graves, 2003). Written words need to express as clearly as possible what the author means. Usually after a writer gives a piece of writing to a reader, the writer loses control of the meaning of the text. It is then the responsibility of the reader to construct meaning, and if the writer hasn't been specific, the reader could misinterpret the author's point.

Most students tend to be poor editors. One of the reasons students aren't very good at cleaning up a piece of writing is that students have had very few chances in their lives to edit writing. The ratio of time students spend speaking and listening is three times greater than the time students spend writing. Most students, therefore, have few opportunities to edit their writings so that they conform to conventional language.

The best way to teach the conventions of language has been debated for over two decades. Writers such as Donald Graves (1983)

encourage teachers to teach students the mechanics of language in the context of their writing. Others suggest that the explicit teaching of conventions also is important. For example, Lisa Delpit (1988) suggests that the ability to write with conventional language can be a gatekeeper for students who do not know the language of power, Standard English. Delpit (1988) recommends that teachers of language minority students should explicitly teach students Standard English. Schuster (2003) agrees that grammar, as one aspect of conventional language, should be taught, but not in the ways that we have taught it in the past. Short, direct lessons of grammar and other conventions can invite students of all backgrounds into the land of power, where Standard English is the norm.

Teaching students to edit their writing and helping them learn how to write in conventional language are important components

Do you agree that most students tend to have a difficult time editing their writing?

of a writing program. Teachers should remember, however, that students need to write so much that only a small percentage of their writing should be edited. This section presents resources, teaching strategies, ideas, and activities to help teach students to edit their writing.

Teaching *1 Strategy*

Section 6.3

EDIT: READY OR NOT?

It takes a while before students reach the editing stage of a piece of writing. Because not every piece of writing students complete will be revised and edited, editing should be reserved for those pieces of writing that will make their way to an audience that expects to read Standard English. Students need to be given multiple opportunities to revise their writing. Only when they have revised as much as they are capable of doing should they begin to edit. With the strategy Edit: Ready or Not? students monitor their progress on a piece of writing to determine whether they need to keep revising, or whether they are ready to edit it.

Directions

1.   Tell students that editing is usually the last stage of the writing process before writers share their work with an audience. Stress the idea that writers often revise their writings several times before they are ready to edit them.

2.   Duplicate and distribute the page Am I Ready to Edit? that follows. Give each student one copy.

3.   Read the questions with students. Make sure all students understand the meanings of the words and phrases on the checklist.

4.   Model editing readiness with a revised draft of your own. Choose a piece of writing that is near completion but not quite ready to edit. Make an overhead transparency of your writing, or if you have written it on a computer, project the copy on a screen using an LCD panel. Read the writing with your students and discuss whether you are ready to edit it.

5.   Divide the class into groups of three or four students. Have students discuss whether their writings are ready to edit.

6.   Answer the questions from the sheet Am I Ready to Edit? Explain why you believe you are ready to edit in some respects and not ready in others.

7.   Tell students that because you could not answer all questions with a "yes" you need to revise your writing before you are ready to edit it.

8.   As students finish revising their writings, have them use the questions on the Am I Ready to Edit? sheet before moving to the editing stage. Set the cutoff point for the number of answers that are "yes" and the number of answers that are "no" based on the writing level of your class, the time you want to devote to this piece of writing, and your expectations of your students.

Name _____ Date _____•

Am I Ready to Edit?

Title _____

1.	I read the writing to myself and it makes sense.	Yes	No
2.	I read the piece to a writing partner and used some of the suggestions.	Yes	No
3.	The purpose of the writing is clear.	Yes	No
4.	My writing style fits my audience.	Yes	No
5.	The writing is focused on one event or idea.	Yes	No
6.	I have enough details to make my writing interesting.	Yes	No
7.	I have included Million Dollar Words.	Yes	No
8.	I have an interesting first sentence.	Yes	No
9.	The title for this writing fits the piece.	Yes	No
10.	The ending has punch.	Yes	No
11.	I corrected as many mistakes as I could find during revising.	Yes	No
12.	I am satisfied with this piece of writing.	Yes	No

There are a number of ways you can approach editing conferences (Danielson & LaBonty, 1994). Students should edit their own writing first. After students have edited their own writing, they should take part in Editing Conferences. Editing Conferences can be held with other student writers, or they can be with you, the teacher. If you choose to hold Editing Conferences with students, you can hold on-the-spot conferences where you walk around the room helping students edit. A second type of conference is an instructional conference, where you bring several students who have the same kinds of writing needs together for small group editing. A third type of conference is an individual Editing Conference where you work with one student to conform the writing to conventional English. The purpose of Editing Conferences is to help students make their revised writings conform more closely to conventional language.

Directions

1. After students have determined that they are ready to edit, they should be assigned to an Editing Conference. Tell students that at an Editing Conference a partner will help them edit their writing. Explain that writers often miss some of their own surface errors and that having a second reader often helps the writer make additional corrections to the paper.

2. Tell students that you will use an Editing Checklist at their Editing Conference. Duplicate and distribute the Editing Checklist that follows. Give a copy to each student.

3. Make a transparency of a piece of writing prepared by a former student or use the Student Example on page 364. Project the writing onto a screen. Read the Editing Checklist, answering the questions as you go. After answering the questions, sign your name in the space for the editor's name and write one or more positive comments about the piece of writing. Explain that you will be using the same process in Editing Conferences.

4. When students have a piece of writing to edit, have them come to an Editing Conference with you. Use the Editing Checklist to help students conform their writings to conventional language. After you have used the Editing Checklist, have students make the appropriate changes to their writings.

Which type of Editing Conference do you prefer?

362

Editing Checklist

Author_____ Date_____

Title _____

1. Spelling is accurate.	Yes	No
2. Capitalization is correct.	Yes	No
3. Punctuation is correct.	Yes	No
4. Subjects and verbs agree.	Yes	No
5. Paragraphs are indented.	Yes	No
6. Margins are appropriate.	Yes	No
7. Sentences are complete.	Yes	No
8. Sentences are clear.	Yes	No
9. Words are used correctly.	Yes	No
10. Writing is legible, or typing is without typos.	Yes	No

Comments _____

_____

_____

Editor's Name _____ *Date* _____

In the Field

In the feild thar was a farm. And in that farm thar was a barn.

And in that farn thar was a stabole. In that stabole thar was a cow.

In that cow thar was a fle. And . . . The cow want Moooo!

That skard the fle that wat our of the . . . Stabol. out of the barn

and out of the farm out of the felde and OUT OUT OUT !!!

Cotē Anne Tracy
First Grade

TEACHER AS COPY EDITOR

Writers rarely compose totally correct text. That's why copy editors play a crucial role in the writing process. Even though writers struggle to write correct copy, they often fall short of the mark. Professional writers know this. They also know that copy editors bring a fresh "read" to a piece of writing and are able to find surface errors that the writer missed. In classrooms, the teacher should be the copy editor for the class. The teacher knows the most about correct writing mechanics, so after the writing process is complete and students have edited their writings, the teacher can put on a copy editor hat and take the writings to their final form.

Directions

1. Tell students that you will copyedit their final writings but that they need to have every possible correction made before you will act as copy editor.

2. Duplicate and distribute the Editing Marks sheet that follows. Give each student a copy of the Editing Marks sheet. Explain that you will copyedit their writings using the symbols on this sheet.

3. Make a transparency of the Editing Marks sheet. Using an overhead projector, show students the editing symbols and discuss each of their meanings. Remind students that you will be using these symbols as you copyedit.

4. Make a transparency of the Unedited Writing Example on page 367 and display it on a screen. Show students the first copy of the writing, the one without marks. Have students read the text to find errors. Encourage students to correct errors using editing marks. Then display a transparency of the Edited Writing Example. Explain each symbol and why it was used.

5. Have a special tray or box in your room marked "For the Copy Editor." Tell students to place their finished writings in the copy editor's tray. Copyedit students' writings as they place them in the tray. You may decide to use different colored pencils for the different editing marks. If you find that you make an exceptional number of editing marks on a student's writing, monitor the student's editing before the future piece of writing goes to copy editing.

6. Tell students that after their writings are copyedited they should make the changes specified by the editing marks before sharing their writing with an audience.

Dr. Grammar

www.drgrammar.org/

This site answers any questions about grammar, usage, punctuation, documentation, and word origins.

Editing Marks

Mark	What It Means	Example
sp.	Correct spelling	I went ⟨fowrard⟩. *sp.*
≡	Change a lowercase letter to a capital letter.	I went to new york.
/	Change a capital letter to a lowercase letter.	In May, I went to the Zoo.
e	Delete or take out letters, words, sentences, lines, and punctuation marks.	I went to my friend's house after I went school.
∧	Add or insert letters, words, or sentences.	My trip fun. *was*
⋁	Add an apostrophe.	I am Dougs friend.
¶	New paragraph.	¶ My friend and I were ready to go.
⊙	Add a period.	The dogs were barking ⊙
∧	Add a comma.	I ran, jumped and played at the park.
#	Add space between two words.	The dog was mine. #
‿	Combine two words.	The dog house was huge.

Wolves are found in cold areas throughout the Northern Hemisphere. Because people have pushed wolves farther into the wilderness they are common only in canada and Alaska. Some wolf species can also be found in Europe and Asia.

Wolves prey on rabbits, game birds, and deer. Some times they eat livestock. Hunters and farmers often object to wolves living in ranching areas because wolves can eat livestock. Many people think that wolves also eat humans, but they don't. Wolves have a bad name, probably because they frequently play the villains roll in fairy tales. Wolves, however, are not bad. They are clever animals that are a part of the natural environment. Wolves are fascinating wild animals.

Edited Writing Example

¶ Wolves are found in cold areas throughout the Northern Hemisphere. Because people have pushed wolves farther into the wilderness, they are common only in canada and Alaska. Some wolf species can also be found in Europe and Asia.

¶ Wolves prey on rabbits, game birds, and deer. Some times they also eat livestock. Hunters and farmers often object to wolves living in ranching areas because wolves can eat livestock. Many people think that wolves also eat humans, but they don't. ¶ Wolves have a bad name, probably because they frequently play the villains roll in fairy tales. Wolves, however, are not bad. They are clever animals that are a part of the natural environment. Wolves are fascinating wild animals.

Teaching Strategy 4

BREAKING THE RULES

Rules are made to be broken. Maybe this well-known saying isn't always true, but it is true when it comes to grammar. In his book, *Breaking the Rules: Liberating Writers through Innovative Grammar Instruction,* Schuster (2003) suggests that some grammar rules can be disregarded in writing, especially for effect. He goes on to say that rules that are necessary for communication should not be broken (e.g., their, there, and they're), but some rules that are *usually* followed should not be *always* followed. Instead, students should be encouraged to use the strategy Breaking the Rules. Sometimes.

Directions

1. Remind students of the many writing rules they have learned over the course of their schooling. Write several of these rules on the chalkboard or on an overhead transparency. Some examples follow.

   Never use a sentence fragment.

   Avoid run-on sentences.

   Each paragraph should have a minimum of three sentences.

   Don't begin a sentence with "because."

2. Ask students to think of additional writing rules that they have learned over the years. Add these rules to your list.

3. Tell students that some of the rules they have listed should not be broken because they would hinder communication. Provide students with examples of rules that they should never break. Explain that word usage, for example, needs to remain constant.

4. Inform students that some rules can be broken. Write the following example on the chalkboard or on an overhead transparency. Help students to understand that the sentence fragment "No" in this paragraph is used for emphasis.

   Tony slipped on his boots and shuffled out into the cold. It was raining outside, a cold rain that arrowed into his bones. In frustration, he picked up the newspaper from the bushes. The paperboy had missed his porch again. Tony decided to call the newspaper office and complain. No. He would give the child one more chance. If it happened once more, Tony would take action.

5. Encourage students to be aware of examples of Breaking the Rules in the books that they read. Explain that authors often break some rules on purpose in order to give their writing more interest.

6. Suggest that students think about Breaking the Rules when they write. Discuss with students the times when Breaking the Rules would be acceptable.

7. Duplicate and distribute the Breaking the Rules sheet that follows. Tell students that if they choose to intentionally break a grammar rule, they should accompany their writing with a Breaking the Rules rationale sheet to explain why they decided to break a grammar rule. Emphasize that this strategy should be used sparingly.

Breaking the Rules

1. What rule do you want to break? _____

   _____

   _____

2. Why do you think your writing will be more effective if this rule is broken? _____

   _____

   _____

   _____

3. Have you used this strategy sparingly? _____

4. Underline the portion of your writing where you have broken a rule. _____

Assessing Writing Style, Voice, and Mechanics

Goal • *To assess students' writing style, voice, and mechanics.*

BACKGROUND

Writing style, voice, and mechanics are important components of writing. Writing that is full of errors is difficult to read. Certainly, young students who are experimenting with writing will write with "invented spelling" and will not use the accepted mechanics of English. However, even young students can learn to rewrite words, sentences, and passages to make their writing more readable. Older students can learn to rewrite so that their writing is clear, interesting, and written in conventional English.

Not all of the writing students complete needs to be rewritten. However, students should learn to rewrite when they have written for an audience. As students rewrite, they need to look for the value in their writing, or what they do well (Hansen, 2001). Students also can be assessed on how well they have learned to use an inter-

esting writing style and how well they have learned to write with conventional English.

There are a number of ways you can assess students' growth as writers. You can use an Analytic Writing Scale such as the one exemplified in Assessment Strategy 1. Using an analytic scale, you can help students pinpoint areas in which they have improved and in which they need to concentrate (Wolcott & Legg, 1998). You also can have students assess their own writing growth as in Assessment Strategy 2, Fix-It. Finally, Assessment Strategy 3 emphasizes Portfolio Assessment, or ways you can assess students' growth using a collection of writings. Each of these assessment strategies should be used as you assess students' growth in developing an engaging writing style and the proper use of the mechanics of writing.

Important Components of Writing

Style
Voice
Mechanics

WRITING SCALE FOR STYLE, VOICE, AND MECHANICS

As students grow as writers, one of the most visible ways in which they improve is through their use of an engaging writing style and the use of conventional mechanics in writing. When students learn how to write with their own unique voice using the conventions of Standard English, their writing becomes increasingly more refined. Teachers and students can use a Writing Scale for Style, Voice, and Mechanics to assess these components of a single piece of writing.

Directions

1. Collect a piece of writing that students have written for an audience. Tell students that this piece of writing should be a finished product, one that has been written with an engaging writing style using Standard English.

2. Duplicate the Writing Scale for Style, Voice, and Mechanics that best matches your students' writing development or adapt the scale so it fulfills your purposes.

3. Complete the Writing Scale for Style, Voice, and Mechanics for each student's writing. After you have completed the scale, conference with students to discuss the strengths and weaknesses of their writing samples.

Writing Scale for Style, Voice, and Mechanics
Younger Students

	Yes	Mostly	No
1. Name and date are correct.	Yes	Mostly	No
2. Title is appropriate.	Yes	Mostly	No
3. Margins are clear.	Yes	Mostly	No
4. Spaces between words are even.	Yes	Mostly	No
5. Capital letters are correct.	Yes	Mostly	No
6. Punctuation is correct.	Yes	Mostly	No
7. Sentences are complete.	Yes	Mostly	No
8. Words are spelled correctly.	Yes	Mostly	No
9. Handwriting is legible.	Yes	Mostly	No
10. Voice is apparent.	Yes	Mostly	No

Writing Scale for Style, Voice, and Mechanics
Older Students

1. Name and date are legible.	Yes	Mostly	No
2. Title is appropriate.	Yes	Mostly	No
3. First sentence is engaging.	Yes	Mostly	No
4. Margins are even.	Yes	Mostly	No
5. Capitalization is correct.	Yes	Mostly	No
6. Punctuation is correct.	Yes	Mostly	No
7. Spelling is correct.	Yes	Mostly	No
8. Sentences are fluent and varied.	Yes	Mostly	No
9. Words are precise and interesting.	Yes	Mostly	No
10. Figurative language is used.	Yes	Mostly	No
11. Paragraphing is correct.	Yes	Mostly	No
12. Handwriting is legible or typos are minimal.	Yes	Mostly	No
13. Voice is evident.	Yes	Mostly	No
14. Concluding sentence is powerful.	Yes	Mostly	No

FIX-IT •

Students can assess their own growth in writing style and mechanics using the Fix-It assessment strategy (Hill, Ruptic, & Norwick, 1998). With the Fix-It strategy, each student saves one or more writing samples that were written early in the year, compares the samples with writing composed at a later date, makes corrections on the earlier drafts, and reflects on his or her learning. Many students are amazed at their growth as writers with these before and after writing samples. Fix-It pairs of writing also can be placed in students' writing portfolios.

Directions

1. Photocopy writing samples from students early in the school year. Save the writing samples in a folder titled Fix-It samples.

2. Write "Fix-It" on a calendar or in a lesson plan book for a time at least four months in the future. Plan to spend a class period at that time for students to participate in the Fix-It assessment strategy.

3. After four or more months, take out the Fix-It folder and distribute the writing samples to students. Ask students to read their writings.

4. Tell students that they have learned many writing skills and strategies during the intervening time period. List two or three of the skills and strategies that students have learned in the past four months, such as writing an engaging first sentence. Have students share other writing skills and strategies that they have learned. Write the list on the chalkboard or on an overhead transparency.

5. Ask students to rewrite their original pieces of writing. Remind students to use the skills and strategies that they have learned in the ensuing months. Tell students that they can write on their original drafts or they can rewrite their entire pieces.

6. After students have completed "fixing" their early writing, ask them to reflect on the ways they have grown as writers. Ask students to write in their personal journals about their writing growth.

7. Save the writing samples for students' portfolios.

PORTFOLIO ASSESSMENT •

Assessment Strategy

Portfolios are a collection of students' writings. With a collection of writings, you can assess students' writing growth over time. In order to determine whether students' writing is improving, you need to have more than one piece of writing. Students might have difficulty writing with style or writing in conventional English on a specific writing sample. However, using a collection of students' writings, you can assess students' growth as writers (Murphy & Underwood, 2000).

Directions

1. Tell students that you will be saving several of their writing samples during the year. Explain that these pieces of writing will not be returned until the end of the year.

2. Provide students with expandable writing file folders. Have students put their names on the files, give their portfolios names, and decorate their files.

3. Every two or three weeks, have students choose a piece of writing to place in their Writing Portfolios. You can choose some pieces of writing to include as well. Label the pieces of writing that your choose "Teacher's Choice."

4. After several months, have students gather their writing portfolios to assess their growth as writers. Duplicate and distribute the list of skills and strategies on the Portfolio Assessment sheet on page 377 to assess students' writing growth.

5. Have students assess their writing growth using the Portfolio Assessment statements by circling the answers that best describe their growth. Then meet with students in small groups or individually to discuss their responses to the statements. Congratulate students on areas of growth and encourage students to continue to improve as writers.

Portfolio Assessment

1. I read my own writing and notice areas to revise.   Often   Sometimes   Rarely

2. I notice areas of strength and weakness in my writing.   Often   Sometimes   Rarely

3. I seek feedback for troublesome passages.   Often   Sometimes   Rarely

4. I use writers' tools such as dictionaries and thesauruses during writing.   Often   Sometimes   Rarely

5. I incorporate suggestions from Writing Partners.   Often   Sometimes   Rarely

6. I incorporate suggestions from Writing Conferences.   Often   Sometimes   Rarely

7. I provide suggestions for other writers.   Often   Sometimes   Rarely

8. I show an interest in improving my writing.   Often   Sometimes   Rarely

9. I revise my drafts several times.   Often   Sometimes   Rarely

10. I use interesting language in my writing.   Often   Sometimes   Rarely

11. I vary my sentence structures.   Often   Sometimes   Rarely

12. I use Million Dollar Words.   Often   Sometimes   Rarely

13. I write in a variety of formats.   Often   Sometimes   Rarely

14. I use conventional English.   Often   Sometimes   Rarely

Comments _____

_____

_____

Appendix

Professional Organizations and Agencies

American Library Association (ALA)
50 East Huron
Chicago, IL 60611
Phone: 800-545-2433
Fax: 312-440-9374
Website: http://www.ala.org
Publications: *Choice Magazine*

Association for Supervision and Curriculum
　　Development (ASCD)
1703 Beauregard Street
Alexandria, VA 22311
Phone: 800-933-ASCD
Fax: 703-575-5400
E-mail: info@ascd.org
Website: http://www.ascd.org
Publications: *Educational Leadership*,
　　Educational Bulletin

Children's Book Council
568 Broadway, Suite 404
New York, NY 10012
Phone: 212-966-1990
Fax: 212-966-2073
E-mail: staff@cbcbooks.org
Website: http://www.cbcbooks.org

International Reading Association (IRA)
800 Barksdale Road
P.O. Box 8139
Newark, DE 19714-8139
Phone:　302-731-1600
　　　　800-336-7323
Fax: 302-731-1057
E-mail: ubinfo@reading.org
Website: http://www.reading.org
Publications: *Reading Research Quarterly, The
　　Reading Teacher, Journal of Adolescent & Adult
　　Literacy, Lectura y vida* (Spanish), *Thinking
　　Classroom*

National Association of the Education of
　　Young Children (NAEYC)
1509 16th St., N.W.
Washington, DC 20036
Phone: 800-424-2460
Fax: 202-328-1846
Website: http://www.naeyc.org
Publications: *Young Children, Early Childhood
　　Research Quarterly*

National Council of Teachers of English (NCTE)
1111 W. Kenyon Road
Urbana, IL 61801
Phone:　217-328-3870
　　　　800-369-6283
Fax: 217-328-0977
E-mail: membership@ncte.org
Website: http://www.ncte.org
Publications: *Language Arts, Primary Voices,
　　English Journal*

National Writing Project
University of California
5511 Tolman Hall #1670
Berkeley, CA 94720-1670
Phone: 510-642-0963
Fax: 510-642-4545
E-mail: nwp@socrates.berkeley.edu
Website: http://www.gse.berkeley.ed/nwp

References

Allen, S., & Lindaman, J. (2003). *Read anything good lately?* Brookfield, CT: Millbrook.

Amis, N. (2003). *The orphans of Normandy.* New York: Atheneum.

Anderson, M. (2003). Reading violence in boys' writing. *Language Arts, 80,* 223–230.

Anderson, N.B., & Anderson, P.E. (2003). *Emotional longevity.* New York: Viking.

Armbruster, B.B. (2000). Responding to informative prose. In R. Indrisano & J.R. Squire (Eds.), *Perspectives on writing: Research, theory, and practice* (pp. 140–160). Newark: DE: International Reading Association.

Armstrong, T. (2003). *The multiple intelligences of reading and writing: Making words come alive.* Alexandria, VA: Association for Supervision and Curriculum development.

Atwell, N. (2002). *Lessons that change writers.* Portsmouth, NH: Heinemann.

Barone, D., & Lovell, J. (1990). Michael the show and tell magician: A journey through literature to self. *Language Arts, 67,* 134–143.

Barrs, M. (2000). The reader in the writer. *Reading, 34,* 54–60.

Belk, E.J., & Thompson, R.A. (2001). *Worm painting and 44 more hands-on language arts activities for the primary grades.* Newark, DE: International Reading Association.

Berger, L.R. (1996). Reader response journals: You make the meaning . . . and how. *Journal of Adolescent & Adult Literacy, 39,* 380–385.

Bottomly, D.M., Henk, W.A., & Melnick, S. (1997/1998). Assessing children's views about themselves as writers using the Writer Self-Perception Scale. *The Reading Teacher, 51,* 286–296.

Bouas, M.J., Thompson, P., & Farlow, N. (1997). Self-selected journal writing in the kindergarten classroom: Five conditions that foster literacy development. *Reading Horizons, 38,* 3–12.

Bradley, D.H. (2001). How beginning writers articulate and demonstrate their understanding of the act of writing. *Reading Research and Instruction, 40,* 273–296.

Bright, R. (1995). *Writing instruction in the intermediate grades: What is said, what is done, what is understood.* Newark, DE: International Reading Association.

Britton, B.K. (1996). Rewriting: The arts and sciences of improving expository instructional text. In C.M. Levy & S. Ransdell (Eds.), *The science of writing: Theories, methods, individual differences, and applications* (pp. 323–345). Mahwah, NJ: Erlbaum.

Britton, J., Burgess, T., Martin, N., McLeod, A., & Rosen, H. (1975). *The development of writing abilities.* London: Macmillan.

Bromley, K. (1999). Key components of sound writing instruction. In L.B. Gambrell, L.M. Morrow, S.B. Neuman, & M. Pressley (Eds.), *Best practices in literacy instruction* (pp. 152–174). New York: Guilford.

Buss, K., & Karnowski, L. (2000). *Reading and writing literary genres.* Newark, DE: International Reading Association.

Buss, K., & Karnowski, L. (2002). *Reading and writing nonfiction genre.* Newark, DE: International Reading Association.

Calkins, L.M. (1994). *The art of teaching writing.* Portsmouth, NH: Heinemann.

Cantrell, R.J., Fusaro, J.A., & Dougherty, E.A. (2000). Exploring the effectiveness of journal writing on learning social studies: A comparative study. *Reading Psychology, 21,* 1–11.

Christian, S. (1997). *Exchanging lives: Middle school writers online.* Urbana, IL: National Council of Teachers of English.

Christenson, T.A. (2002). *Supporting struggling writers in the elementary classroom.* Newark, DE: International Reading Association.

Clay, M.M. (1975). *What did I write?* Portsmouth, NH: Heinemann.

Cohle, D.M., & Towle, W. (2001). *Connecting reading and writing in the intermediate grades.* Newark, DE: International Reading Association.

Collins, J.L. (1998). *Strategies for struggling writers.* New York: Guilford.

Csak, N.L.B. (2002). "What's important when you're six?" Valuing children's oral stories. *Language Arts, 79,* 488–497.

Culham, R. (2003). *6+1 traits of writing.* New York: Scholastic Professional Books.

Dahl, K.L., & Farnan, N. (1998). *Children's writing: Perspectives from research.* Newark, DE: International Reading Association.

Danielson, K.D., & LaBonty, J. (1994). *Integrating reading and writing through children's literature.* Boston: Allyn and Bacon.

De La Paz, S., Owen, B., Harris, K.R., & Graham, S. (2000). Riding Elvis's motorcycle: Using self-regulated strategy development to PLAN and WRITE for a state writing exam. *Learning Disabilities Research & Practice, 15,* 101–109.

Delpit, L.D. (1988). The silenced dialogue: Power and pedagogy in educating other people's children. *Harvard Educational Review, 58,* 280–298.

Doherty, C., & Mayer, D. (2003). E-mail as a "contact zone" for teacher-student relationships. *Journal of Adolescent & Adult Literacy, 46,* 592–600.

Donovan, C. (2001). Children's development and control of written story and information genres: Insights from one elementary school. *Research in the Teaching of English, 35,* 394–447.

Dorn, L.J., French, C., & Jones, T. (1998). *Apprenticeship in literacy: Transitions across reading and writing.* York, ME: Stenhouse.

Dyson, A.H. (2001). Introduction . . . and a warning. *The Elementary School Journal, 101,* 379–383.

Dyson, A.H., & Freedman, S.W. (1991). Writing. In J. Flood, J.M. Jensen, D. Lapp, & J.R. Squire (Eds.), *Handbook of research on teaching the English language arts* (pp. 754–774). New York: Macmillan.

Elbow, P. (1981). *Writing with power.* New York: Oxford.

Emig, J. (1971). *The composing process of twelfth graders.* Urbana, IL: National Council of Teachers of English.

Farnan, N., & Dahl, K. (2003). Children's writing: Research and practice. In J. Flood, D. Lapp, J.R. Squire, & J.M. Jensen (Eds.), *Handbook of research on teaching the English language arts* (2nd ed.) (pp. 993–1007). Mahwah, NJ: Erlbaum.

Fearn, L., & Farnan, N. (2001). *Interactions: Teaching writing and the language arts.* Boston: Houghton Mifflin.

Fletcher, R., & Portalupi, J. (1998). *Craft lessons: Teaching writing, K–8.* Portland, MA: Stenhouse.

Fletcher, R., & Portalupi, J. (2001). *Writing workshop: The essential guide.* Portsmouth, NH: Heinemann.

Fradin, D., & Fradin, J. (2001). *Ida B. Wells: Mother of the Civil Rights Movement.* New York: Clarion Books.

Frank, C.R. (2003). Mapping our stories: Teachers' reflections on themselves as writers. *Language Arts, 80,* 185–195.

Freedman, R. (1983). *Children of the wild west.* New York: Scholastic.

Freire, P., & Macedo, D. (1987). *Literacy: Reading the word and the world.* South Hadley, MA: Bergin & Garvey.

Frost, H. (2001). *When I whisper, nobody listens.* Portsmouth, NH: Heinemann.

Fulkerson, R. (1996). *Teaching the argument in writing.* Urbana, IL: National Council of Teachers of English.

Fulwiler, T. (1987). *The journal book.* Portsmouth, NH: Heinemann.

Furr, D. (2003). Struggling readers get hooked on writing. *The Reading Teacher, 56,* 518–525.

Gambrell, L.B. (1985). Dialogue journals: Reading-writing interaction. *The Reading Teacher, 38,* 512–515.

Gambrell, L.B. (1996). Creating classroom cultures that foster reading motivation. *The Reading Teacher, 50,* 14–25.

Gardner, H. (1993). *Multiple intelligences.* New York: BasicBooks.

Giorgis, C. (2002). Jack Gantos—Journal keeper extraordinaire. *Language Arts, 79,* 272–276.

Graves, D.H. (1975). An examination of the writing processes of seven-year-old children. *Research in the Teaching of English, 9,* 227–241.

Graves, D.H. (1983). *Writing: Teachers and children at work.* Portsmouth, NH: Heinemann.

Graves, D.H. (1994). *A fresh look at writing.* Portsmouth, NH: Heinemann.

Graves, D.H. (2002). *Testing is not teaching: What should count in education.* Portsmouth, NH: Heinemann.

Graves, D.H. (2003). *Writing: Teachers & children at work.* Portsmouth, NH: Heinemann.

Hansen, J. (2001). *When writers read* (2nd ed.). Portsmouth, NH: Heinemann.

Harris, T.L., & Hodges, R.E. (Eds.). (1995). *The literacy dictionary: The vocabulary of reading and writing*. Newark, DE: International Reading Association.

Harste, J.C., Woodward, V.A., & Burke, C.L. (1985). *Language stories and literacy lessons*. Portsmouth, NH: Heinemann.

Hart, D. (1994). *Authentic assessment: A handbook for educators*. Parsippany, NY: Dale Seymour.

Harwayne, S. (2001). *Writing through childhood: Rethinking process and product*. Portsmouth, NH: Heinemann.

Harvey, S. (1998). *Nonfiction matters: Reading, writing, and research in grades 3–8*. York, ME: Stenhouse.

Hayes, J.R. (1996). A new framework for understanding cognition and affect in writing. In C.M. Levy & S. Ransdell (Eds.), *The science of writing: Theories, methods, individual differences, and applications* (pp. 1–27). Mahwah, NJ: Erlbaum.

Hayes, J.R., & Nash, J.G. (1996). On the nature of planning in writing. In C.M. Levy & S. Ransdell (Eds.), *The science of writing: Theories, methods, individual differences, and applications* (pp. 29–55). Mahwah, NJ: Erlbaum.

Heard, G. (2002). *The revision toolbox: Teaching techniques that work*. Portsmouth, NH: Heinemann.

Hill, B.C., Ruptic, C., & Norwick, L. (1998). *Classroom based assessment*. Norwood, MA: Christopher-Gordon.

Hillocks, G. (2002). *The testing trap: How state writing assessments control learning*. New York: Teachers College Press.

Holdaway, D. (1970). *The foundations of literacy*. New York: Ashton.

Hubbard, R. (1985). Second graders answer the question 'Why publish?' *The Reading Teacher, 38,* 658–662.

Hughey, J.B., & Slack, C. (2001). *Teaching children to write: Theory into practice*. Upper Saddle River, NJ: Prentice-Hall.

International Reading Association & National Association for the Education of Young Children. (1998). Learning to read and write: Developmentally appropriate practices for young children. *The Reading Teacher, 52,* 193–211.

International Reading Association & National Council of Teachers of English. (1994). *Standards for the assessment of reading and writing*. Newark, DE and Urbana, IL: Author.

International Reading Association & National Council of Teachers of English. (1996). *Standards for the English language arts*. Newark, DE and Urbana, IL: Author.

Jago, C. (2002). *Cohesive writing: Why concept is not enough*. Portsmouth, NH: Heinemann.

Kawakami-Arakaki, A., Oshiro, M., & Farran, S. (1989). Research to practice: Integrating reading and writing in a kindergarten curriculum. In J. Mason (Ed.), *Reading and writing connections* (pp. 199–218). Boston: Allyn and Bacon.

Kear, D.J., Coffman, G.A., McKenna, M.C., & Ambrosio, A.L. (2000). Measuring attitude toward writing: A new tool for teachers. *The Reading Teacher, 54,* 10–23.

Kern, D., Andre, W., Schilke, R., Barton, J., & McGuire, M.C. (2003). Less *is* more: Preparing students for state writing assessments. *The Reading Teacher, 56,* 816–826.

Lancia, P.J. (1997). Literary borrowing: The effects of literature on children's writing. *The Reading Teacher, 50,* 470–475.

Learning Media. (1992). *Dancing with the pen: The learner as writer*. Wellington, New Zealand: Ministry of Education.

Lenski, S.D., & Johns, J.L. (1997). Patterns of reading-to-write. *Reading Research and Instruction, 37,* 15–38.

Lenski, S.D., Wham, M.A., & Johns, J.L. (2003). *Reading & learning strategies: Middle grades through high school*. Dubuque, IA: Kendall/Hunt.

Levine, K. (2003). *Hana's suitcase*. Morton Grove, IL: Albert Whitman.

Lipson, M.Y., Mosenthal, J., Daniels, P., & Woodside-Jiron, H. (2000). Process writing in the classrooms of eleven fifth-grade teachers with different orientations to teaching and learning. *The Elementary School Journal, 101,* 209–231.

Luse, P.L. (2002). Speedwriting: A teaching strategy for active student engagement. *The Reading Teacher, 56,* 20–21.

Mackey, M. (1997). Good-enough reading: Momentum and accuracy in the reading of complex fiction. *Research in the Teaching of English, 31,* 428–458.

MacLachlan, P. (1985). *Sarah, plain and tall*. New York: Harper and Row.

Mallon, T. (1984). *A book of one's own: People and their diaries*. New York: Ticknor & Fields.

Mariage, T.V. (2001). Features of an interactive writing discourse: Conversational involvement, conventional knowledge, and internalization in "Morning Message." *Journal of Learning Disabilities, 34,* 172–196.

McElveen, S.A., & Dierking, C.C. (2000/2001). Children's books as models to teach writing skills. *The Reading Teacher, 54,* 362–364.

McIntosh, M. (1997). 500 writing formats. *Mathematics Teaching in the Middle School, 2,* 354–357.

Mohr, M.M. (1984). *Revision: The rhythm of meaning*. Upper Montclair, NJ: Boynton/Cook.

Monahan, M.B. (2003). "On the lookout for language": Children as language detectives. *Language Arts, 80,* 206–214.

Murphy, S., & Underwood, T. (2000). *Portfolio practices: Lessons from schools, districts and states*. Norwood, MA: Christopher-Gordon.

Murray, D. (1982). *Learning by teaching: Selected articles on writing and teaching*. Upper Montclair, NJ: Boyton/Cook.

Murray, D.M. (1991). *The craft of revision*. Fort Worth, TX: Holt.

Nelson, P. (2002). *Left for dead*. New York: Delacorte Press.

Newkirk, T. (1989). *More than stories: The range of children's writing*. New York: Teachers College.

Newman, J. (1983). On becoming a writer. *Language Arts, 60,* 860–870.

Odgers, S. (1990). *Drummond*. New York: Holiday House.

Ogle, D.M. (1986). K-W-L: A teaching model that develops active reading of expository text. *The Reading Teacher, 39,* 564–570.

Ollmann, H.E. (1991/1992). The voice behind the print: Letters to an author. *Journal of Reading, 35,* 322–324.

Ollmann, H.E. (1996). Creating higher level thinking with reading response. *Journal of Adolescent & Adult Literacy, 39,* 576–581.

Parsons, L. (2001). *Response journals revisited: Maximizing learning through reading, writing, viewing, discussing, and thinking*. Portland, ME: Stenhouse.

Pinnell, G.S., & McCarrier, A. (1994). Interactive writing: A transition tool for assisting children in learning to read and write. In E. Hiebert & B. Taylor (Eds.), *Getting reading right from the start: Effective early literacy interventions* (pp. 149–170). Needham, MA: Allyn and Bacon.

Pollington, M.F., Wilcox, B., & Morrison, T.G. (2001). Self-perception in writing: The effects of writing workshop and traditional instruction on intermediate grade students. *Reading Psychology, 22,* 249–265.

Powell, R., Cantrell, S.C., & Adams, A. (2001). Saving Black Mountain: The promise of critical literacy in a multicultural democracy. *The Reading Teacher, 54,* 772–781.

Raines, S.C., & Canady, R.J. (1990). *The whole language kindergarten*. New York: Teachers College.

Ray, K.W., with Laminack, L.L. (2001). *The writing workshop: Working through the hard parts (and they're all hard parts)*. Urbana, IL: National Council of Teachers of English.

Rhodes, L.K., & Shanklin, N.L. (1993). *Windows into literacy: Assessing learners K–8*. Portsmouth, NH: Heinemann.

Richards, J.C., & Gipe, J.P. (1995). What's the structure? A game to help middle school students recognize common writing patterns. *Journal of Reading, 38,* 667–669.

Rief, L. (1999). *Vision & voice: Extending the literacy spectrum*. Portsmouth, NH: Heinemann.

Rog, L.J. (2001). *Early literacy instruction in kindergarten*. Newark, DE: International Reading Association.

Rosenblatt, L. (1985). Language, literature, and values. In S.N. Tchudi (Ed.), *Language, schooling, and society* (pp. 64–80). Upper Montclair, NJ: Boyton/Cook.

Rothstein, E., & Lauber, G. (2000). *Writing as learning: A content-based approach*. Arlington Heights, IL: Skylight.

Routman, R. (1991). *Invitations: Changing as teachers and learners, K–12*. Portsmouth, NH: Heinemann.

Rubenstein, S. (1998). *Go public! Encouraging student writers to publish*. Urbana, IL: National Council of Teachers of English.

Rubin, D.L. (1998). Writing for readers: The primacy of audience in composing. In N. Nelson & R.C. Calfee (Eds.), *The reading-writing connection* (pp. 53–73). Chicago: University of Chicago.

Ryder, R.J. (1994). Using frames to promote critical writing. *Journal of Reading, 38*, 210–218.

Santa, C.M., Havens, L., & Harrison, S. (1989). Teaching secondary science through reading, writing, studying, and problem-solving. In D. Lapp, J. Flood, & N. Farnan (Eds.), *Content area reading and learning: Instructional strategies* (pp. 137–151). Englewood Cliffs, NJ: Prentice Hall.

Schneider, J.J. (2003). No blood, guns, or gays allowed!: The silencing of the elementary writer. *Language Arts, 78*, 415–425.

Schneider, J.J., & Jackson, S.A.W. (2000). Process drama: A special space and place for writing. *The Reading Teacher, 54*, 38–51.

Schuster, E.H. (2003). *Breaking the rules: Liberating writers through innovative grammar instruction.* Portsmouth, NH: Heinemann.

Sharples, M. (1996). An account of writing as creative design. In C.M. Levy & S. Ransdell (Eds.), *The science of writing: Theories, methods, individual differences, and applications* (pp. 127–148). Mahwah, NJ: Erlbaum.

Smith, F. (1988). *Joining the literacy club.* Portsmouth, NH: Heinemann.

Smith, F. (1990). *To think.* New York: Teachers College Press.

Spandel, V., & Stiggins, R.J. (1997). *Creating writers: Linking writing assessment and instruction* (2nd ed.). New York: Longman.

Stauffer, R.G. (1970). *The language-experience approach to the teaching of reading.* New York: Harper and Row.

Stotsky, S. (1995). The uses and limitations of personal or personalized writing in writing theory, research, and instruction. *Reading Research Quarterly, 30*, 758–776.

Straub, R. (1997). Students' reactions to teacher comments: An exploratory study. *Research in the Teaching of English, 31*, 91–118.

Strickland, D.S., Bodino, A., Buchan, K., Jones, K.M., Nelson, A., & Rosen, M. (2001). Teaching writing in a time of reform. *The Elementary School Journal, 101*, 385–397.

Sulzby, E., Teale, W.H., & Kamberelis, G. (1989). Emergent writing in the classroom: Home and school connections. In D.S. Strickland & L.M. Morrow (Eds.), *Emerging literacy: Young children learning to read and write* (pp. 63–79). Newark, DE: International Reading Association.

Tchudi, S. (Ed.). (1997). *Alternatives to grading student writing.* Urbana, IL: National Council of Teachers of English.

The National Writing Commission. (2003). www.writingcommission.org. Available.

Topping, K., Nixon, J., Sutherland, J., & Yarrow, F. (2000). Paired writing: A framework for effective collaboration. *Reading, 34*, 79–89.

Van Allsburg, C. (1984). *The mysteries of Harris Burdick.* Boston: Houghton Mifflin.

Van Sluys, K. (2003). Writing and identity construction: A young author's life in transition. *Language Arts, 80*, 176–184.

Vasquez, V., with Muise, M.R., Adamson, S.C., Heffernan, L., Chiola-Nakai, D., & Shear, J. (2003). *Getting beyond "I like the book": Creating space for critical literacy in K–6 classrooms.* Newark, DE: International Reading Association.

Viorst, J. (1972). *Alexander and the terrible, horrible, no good, very bad day.* New York: Simon and Schuster.

Vygotsky, L.S. (1962). *Thought and language.* Cambridge, MA: MIT.

Wolcott, W., & Legg, S.M. (1998). *An overview of writing assessment: Theory, research, and practice.* Urbana, IL: National Council of Teachers of English.

Wolf, S.A., & Wolf, K.P. (2002). Teaching *true* and *to* the test in writing. *Language Arts, 79*, 229–240.

Wollman-Bonilla, J. (2000). *Family message journals: Teaching writing through family involvement.* Urbana, IL: National Council of Teachers of English.

Wray, D., & Lewis, M. (1997). Teaching factual writing: Purpose and structure. *The Australian Journal of Language and Literacy, 20*, 131–138.

Yell, M.M. (2002). Putting gel pen to paper. *Educational Leadership, 60*, 63–66.

Yolen, J. (2003). *Hoptoad.* San Diego, CA: Silver Whistle.

Zaragoza, N., & Vaughn, S. (1995). Children teach us to teach writing. *The Reading Teacher, 49*, 42–47.

Ziefert, H., & Doughty, R. (2003). *31 uses for a mom.* New York: Putnam's Sons.

Index